THE ARCH OF
CONSTANTINE

THE ARCH OF CONSTANTINE

INSPIRED BY THE DIVINE

IAIN FERRIS

AMBERLEY

Once more dedicated to Lynne with love.

First published 2013

Amberley Publishing
The Hill, Stroud
Gloucestershire, GL5 4EP

www.amberley-books.com

British Library Cataloguing in Publication Data.
A catalogue record for this book is available from the British Library.

ISBN 978 1 4456 0129 8

Typeset in 10pt on 12pt Sabon.
Typesetting and Origination by Amberley Publishing.
Printed in the UK.

Contents

Acknowledgements

In putting this book together I have received help from a number of individuals and organisations and I would like to take the opportunity to thank them all here. Firstly, for help in obtaining photographs for reproduction in the book I would like to thank Graham Norrie, formerly of Birmingham University, and Daria Lanzuolo of the Photo Archives of the Deutsches Archäologisches Institut Rom (DAIR). I am also indebted to Julian Parker for sourcing a number of historical images for me and turning them into digital prints suitable for reproduction here and to John Boden for help with information about certain coin issues. Dr Sandra Knudsen and Dr Ann Kuttner very kindly replied in detail to my queries about their future publication plans with regard to the arch.

The staff of the Institute of Classical Studies library, London, the Institute of Archaeology (UCL) library, London University, the British Library, London, the Society of Antiquaries of London library, Swansea University library, and the library of University of Wales Trinity St David's, Lampeter, were unfailingly helpful in obtaining books and journals for my reference while researching this book.

As always, my colleague and wife Dr Lynne Bevan read and commented on a draft of the book, much to the benefit of the finished work. At Amberley Publishing I would like to thank Alan Sutton and Peter Kemmis Betty for commissioning this book in the first place and Christian Duck for her editorial work and advice.

Preface

The Arch of Constantine (plate 1), built between AD 312 and 315, stands at what was once the beginning of the Via Triumphalis in Rome. Built to celebrate ten years of the Emperor Constantine's reign and his victory over 'the tyrant' Maxentius at the Battle of the Milvian Bridge (plate 2), the arch is undoubtedly the most impressive civic monument in Rome surviving from Late Antiquity. The complex decorative programme of sculpture adorning the arch includes both contemporary, or at least Late Antique, carved scenes, and historic *spolia* – carefully selected and curated relief sculpture and architectural fragments from demolished monuments of earlier emperors' reigns. The arch is the last such commemorative arch built in the Roman world, and academic debate today rages around the origins and meaning of the arch and its adorning artworks.

This study, the first book in English on the monument since Bernard Berenson's idiosyncratic 1954 book *The Arch of Constantine or the Decline of Form*, includes an analysis of the arch and of the reign of Constantine himself, a survey of other Constantinian artworks such as portrait sculptures and decorated carved gemstones and cameos, and a discussion of the widespread late Roman use of *spolia*, all set against the broader geographical, chronological, and cultural context of the world of Late Antiquity. It also includes a broader discussion of Constantine's Rome, of the emperor's impact on the very fabric and geography of the city. Did Constantine oversee or support the transformation of Rome from a pagan city to a Christian city between AD 312 and 326 and, if so, does the Senate-sponsored Arch of Constantine tell us anything about this process? Consideration is also given to the question of whether much of Constantine's impact on Rome through new building projects was simply an act of serendipitous adoption of many schemes set in train but uncompleted under Maxentius, or completed by Maxentius but co-opted as his achievement by Constantine through rededication ceremonies and inscriptions.

The general reader might have thought that more or less everything about the Arch of Constantine was now known after hundreds of years of its study by archaeologists, ancient historians, and architectural historians. However, this is not in fact the case; indeed, far from it, and it is this air of uncertainty about so many aspects of the monument that makes its study so exciting and so highly pertinent today. In the last fifteen years or so there has been a fierce academic debate about whether the arch should indeed be known as the Arch of Constantine at all, and various camps of scholars first formed around the idea that the arch was an earlier Hadrianic arch revamped in the era of Constantine, and then around the theory that the arch was started by Constantine's enemy Maxentius and subsequently taken over by Constantine after Maxentius's death. The opening of this Pandora's Box over dating has also released, set in motion, or reignited other debates about the interpretation of the reused artworks or *spolia* on the arch and about the significance of the setting of the arch within the broader urban topography of Rome.

When I first took a course in Roman art at the Institute of Archaeology, London University, in the mid-1970s, under Dr Malcolm Colledge, along with my fellow students I was surprised and disappointed at how few introductory books there were in English focusing on the major individual monuments of Rome and suitable for undergraduate use. To some extent surprisingly, this is still the case today, with the very obvious exceptions being the ever-growing number of books available about Trajan's Column and Augustus's Ara Pacis monument. In 2009 my book *Hate and War: The Column of Marcus Aurelius* was published and this present book should be seen in some ways as a companion volume to that earlier work, intended to serve the selfsame purpose: to explain the monument. As I did with Marcus Aurelius in *Hate and War* I intend here to also do with Constantine: to examine his life and times; describe his major monument, the arch that bears his name, in the context of the art and architecture of his reign; and review the main scholarly debates about the monument's history and significance.

The book consists of seven chapters, including an introductory chapter on the life and reign of the Emperor Constantine and an examination of his image as portrayed in contemporary art; a chapter on the form and build of the Arch of Constantine; two chapters analysing the decorative sculptural programme of the monument; a chapter on other Constantinian monuments in or around Rome; a chapter investigating the phenomenon of the widespread late Roman use of *spolia* – reused architectural or sculptural fragments – in various contexts, including on the Arch of Constantine, with a discussion of the arch as a work of collage; and a final chapter examining the arch and its decoration in the broader geographical, chronological, and cultural context of the world of Late Antiquity and looking at the way that later artists, from the Renaissance into the twentieth century, have been inspired by and interacted with the arch as a subject. While the book is not intended to be a guidebook of any kind, I have also provided a short appendix about visiting Constantine's Rome in the form of a list of monuments and museums that the interested cultural tourist might want to take in, perhaps inspired by reading this or other books about Constantine. The book also includes academic notes and a full bibliography, which should allow students to further pursue themes and arguments only touched upon in the main text. Almost inevitably I have had to use a number of Latin words and terms in the text and hope that this is not off-putting to those who have not studied the language; for the benefit of such readers I have included, towards the end of the book, a short glossary of Latin words used. By necessity, the book is well illustrated, with both black-and-white and colour images, whose presence here is intended to facilitate the interpretation and understanding of the nature of the monument.

In the process of dealing with these major topics a number of other diverse themes are explored that cut across the individual chapter boundaries. These include: a consideration of the relationship between art and memory; an examination of the concept of the past in the past, particularly in the Roman world; an analysis of the theoretical underpinnings of the art of collage and how this artistic technique can be used to conflate past and present; and an exploration of how art, propaganda and ceremony were to some extent fused in Late Antiquity into a new form of Roman imperial ideology and image. The reception of the arch in later periods is also considered in terms of the way the monument has been represented by artists from the Renaissance up to the twentieth century.

Much of the book was completed by the autumn of 2012 and I had been intending for this to be the cut-off point for including new references in the academic notes and bibliography. However, a final period of library research was undertaken in early December 2012 and has therefore allowed me to make reference to a number of brand-new, hot-off-the-press articles on the arch included in the most recent volume of the transactions of the Norwegian Institute in Rome – the *Institutum Romanum Norvegiae*.[1] In particular, the articles in this volume on the arch, by Siri Sande and Marina Prusac, centred on discussion of memory, continuity and commemoration; they very much reflect and echo some of the ideas that I had developed independently during my own research and run parallel to various sections of discussion I had already written for this book. I am therefore very pleased to be able to cite their articles here.

The book is intended as a general work for undergraduate students of Roman art and archaeology and an informed lay audience interested in the Roman world in general. It aims to demonstrate how close readings of the artworks on the Arch of Constantine and an examination of the structure of the arch itself can enable certain aspects of the past history of Rome in Late Antiquity to be reconstructed, and allow for some sense to be made of the nature of this rapidly changing city and society. The year 2012 marked the 1,700th anniversary of Constantine's Christian vision and his victory at the Battle of the Milvian Bridge, an important anniversary for those interested in the history of Rome and of Christianity. In all probability 2013, the year of publication of this book, marks the 1,700th anniversary of the design and commissioning of the Arch of Constantine by the Senate of Rome, an apposite time perhaps for the appearance of this study.

I. M. Ferris, March 2012 – January 2013.
Pembrey, Carmarthenshire, Wales.

1
Life and Times

In order to understand the significance of the Arch of Constantine in Rome it will first be necessary to understand something of Constantine the man. Constantine I, or Constantine the Great as he has become known, ruled between AD 306 and 337, being sole emperor for the latter part of his reign between 324 and 337 (plate 3). He is perhaps best known to many in the west today as 'the first Christian emperor', though it might be fairer to say that he was the first Roman ruler not to actively persecute or ignore Christians and to harness certain aspects of the Christian doctrine to help strengthen his power and authority in his capacity as a Roman emperor. Indeed, his embrace of Christianity was inseparable from his wielding of imperial power (fig. 1). He recognised that Christianity could better serve the cause of social cohesion within the structures underpinning empire if it weren't opposing it from the outside. Constantine's reign marks the point at which the power of the Christian Church reached a historical tipping point from which there was no return.

This study will be introduced by a summary of the main events in the life of Constantine, as far as they relate to his personal and political biography.[1] His later reign was to become very much taken up with dealing with the minutiae of Church affairs and such issues will to some extent be glossed over in the account that follows, as their details are not strictly relevant to the elucidation of his life story. The historical accounts of Constantine's life that have come down to us provide a coherent image of his character, if not necessarily of his motivations, and in the second part of this chapter an examination will be made of the officially endorsed portraits of Constantine created in various media during his lifetime and presented to the Roman people and the peoples of the wider empire as the image of their emperor.

We are extremely fortunate to have a surviving contemporary literary work describing the life of the emperor and situating his religious policies within the history of the Christian Church and its followers. Written by Eusebius, Bishop of Caesarea in Palestine, the *Vita Constantini*, or *Life of Constantine*, cannot be taken as a literal historical biography of its subject, nor can it be accepted as being otherwise unbiased in its narrative and concerns.[2] As long as this is accepted as being the case, the *Vita Constantini*, though an unfinished work at its author's death, provides us with an unrivalled insight into the history of its age, and will be used here as the principal primary source for the biographical exposition in this chapter. Eusebius died in AD

1. A bronze *nummus* of Constantine. Constantinople mint AD 327. Obverse: bust of emperor, reverse: Christogram topped standard – the *labarum* – with shaft piercing serpent. British Museum, London. (Photo: Copyright Trustees of the British Museum)

339, having started the first version of his work around AD 324. While he is known to have met Constantine at least once, at the Council of Nicaea in AD 325, he cannot be considered to have had an intimate knowledge of the emperor as a person, nor can he be viewed to be an insider within the court. His motives for writing the *Vita* may have been linked to Church politics of the time, and a need, as he possibly saw it, to commend and urge the continuance of Constantine's policies in relation to the Christian Church.[3]

The account of the emperor's life in the *Vita Constantini* can be fleshed out with reference to a number of other, lesser but no less important, sources, including Lactantius's *De Morte Persecutorum* or *On the Deaths of the Persecutors*, the anonymous *Origo Constantini Imperiatoris* or *Lineage of the Emperor Constantine*, Zosimus's *Historia Nova* or *New History*, and five of the panegyrics collected in *Panegyrici Latini*.

As I have already noted, in the summary account of Constantine's life that follows I have had to simplify parts of the narrative. In particular the account of the breaking up of the Tetrarchic system of imperial governance, from which events Constantine was eventually to emerge as sole emperor, has had to be purged of the almost bewildering detail surrounding the pacts, broken pacts, shifting allegiances, duplicitous conduct, lying, cheating, prevaricating, and betrayal that marked the behaviour of the clique of powerful, ruthless men who were chosen to oversee the affairs of the empire in the later third and early fourth centuries. In addition, the account of the highly complex theological and liturgical quandaries and arguments which Constantine and the leaders of the Christian Church were debating in the years following the Edict of Milan of AD 313 has been, by necessity, largely glossed over, as it has little direct bearing on the main topic of this book. In so doing I hope I have not oversimplified matters too much.

A Privileged Life

Constantine – Flavius Valerius Constantinus – was born at Naissus (Niš) in the Roman province of Moesia Superior in present-day Serbia in around AD 272/273, the son of the future Emperor Constantius I, also known as Constantius Chlorus, and his first wife, Helena. Constantius was to divorce Helena in AD 289 to marry Theodora, daughter of Maximian, though Theodora was to feature little in Constantine's life.

The bald facts of Constantine's life are simple. He married twice, first to Minervina, who bore their son Crispus, and in AD 307 to Fausta, daughter of Maximian and Eutropia. Together they had five children: the sons (and future Caesars and Augusti) were Constantine II, Constantius II, and Constans, and the daughters were Constantina and Helena. Constantine had been groomed for power since childhood and became one of the Tetrarchic emperors in AD 306. Following the violent break-up of the Tetrarchy, due in no small part to Constantine's own unfettered ambition, he became sole emperor in AD 324, and was to reign as such till his death at Nicomedia in AD 337. This curt biography does not do justice to the complexities of the time in which Constantine lived and it will be necessary to present a more detailed background to the emperor's life.

By the time Constantine was around twenty years of age, in AD 293, the then emperor Diocletian had created a new form of imperial governance – the Tetrarchy, or 'rule of four', which relied on a team of emperors to rule the Roman Empire in the form of two senior emperors, each called an Augustus, and two junior emperors, each called Caesars, to assist them and learn from them. The rule of a sole emperor or more recently of joint emperors had proven to be a recipe for political and military instability in the third century, and Diocletian's Tetrarchic system was seen as a solution to the empire's social troubles. However, this system lasted only about twenty years, and with Diocletian's retirement in AD 304 internecine imperial power struggles were set in motion which were to blight the functioning of the Roman political system for the next two decades. The first Tetrarchy consisted of Maximian and Diocletian, with respective subordinate Caesars Constantius, based in Milan in the west, and Galerius at Nicomedia in the east.

Constantine served under Diocletian and Galerius from AD 293 and was with Diocletian in Nicomedia until 305 when not campaigning. Constantine certainly took part in Galerius's military campaign in Mesopotamia, which led to the defeat of the Persian king Narses, the capture of Ctesiphon in AD 297/298, and he is also recorded as accompanying Diocletian to Syria, Palestine, and Egypt in AD 301–2. Less certain is whether Constantine was part of the imperial party that travelled to Rome in AD 303 for the celebrations accompanying Diocletian's *vicennalia* or 'twenty-year reign' in the city.

In AD 305 both Diocletian and Maximian abdicated, perhaps as a gesture to demonstrate that the Roman state was more significant than the rule of individual emperors, and the Second Tetrarchy was formed, with Constantius and Galerius as Augusti working with Caesars Severus at Milan and Maximinus Daza at Nicomedia. This Second Tetrarchy was to be very short-lived indeed. For some reason, Constantine chose to leave the eastern court in AD 305, and after receiving permission to do so is recorded as accompanying his father Constantius to Britain. It would appear that although Constantine was not yet a junior emperor he was very much a member of the upper echelon of the ruling Roman elite, being groomed for future power. He may have considered this an apposite moment to distance himself from the controversial and divisive figure of Galerius.

It is evident from a contemporary panegyric that Constantius undertook a military campaign beyond the northern frontier of Britain against the Pictish tribes of Scotland and that he returned south to York to regroup and resupply his forces. However, he was to die there in a matter of months. On his father's death in July AD 306, Constantine was declared emperor by the troops at York, but such an acclamation gave no official authority to this popular promotion. The more formal official process first led to him being made Caesar by Galerius and then Augustus by Maximian in AD 307. Elsewhere in the empire, Constantius's death had led to the rapid promotion of Severus to Augustus in AD 306, but late in the same year Maxentius seized power in Rome with help from his father Maximian, the retired former Tetrarch, and they defeated Severus, who subsequently abdicated at Ravenna in AD 307, to be killed in Rome some months later. This pattern of an empire riven by shifting alliances and political machinations among the Tetrarchs and their would-be rivals was to repeat itself again and again in the next twenty years or so.

Having been made Augustus by Maximian in AD 307, Constantine had sealed his relationship with him by marrying Maximian's daughter Fausta at Trier in the same year. Constantine, now based principally at Trier, is recorded as campaigning against the Germans between AD 307 and 310, and also appears to have been in Britain again in AD 307, 310 and 313. These campaigns may have distracted him from the jockeying for position among his fellow Tetrarchs, or he may have deliberately absented himself from the political intrigue by seeking to build his reputation as an old-style soldier emperor concerned with matters of state rather than with pursuing petty rivalries to the detriment of the empire. Attempts were now made by Galerius as senior Tetrarch to bring order to this increasingly chaotic political situation, first by unsuccessfully entering Italy with military forces in 307, and in the next year by calling a conference at Carnuntum, at which Maximian was persuaded to abdicate for a second time and remove himself from the fractious situation into which he had been dragged. His son-in-law Constantine was not forced out, perhaps as an incentive to Maximian to remove himself from the field, and Licinius was made Augustus.

For a short time things held steady, but all hell was to break loose in AD 310–11. First Maximinus declared himself Augustus, a bold move, quickly neutered by Galerius renaming all the four Tetrarchs as Augusti. Maximian moved against Constantine, who was forced to lead an army against him, which then defeated Maximian's forces at *Massilia* (Marseilles). Maximian then either committed suicide or was murdered. According to a panegyric, a legend subsequently grew up concerning Constantine's vision of Apollo at a temple in Gaul, and it may be that the subsequent reporting of a Christian vision only two years later was a strategy to counteract this mysterious pagan event. It is possible that the story linking Constantine to Apollo, a sun god, was part of a then current strategy to identify Constantine with Augustus, who had enjoyed a special relationship with that particular deity. For many years after AD 310, the year of his 'pagan vision' of Apollo, the legend *Soli invicto* – to the unconquered sun – appeared on Constantine's coins.[4] Finally, with the death of Galerius in 311, Maximinus and Licinius divided his eastern territories between them. Though he had not been directly involved in imperial affairs for many years, the death of Diocletian at Split late in 311 probably seemed quite portentous at the time, symbolically bringing the Tetrarchic experiment to an end and freeing its present incumbents from any lingering feelings of loyalty they might have had towards Diocletian and his great, now failed, idea. Within a year Constantine had finally determined to make his move, and did so by invading Italy and moving against Maxentius, who was still clinging on to his power base in Rome. Maxentius was to die at the major battle at the Milvian Bridge on 28 October AD 312.

Eusebius of Caesarea's account of Constantine's military and political manoeuvrings after his father's death paints a picture of a man righting wrongs according to a pre-prepared plan rather than a pragmatic individual taking advantage of individual opportunities to seize power in a piecemeal fashion, as is suggested by the bare bones of the historical narrative of events between AD 306 and AD 312, as summarised above. According to Eusebius, 'next [Constantine] became aware that the head of the whole, the imperial city of the Roman Empire, lay oppressed by bondage to a tyrant, he first gave opportunity for those who governed the other parts to rescue it, inasmuch as they were senior in years; but when none of these was able to give aid, and even those who did make the attempt had met a shameful end, he declared that his life was not worth living if he were to allow the imperial city to remain in such a plight, and began preparations to overthrow the tyranny'.[5] Eusebius states that it was now that Constantine sought God to help him, rather than the false pagan gods whose help had proved useless against the tyrant for others.

In contrast, the *Vita Constantini* by Eusebius paints a vivid picture of a truly wicked Maxentius; he is portrayed as a man with a thirst for power and uncontrolled lusts for female flesh.[6] His murderous reign was painted as being positively gothic in its horrors, it would seem:

At their peak the tyrant's crimes extended to witchcraft, as for magical purposes he split open pregnant women, sometimes searched the entrails of new-born babies, slaughtered lions, and composed secret spells to conjure demons and to ward off hostilities. By these means he hoped he would gain the victory. Ruling by these dictatorial methods in Rome he imposed on his subjects unspeakable oppression, so that he brought them finally to the utmost scarcity and want of necessary food, such as our generation never remembers happening in Rome at any other time.[7]

The sequence of events in AD 312 that led to the Battle of the Milvian Bridge, the *Pons Mulvius*, just outside Rome, on 28 October AD 312, is reflected in the Constantinian historical frieze on the Arch of Constantine. Firstly Constantine marched against Maxentius (plate 4), defeated his forces at Turin, rested his army in Milan, and then went on to win further victories at Verona and in other parts of Northern Italy, winning a final decisive victory over him at the Milvian Bridge (plate 2). He then entered Rome. A legend concerning a Christian vision now grew up around the person of Constantine and subsequently around his victory at the Milvian Bridge, in particular, and in what is perhaps the most famous passage in the *Vita Constantini*, Eusebius describes this pivotal event, though he does not place the vision at a time before this particular battle:[8]

As he made [these] prayers and earnest supplications there appeared to the Emperor a most remarkable divine sign … About the time of the midday sun, when day was just turning, he said he saw with his own eyes, up in the sky and resting over the sun, a cross-shaped trophy formed from light, and a text attached to it which said, 'By this conquer'. Amazement at the spectacle seized both him and the whole company of soldiers which was then accompanying him on a campaign he was conducting somewhere, and witnessed the miracle … as he slept, the Christ of God appeared to him with the sign which had appeared in the sky, and urged him to make himself a copy of the sign which had appeared in the sky, and to use this as a protection against the attacks of the enemy. When day came he arose and recounted the mysterious communication to his friends. Then he summoned goldsmiths and jewellers, sat down among them, and explained the shape of the sign, and gave them instructions about copying it in gold and precious stones.[9]

Eusebius then claimed that in a meeting with the emperor, at which the story of the vision was vouchsafed to him, he was shown the manufactured banner:

It was constructed to the following design. A tall pole plated with gold had a transverse bar forming the shape of a cross. Up at the extreme top a wreath woven of precious stones and gold had been fastened. On it two letters, intimating by its first characters the name 'Christ', formed the monogram of the Saviour's title, rho being intersected in the middle by chi. These letters the Emperor also used to wear upon his helmet in later times. From the transverse bar, which was bisected by the pole, hung suspended a cloth, an imperial tapestry covered with a pattern of precious stones fastened together, which glittered with shafts of light, and interwoven with much gold, producing an impression of indescribable beauty on those who saw it. This banner then, attached to the bar, was given equal dimensions of length and breadth. But the upright pole, which extended upwards a long way from its lower end, below the trophy of the cross and near the top of the tapestry delineated, carried the golden head-and-shoulders portrait of the Godbeloved Emperor, and likewise of his sons. This saving sign was always used by the Emperor for protection against every opposing and hostile force, and he commanded replicas of it to lead all his armies.[10]

The writer Lactantius[11] records the soldiers of Constantine's victorious army as having the Christian Chi Rho symbol painted on their shields, but this detail might represent a later embellishment of the story. At the Milvian Bridge, Eusebius paints a vivid picture of the decisive moment of victory:

> Maxentius and the armed men and guards about him 'sank to the bottom like a stone', when, fleeing before the force which came from God with Constantine, he went to cross the river lying in his path. When he himself joined its banks with boats and bridged it perfectly well, he had built an engine of destruction for himself, intending thus to catch the friend of God. But the latter had his God present at his right hand, while Maxentius constructed in his cowardice the secret engines of his own destruction. Of him it could also be said that 'he dug a hole and excavated it, and will fall into the pit he made. His labour will return on his head, and on his pate will his wickedness fall'. Thus then by God's will the mechanism in the link and the device concealed in it gave way at a time which was not intended, the crossing parted, and the boats sank at once to the bottom with all their men, the coward himself first of all, and then the infantry and guards about him.[12]

Most significant, in the context of this present book, is Eusebius's description of the celebrations accompanying Constantine's victorious entry into Rome, and particularly the monument erected to celebrate that victory:

> All the members of the Senate and the other persons there of fame and distinction, as if released from a cage, and all the people of Rome, gave him a bright-eyed welcome with spontaneous acclamations and unbounded joy. Men with their wives and children and countless numbers of slaves with unrestrained cheers pronounced him their redeemer, saviour and benefactor.

Constantine, he continued,

> announced to all people in large lettering and inscriptions the sign of the Saviour, setting this up in the middle of the imperial city as a great trophy of victory over his enemies, explicitly inscribing this in indelible letters as the salvific sign of the authority of Rome and the protection of the whole empire. He therefore immediately ordered a tall pole to be erected in the shape of a cross in the hand of a statue made to represent himself, and this text to be inscribed upon it word for word in Latin: 'By this salutary sign, the true proof of valour, I liberated your city, saved from the tyrant's yoke; moreover the Senate and People of Rome I liberated and restored to their ancient splendour and brilliance.'[13]

Eusebius does not relate the story of the fate of the recovered body of the drowned Maxentius, which would appear to have been little different in its casual savagery from that of the Dacian king Decebalus just over 200 years before. Maxentius's head was cut off his body when dragged from the Tiber, and carried through the streets of Rome to universal public derision, if contemporary Panegyric is to be believed.[14] It was then sent on to Carthage, presumably brined or otherwise pickled, to demonstrate to the citizens there that 'the tyrant' was truly dead.

Neither is there a mention in Eusebius's account of the building and dedication of the Arch of Constantine or indeed of its existence at all, though as has been noted there is a striking resemblance between the inscription said to have been set up by the emperor in the centre of the city and the one eventually set up on the arch by the dedicating Senate. In the arch inscription, though, there is no mention of a saviour or of the sign or vision. As to the statue of the emperor into whose hands the sign-bearing pole/cross was placed, this cannot be identified, if indeed it ever actually existed, and certainly it is unlikely to have been the famous colossal statue of the emperor, parts of which are now on display in the courtyard of the Palazzo dei Conservatori in Rome and which will be discussed in detail below.

In the context of the time Constantine's 'conversion' is not altogether surprising. In moving to destroy the Tetrarchic system and patiently waiting for his opportunity to seize sole control of the empire, Constantine had demonstrated a singular drive and vision that valued pragmatism and expediency over compromise. The Christian community in Rome by this time constituted no more or less than a state within a state, with Christians being overtly prominent in public affairs, as senators and military and political officials, and in the social and economic life of the city. This pattern was repeated in cities across the empire, though in varying degrees of intensity. The strength of Roman Christianity in the later third to early fourth centuries accounted for the power of the counter persecution of the Christians launched by successive emperors, from the time of Trajan Decius (249–51) up to Diocletian and particularly by Galerius in the east. What better way for Constantine to distance himself from Diocletian and the Tetrarchy, the last group of persecutors of the Christian faith, than by embracing or at least co-opting that faith into the structures of the governance of the Roman Empire.[15]

Constantine now focused his attention on his relations with the Senate and people of Rome. He was hailed by the Senate as senior Augustus, and probably promised a significant triumphal monument to be erected in his honour quite early on in the process of *rapprochement* with the city's leading politicians. Constantine would appear to have cemented his authority by disbanding the Praetorian Guard that had so actively supported Maxentius, and his popularity by not further pursuing a root-and-branch wheedling out of Maxentius's other supporters. He granted restitution of property, land, and monies to Christians persecuted under Maxentius, and enabled the political and religious climate to clear such as to allow work to begin on the building of the Church of Christ the Saviour at the Lateran. He also appears to have focused on his relationship with Licinius, and the outcomes of their meeting in Milan in AD 313 were both political and personal, with the issuing of the Edict of

Milan, a statement on religious toleration, and the marriage of Constantine's sister Constantia to Licinius.

For a while these actions allowed Constantine to turn his attention to other political and religious matters in the empire – firstly possibly restoring 'the christians to their worship and their God'[16] – in particular the problems among Christians in North Africa, addressed by councils called at Rome in AD 313 and Arles in 314. Constantine and Licinius became sole emperors in AD 313 (fig. 2), after Licinius's defeat of Maximinus at the Battle of Adrianople, and his killing of other members of the Tetrarch's families. Maximinus, having fled east, died at Tarsus later that year. In Rome church building began and in AD 315 Constantine celebrated his *decennalia* in the city, having campaigned again against the Germans in 314. Constantine, perhaps because of his desire to be recognised as a soldier emperor in the vein of Trajan, always viewed his accession as 25 July 306, the day he was proclaimed emperor by his troops at York, and not the formal awarding of the title Augustus on his wedding to Fausta in or around September 307. Thus, he chose to celebrate his *decennalia* in the year July 315 to July 316. His triumphal arch, dedicated to him by the Senate, was probably inaugurated on this occasion. However, the emperor, on leaving Rome after only two months there, was not to return until over a decade later in AD 326.

However, it was almost inevitable that the co-emperors found that they could not work together. A cycle of battles and confrontations, a civil war to all intents and purposes, raged from AD 316 when Constantine invaded Licinius's territory until the

2. A portrait head of Licinius recarved from the head of Hadrian on the Sacrifice to Hercules *tondo*. The Arch of Constantine, Rome. (Photo: Deutsches Archäologisches Institut Rom. Faraglia, DAIR 32.42)

latter's death, along with his son, in September AD 324, after a lull in hostilities. One later historian painted this situation as being down to their differing temperaments and characters, that Constantine 'possessed great qualities', while Licinius was cursorily dismissed as having had only 'frugality, and that, to be sure, of merely a rustic nature'.[17] The major events between these two dates were many. The Battle of Cibalae (Vinkovci in Croatia) in AD 316 and the Battle of Mardia or Campus Ardiensis (Harmanli in Bulgaria) in AD 317 both resulted in victory for Constantine. The subsequent brokered peace included the proclamation of Constantine's sons Crispus and Constantine and Licinius's son Licinius as Caesars in AD 317. Constantine is recorded as campaigning against the Sarmatians in Gaul in AD 323, and it was supposedly in pursuit of Sarmatian raiders that Constantine crossed over into Licinius's territory, thus setting up further bloody confrontation between the two. These renewed hostilities, following the depiction of Licinius as a persecutor of Christians, culminated in the Constantinian victories at the Battle of Adrianople, Bulgaria; the Battle of the Hellespont in July AD 324; and the Battle of Chrysopolis, Chalcedon, in September of that year. Finally, the abdication of Licinius was brokered by Constantia, but he was subsequently executed in early 325 at Thessalonica as was his son just a year later. Constantine then became the sole Augustus in the autumn of 324, with his son Constantius II proclaimed Caesar and Helena and Fausta made Augustae.

Thus, from AD 324 to 337 Constantine reigned as sole emperor in both western and eastern empires. It had been some time since a single individual had held so much power in the Roman world and displayed such overt dynastic ambitions for the Roman Empire's future, if not necessarily for the city of Rome itself. Indeed, in AD 324 Constantinople was founded by him as a new capital, a new Rome in the East, on the site of Byzantium. Much of Constantine's time and indeed most of his political energy were subsequently spent on the development of the new city, whose dedication he attended in May AD 330. His links with Rome were now few, though he is known to have provided endowments of land and property in the east to the new St Peter's church then being built in Rome in 326. According to Eusebius,[18] Constantine made provision for church building to be funded by the imperial treasury and expected cooperation from provincial governors and bishops in implementing this policy. Bishops were indeed actively encouraged to build new churches or to restore or enlarge existing ones.

At the Council of Nicaea in Bithynia in AD 325, where he also celebrated the start of his *vicennalia*, or twenty years' reign, Constantine attempted to forge a consensus among the assembled bishops on various ecumenical issues, including the definition of the relationship between Jesus and God, the composition of the first part of what came to be known as the Nicene Creed in situations of worship, the date of Easter, and the formulation of certain tenets of canon law. The emperor then travelled on to Rome and in July AD 326 he concluded the celebration of the *vicennalia* there. However, either just before or around the same time as this, a bizarre sequence of deaths occurred linked to familial intrigue at the imperial court or, as some later sources would have it, linked to the forming of an unnatural relationship between Constantine's first son Crispus and Crispus's mother Fausta. Whatever the reason, Crispus was tried, condemned, and put to death in Pola, Istria, and Fausta died in mysterious circumstances, reportedly in an over-hot bath. Perhaps more predictable was the death, probably murder, of the younger Licinius, son of the late emperor, nephew of Constantine and once a Caesar himself. His death, coming so soon after those of Crispus and Fausta, suggests the linking of the three together in some plot against Constantine. Nevertheless the sheer ferocity and ruthlessness of the emperor's response sits uneasily with his newly forged image as a wise, benevolent statesman. His youngest surviving son, Constans, was to be proclaimed Caesar in AD 333, perhaps an event that Constantine was clearing the way for well in advance by disposing of Crispus.

Helena, his mother, who may have had some hand in the murky events surrounding Crispus and Fausta, became more prominent in imperial life after being made Augusta in AD 324. She founded churches in the Holy Land and died in AD 328 after her return from there. The emperor is also reported to have taken a great interest in the location of the site of the Holy Sepulchre in Jerusalem and was instrumental in the building of a church there. Her search for fragments of the true cross has come down to us as first related by Aurelius Ambrosius – Bishop Ambrose of Milan – in his *De Obitu Theodosii* (*On the Death of Theodosius*), and Rufinus of Aquilea in his notes accompanying his translation of Eusebius's history. Helena was buried in a porphyry sarcophagus placed in a mausoleum on the Via Labicana in Rome, a mausoleum which Constantine may have originally intended for himself, as will be discussed further below in Chapter Five. Eusebius tells us that 'even the temporal dwelling of the blessed one [Helena] deserved no ordinary care, so with a great guard of honour she was carried up to the imperial city, and there laid in the imperial tombs.'[19]

With Constantine's considerable commitments to the running of the empire, the business of the Christian Church, his continuing attendance upon affairs in Constantinople in particular, and his having to contend with enemies within the imperial court, it is easy to forget that all of this was taking place against a backdrop of severe crisis on many of the frontiers of the empire. The pressure being exerted by movements of people from outside the borders and the growing instability within were conspiring to destabilise the very regions that Rome needed to act as buffers against attacks and incursions from disgruntled or opportunistic barbarian war bands. It is therefore no surprise that Constantine is recorded as having campaigned against the Goths in AD 332, the Sarmatians once more in AD 334, and north of the Danube in AD 336. The latter campaign is of particular interest, given that there is a great deal of Dacia-related imagery from the reigns of earlier emperors reused on the Arch of Constantine and, as will be discussed in Chapter Three, perhaps not all of this was added to the arch when first constructed. The cross-Danubian campaigns saw the construction of a new bridge across the river at Transmarisca–Daphne in Lower Moesia and another at Oescus–Sucidava in Dacia itself, as well as road construction. So important was this frontier restoration seen to be that the emperor claimed the title 'Dacicus Maximus' – Great Victor over the Dacians – as a result, and a medallion was struck that depicts the bridge over the Danube.

In AD 335 the Church Council of Tyre was held, principally to deal with issues surrounding Athanasius, Bishop of Alexandria, but it need not concern us further here. The council was immediately followed by the dedication of the church built at the supposed site of the Holy Sepulchre in Jerusalem in September of that year. Eusebius describes this event at great length and details the excavation of the purported burial cave of Christ ahead of the erection of the new temple.[20] Later in the same year Constantine's nephew Dalmatius was proclaimed Caesar, further cementing dynastic succession well into the future and perhaps suggesting an pre-emptive act by a man who perhaps realised that he did not have many more years to live. An opportunity to take stock of his life and reign, of his political and religious achievements, and to celebrate the dynastic future was provided by the celebration of Constantine's *tricennalia* – thirty years' reign – at Constantinople. A suitably effusive panegyric was delivered by the emperor's biographer and Church historian Eusebius of Caesarea. Constantine died the next year, in Nicomedia on 22 May AD 337, aged either sixty-four or sixty-five. Before his death he had arranged to be baptised on his sickbed by Eusebius, Bishop of Nicomedia. Constant alertness to the necessities of the affairs of state meant that on his death preparations were reported as being underway for a campaign against the Persians. His body was taken to his new city of Constantinople, where it lay in state before its interment in a mausoleum in the Church of the Holy Apostles, following a Christian ceremony. He received the honour of a *consecratio* in Rome and was deified, being given the title of *divus*.

Eusebius describes the news of his death reaching Rome:[21]

> The inhabitants of the imperial city and the Senate and People of Rome, when they learned of the emperor's decease, regarding the news as dreadful and the greatest possible disaster, fell into unrestrained grief. Baths and markets were closed, as were public spectacles and all the customary leisure activities of happy people. The previously easygoing went about dejected, and together they all praised the Blessed One, the Godbeloved, the one who truly deserved the Empire. Not only did they voice such cries, but took steps to honour him in death as if he were alive with dedications of his portraits. They depicted heaven in coloured paintings, and portrayed him resting in an aetherial resort above the vaults of heaven.

The *consecratio* coin issued after his death shows on the obverse the veiled head of the deceased emperor, and on the reverse Constantine in a chariot ascending to heaven, with the hand of God reaching down towards him from above. The legend *divus* or *divo* – god – also appears on this issue.[22] This image will be considered further below.

Even though Constantine had set in place plans for a smooth dynastic succession, political confusion reigned for a short time after his death, with his brothers and nephews murdered before his three surviving sons, Constantine II, Constantius II, and Constans, were formally declared Augusti. Through them, and indeed through their very names and his successors' almost interchangeable portrait types, Constantine lived on, though it was not until after the death of Eusebius of Caesarea in 339 that the posthumously published *The Life of Constantine* presented a formal account of his life and beliefs to the wider Late Antique Roman world. Until that time the character of Constantine had been presented to the Roman world in a series of images whose construction, intent, and impact will now be considered.

Forging an Image

During Constantine's reign his image was presented to the more literary-inclined sections of the Roman people through panegyric literature, which created a complex web of imagery around the person of the emperor. After his death the public image of Constantine would become very much the version propagated by Eusebius in his *Life*. Visual imagery was also, of course, important in helping to create and put across an imperial persona and such imagery, dependent on context, would be aimed at both the literate and the word-illiterate but visually literate of Rome, Italy and the provinces. As is usual for a Roman emperor, Constantine left to us a number of images of himself in various media, which help us to establish a good picture of how he wished to be presented to the Roman people and more widely throughout the empire. Official sanction of these images must be considered to have taken place in the majority of cases. Portraits of the emperor appear on coin issues and on medallions, on cameos and gemstones, and, of course, in the form of statuary, both bronze and in stone.

The period after Diocletian's establishment of the Tetrarchy saw a new, highly formal style of imperial portraiture emerge, in which formality and the position of emperor became more significant than the individuals holding office. However, this somewhat anonymising style existed side by side with more traditional personal images.[23] There was a great deal of experimentation in portrait types delivered to the Roman people and the peoples of the broader empire at this time, a positive plethora of imperial images, some conservative, some reactionary, some innovative, and others quite plainly indicative of the kind of hypermasculine posturing that had also underpinned many of the portrait types of the soldier emperors of the third century. It is possible that the young Constantine (when he was Caesar) appeared in Tetrarchic scenes on the Arch of Galerius in Thessalonica, Greece, and on the Decennalia Monument of Diocletian in Rome, but as these figures are all missing their faces and, in some cases, heads, this cannot be proven.

Constantine's portraits span a period of thirty years, from his coming to power in his mid-twenties or early thirties in AD 306 to his death in AD 337. This is the longest reign of any emperor since Augustus and it provides a sufficiently lengthy time to allow the evolution and development of his portrait types to be analysed in some detail and for an examination to be made of how he and others might have manipulated time and the ageing process to present an older appearance than might have been expected towards the start of his reign and a younger appearance towards the end. Such manipulation of portrait age by Roman emperors is well attested, the two most blatant exponents of this tactic being Augustus and Trajan. The interruption of the linearity of time and thus the consequent falsification of memory and its relationship with contemporary reality are also marked characteristics of the intention of the decorative scheme on the Arch of Constantine, as will be seen in the chapters that follow.

However, despite the length of his reign, the number of portraits that have come down to us is quite small, perhaps around fifty.[24] A chronological framework for defining the portrait types is provided by an analysis of contemporary coin issues, which have the advantage of providing dates for any significant changes or variations.[25] These will be discussed here first, followed by an analysis of the best surviving sculptural portraits of the emperor, and finally by a discussion of miniature portraits of the emperor and members of the imperial family on cameos and gemstones.

Soon after AD 306 Constantine's portrait head appeared on coin issues at Rome in the form of a mature man, very much indicative of Constantine's real age then, thirty-four or thirty-five. The portrait shows a dependable, interchangeable Tetrarch, with a square head, short, cropped hair and a beard. However, coins from his own Trier mint bore a very different representation of the emperor as a more youthful figure. Although depicted with cropped hair and a stubble beard, or on occasions with a clean-shaven face and pronounced sideburns, he was nevertheless quite boyish in appearance and not at all jaded and world-weary, as his image appeared on the coin issues from the Rome mint. The Trier coin portrait type (fig. 3) was to be the forerunner of a youthful portrait type that would coalesce around a carefully concocted suite of stylistic face, hair, and body traits from around AD 310 onwards and would appear on both the more common profile coin and medallion portraits, and on the rarer frontal coin portraits that had become acceptable under the Tetrarchy, and which indeed were markers of the style of the age.

Thinner and taller in the face than before, the clean-shaven Constantine now appeared on his coins both youthful and handsome, with a very distinctive arched fringe of hair over his brow. A more than passing resemblance to images of the mid-period (but still youthful) Augustus was unlikely to have been a mere coincidence, and the significance of this likeness would surely not have been lost on the more visually literate citizens of Rome. It may also have rung alarm bells among Constantine's fellow Tetrarchs with regard to setting out the limits of his ambition here. This was surely a deliberately deployed distancing device between Constantine and the other

3. A silver *argenteus* of Constantine, Trier mint, AD 306–7. Obverse: bust of emperor, reverse: fort gateway. British Museum, London. (Photo: Copyright Trustees of the British Museum)

Tetrarchs and soldier emperors, whose stolid, sometimes intimidatingly aggressive, portraits defined the era of crisis of the third and fourth centuries. This is not to say that Constantine somehow feminised his image. Indeed, if all visual images of the emperor from portraits and other artworks, including the Arch of Constantine, are put together and examined as a group alongside literary images of the emperor from contemporary panegyrics, and historical accounts, then he can be seen to be no less hypermasculine an imperial figure than other emperors of the third and fourth centuries.

This Augustan-style, classicising image on gemstones, coins, and medallions was also to become the template for sculptural portraits in both bronze and stone, and most surviving sculpted portraits of Constantine present minor variations on the image of a mature but youthful civilian emperor with idealised features. Of course, an exception is known and will be discussed further below. Later in his reign the portrait head on coins acquired a regal diadem, not unlike the diadem of Alexander the Great adopted by Augustus and successor emperors of the Julio-Claudian dynasty, and for a while Constantine on coins adopted the bearing of a Hellenistic king before resorting to the earlier Augustan model, albeit with a more elaborate style of hair.

After the defeating of Maxentius at the Battle of the Milvian Bridge in AD 312 Constantine would have been able to directly oversee or at least approve the portrait type presented on coins issued by the mints at Rome and Ostia, which would now have fallen under his control. Certainly this would have allowed the Augustan-styled portrait types of coins to become better circulated in Rome itself. From the period when Constantine was obliged to at least maintain the impression of solidarity with Licinius in the virtual Dyarchy – rule of two – that existed between AD 312 and 325, he was not averse to reverting to the use of a more military portrait on some of his coin issues, appearing in profile in a cuirass with the god Sol as protector, or in a high-crested helmet, or in full-frontal pose in military dress like other former Tetrarchs. On the obverse of the gold Ticinum medallion of AD 313 in the Cabinet des Médailles, Bibliothèque Nationale, Paris, Constantine appears in profile accompanied by Sol, identifiable by reason of his rayed crown. Constantine is youthful, wears a laurel crown, and is dressed in a cuirass. He holds a spear over his shoulder and a shield decorated with an image of a solar chariot in his other hand. On the reverse there is depicted the imperial arrival, with the mounted emperor accompanied by a winged victory holding a laurel wreath, and a soldier with a standard.

Once he was sole emperor, he adopted a range of coin portraits that shared the aim of presenting him as some kind of idealised Hellenistic ruler, crossed, of course, with Augustus. However, some authorities see a change in some of the coin and medallion portrait types after AD 333, when Constantine would have been in his sixties, with the lean, youthful appearance finally usurped by a face that bears some evidence of the passage of time, even if the heavier jaw, fleshiness, and pronounced jowls are those of a middle-aged man rather than a more elderly one as he would have been then. The posthumously issued *consecratio*, or consecration, coins also depict the late emperor as an early middle-aged man with a veiled head on the obverse, and on the reverse Constantine in a *quadriga*, or four-horse chariot, being welcomed to heaven by the hand of God (fig. 4). The coins' legends stress not only his consecration as a god but also his revered memory, and the important fact in terms of supporting the dynastic accession of his sons that he was *Pater Augusti* – father of the Augusti. Just as family lineage was stressed here and on the Ada Cameo which will be discussed below, it must be remembered that this theme also appeared on a number of the coin issues. In one example Constantine stands between two of his sons who are being crowned by Virtus and Victory while their father is being crowned by the hand of God emerging from a cloud, and in another he is seated on a throne between his two sons. The emperor is nimbate and all three hold spears, showing their solidarity in protecting Rome and her empire. Constantine even appears on coins with his first son Crispus, who was to be executed on his father's orders only a few years later (fig. 5).

Now that the chronological framework for dating the various portrait styles adopted by Constantine has been discussed, attention will be turned towards an examination of the portrait sculpture of the emperor.[26] Maybe a dozen sculptural portraits of Constantine are recognised today, a number of them being idealised in a manner already seen on the coins and medallions. The most significant portrait sculptures will be discussed here, including the colossal stone statue of Constantine that would have been placed in the remodelled Basilica Nova; the head of another colossal stone statue of the emperor from York, a fitting place for such a statue given that this is where he was proclaimed emperor by his troops while on campaign in Britain; a huge bronze head of the emperor and other fragments from the same statue in the collections of the Musei Capitolini in Rome; a full-length stone statue of a cuirass-wearing Constantine that now stands on the balustrade around the Campidoglio in Rome; a stone portrait head in the Metropolitan Museum of Art, New York; another stone portrait head in the Musée du Bardo, Tunis; and a bronze head from Naissus, Constantine's birthplace, in Serbia, which is now in the National Museum, Belgrade. A further small alabaster head of Constantine from the collections of the British Museum is also illustrated here. An attempt will be made to discuss these portraits in chronological order, as far as that is strictly possible.

The York head is often omitted from general discussions of Constantine's portraits, perhaps because of its finding in such a remote outpost of the empire as northern Britannia, with a hint and taint of provincialising style attached to it, and yet it is probably the earliest portrait head of the emperor that has come down to us (plate 5). This twice life-size head that would have been part of a larger statue, not necessarily all of stone, is today quite seriously damaged by water erosion, but is otherwise intact. It was found in the nineteenth century, close to the site of the *principia*, or headquarters building, within the Roman legionary fortress, and it is likely that the statue of the emperor from which this head derived was set up there in commemoration of Constantine's declaration as emperor at York, perhaps inside or outside that very building, perhaps in that very year AD 306 or shortly thereafter. The portrait is of a clean-shaven man with a noticeably thick neck and plump chin, well-defined cheekbones, smooth features, small ears and large but not pronounced eyes. His nose is unfortunately damaged. His hair is cut short but comes partially over the ears and is combed over the forehead in a fringe reminiscent of the hairstyle

4. A gold *solidus* of Constantine. Rome mint, AD 337. Obverse: bust of veiled emperor, reverse: Constantine ascending to heavens in a chariot. British Museum, London. (Photo: Copyright Trustees of the British Museum)

5. A gold *solidus* of Constantine. Siscia mint, AD 317. Obverse: bust of emperor, reverse: Constantine and Crispus. British Museum, London. (Photo: Copyright Trustees of the British Museum)

of Augustus. He wears what appears to be an oak-leaf crown or *corona civica*. Thus we appear to have here a portrait that crosses the standardised image of the bull-necked military emperor, so common in the third century and occasionally borrowed as a style in Tetrarchic portraiture, and the classicising image of Augustus. Even by the time of his *quinquennalia*, or five years' reign, the coin portraits had not entirely moved on from referencing Tetrarchic types, as well as Augustus. Indeed, the fine, 2-foot-high Carrara marble portrait head of Constantine found in a Roman sewer during excavations in the Forum in 2005 would appear to be a recarved head of the *quinquennalia* type.[27]

It has been suggested that the colossal stone statue of a 30-foot-tall seated Constantine, which would have been placed in the remodelled Basilica of Maxentius, the Basilica Nova, could be a reworked statue of Maxentius that itself had originally been a portrait of Hadrian.[28] The statue would have been what is called acrolithic, that is a figure with only the extremities made of stone, the main body either being wooden or, as in this case, draped with bronze. The surviving parts of the statue still contrive to indicate just what a powerful piece of sculpture this would have been, and consist of the head and neck, a foot, part of a leg, part of an arm, a hand with pointed finger, and part of the chest in the form of the left breast. The larger pieces are displayed in the courtyard of the Museo del Palazzo dei Conservatori, off Campidoglio in central Rome, where they are much photographed by visitors to the museum (figs 6, 7, 8, see also plate 38). The statue fragments were found in the fifteenth century during clearance work in the west apse inside the shell of the Basilica Nova, and most probably date to the rededication of the building around AD 313.

6. Fragments of a colossal statue of Constantine. Museo del Palazzo dei Conservatori, Rome. (Photo: Author)

7. The head of a colossal statue of
Constantine. Museo del Palazzo dei
Conservatori, Rome. (Photo: Author)

8. A foot from a colossal statue of Constantine. Museo del Palazzo dei Conservatori, Rome.
(Photo: Author)

The Basilica Nova giant head of Constantine is more or less unique among the surviving portraits, and not only because of its sheer size. Everything about it is somehow exaggerated. Perhaps the most striking aspects of the rather rectangular head are the rendering of the immense, forward-staring eyes – with their deep-set pupils and irises and pronounced upper and lower lids that make them the focal point of the face – and the pronounced nose, with its flaring nostrils. In contrast, the mouth is small, almost pursed; the chin strong and jutting. There is no facial hair, other than the stylistically rendered eyebrows. The head is capped with an improbably full cap of hair, its deeply drilled bunches of locks making it look more like a kind of skullcap rather than a natural but styled growth. It is possible that the need to create a recognisable image almost in shorthand, given the problems with viewers at some distance removed from the statue's head, might have led to a necessary simplification of the emperor's physiognomy and the creation of an image much noted today for its direct, almost hypnotised gaze forward into an uncertain future. It is likely that many of the modern viewers of the head are familiar with it from photographs where the photographer has taken the shot from directly in front, emphasising the forward-looking glance of the eyes. Often, reproduced photographs are shot from a height equal to the mid-point of the face, again perhaps over stressing the frontality of the portrait and thus its other-worldliness. Ancient viewers would, of course, have been looking up at this face from any number of different viewpoints – from in front of the statue or from the sides – and it may be that its transcendent vacuity is something of a modern construct.

The head was traditional for the time in that it incorporated some elements of the abstract anonymity of Tetrarchic portraiture, yet it also incorporated enough in the way of individual facial features, like the large nose and the tell-tale hairstyle, to allow the viewer to identify this as a likeness in some way of Constantine. In contrast to the head, with its abstract appearance, the parts of the surviving hands and limbs are quite naturalistic, with tensing muscles present and the implied rendering of the bones beneath the skin.

There is a general consensus that the Basilica Nova statue took the form of a seated, bare-chested Constantine in the guise of Jupiter.[29] The statue obviously held something in its hand but we do not know what. It is possible that it held a sceptre with Christian insignia but this is unlikely, though this could be the very statue that Eusebius discusses in his *Life*. Holes in the head of the statue for the attachment of a diadem suggest that the statue was altered, indeed updated, sometime after AD 324 when this item became a standard feature of Constantine's image.

Given the great significance that seems to have been attached to colour in the art of the Constantinian period it is highly likely that the white marble of the statue's head, breast, arms, and legs was intended to contrast with a draped mantle, cast in bronze. Some authorities believe that a patina was applied to the exposed flesh areas of the statue to make it appear as if it was made of ivory, and that the draped robe and attached accoutrements would have been gilded. The textural effect of the mixing and blending of these two different raw materials would also have added a new element to the overall appreciation of the work, and its lighting would have afforded further opportunities for the theatrical aspects of the statue to be emphasised through the exploration of its very materiality. It has been suggested that, while at first glance the surviving individual marble pieces of this statue appear to be the same, there is actually a difference between some of them, in terms of the colour and graining of the marble, such that the viewer might have been able to notice. This once more suggests a deliberate strategy of incorporating the happy accidents in marble variation that is an element in the appearance of parts of the Arch of Constantine, as will be seen below in Chapter Two.

Even though the head of the statue has been recarved once, if not twice, it is nevertheless an astonishingly powerful work of art. The recarving of portrait heads of former emperors to produce portraits of Constantine always seems to have been undertaken with a great deal of skill, demonstrated firstly in the careful selection of appropriate original models from which to work and secondly in terms of the sheer quality of the finished product. This rather argues against the old theory that there was a shortage of highly skilled sculptors in Late Antiquity and that this largely accounts for the 'decline' in the form and quality of art at this time.

The distant, faraway look of the emperor in the colossal portrait head and to some extent on the York head is part of a Late Antique strategy for presenting the imperial personage as transcendent. This image, linked to the broader presentation of the figure of the emperor through the theatre of formally conducted and strictly coordinated ceremony, is well illustrated by Ammianus's well-known account of Constantius II's ceremonial arrival, or *adventus*, in Rome:

> He kept the gaze of his eyes straight ahead and turned his face neither to right nor to left but (as if he were a statue) neither did he nod when the wheel jolted nor was he ever seen to spit, or to wipe or rub his face, or move his hands about.[30]

Of course, Constantine's portrait also appears on the arch around about the same time (figs 9 and 10). On the boar hunt *tondo* his portrait is recut from a head of Hadrian, and indeed this is the best surviving image of the emperor's face on the arch. There are two further portraits recut from heads of Hadrian, two from heads of Trajan, and one original in the Constantinian Siege of Verona scene. The other figures of Constantine in the contemporary reliefs have all lost their heads. The images of Marcus Aurelius reused on the arch today bear relatively modern heads, and these repairs confusingly make him appear like Trajan, when the first recarving would have transformed him, too, into Constantine. The boar hunt *tondo* Constantine is quite youthful-looking, despite then being in his forties, with a lean face and his short hair combed over his brow, and, perhaps most significantly, he is clean-shaven.

A stone portrait head in the Musée du Bardo, Tunis, most closely resembles the images of Constantine in the surviving recarved heads on the arch and on coins of the period AD 312–24, and therefore must itself date from this time. Another surviving example of this type is known from Rome and others are in collections in Madrid and Copenhagen.

The full-length stone statue of an armed, cuirass-wearing Constantine wearing an oak-leaf crown, or *corona civica*, that now stands on the balustrade around the

Above left: 9. The head of Hadrian recarved as Constantine, boar hunt *tondo*. The Arch of Constantine, Rome. (Photo: Deutsches Archäologisches Institut Rom. Faraglia, DAIR 32.36)

Above right: 10. The head of Trajan recarved as Constantine, west wall of central passageway. The Arch of Constantine, Rome. Plaster cast from the Museo della Civiltà Romana, Rome (Photo: Deutsches Archäologisches Institut Rom. Schwanke, DAIR 82.1106)

Campidoglio in Rome probably dates to the period after AD 317 when Crispus and Constantine II became Caesars (plate 8). It is unusual in the canon of Constantine's statue portraits in that it is full length and that it is militaristic. It has been suggested that this statue, along with the one of Constantine II – also on the balustrade – and a third statue of Constantius II at the Lateran, was recut from three out of four statues of Tetrarchs, and they were subsequently displayed together, perhaps as a rare dynastic group, possibly in Constantine's baths on the Quirinal Hill, put there in AD 326 to honour his *vicennalia*. Another Constantinian dynastic group, this time made of porphyry, may have been set up in Alexandria in the AD 330s.

The Tetrarchic vision that every emperor looked the same – as demonstrated, for instance, by the Tetrarchic porphyry statue group now built into the outer wall of the basilica in Piazza San Marco in Venice, relocated there from the Philadelphion in Constantinople – was intended as a means to suggest solidarity among the Augusti and Caesars, and stability by their similarity to each other and, by implication, to other, future Tetrarchs. Thus perhaps Constantine can become Trajan on the arch sculptures; alternatively he could become Hadrian, or Marcus Aurelius. The Roman viewer had perhaps become accustomed in a relatively short space of time to the easy interchangeability of emperors' images.

That there was a certain amount of interchangeability in appearance between a number of the Tetrarchic emperors, and subsequently between Constantine and his sons and successors, is reflected in the confusion among academics about the specific identities of some of the images just discussed above, with the Lateran statue often misidentified as Constantine rather than Constantius II. Again, the colossal bronze head in the Museo del Palazzo dei Conservatori in Rome discussed below is sometimes identified as being of Constantius II rather than his father Constantine.

Returning to the chronological survey of Constantinian portrait sculptures, the next significant work in line is probably the stone portrait head in the Metropolitan Museum of Art, New York (plate 6). Here we see a youthful, thin-faced emperor but with quite pronounced, large eyes, especially the pupils and lower lids, and with a very prominent nose. The hair of the eyelids is rendered in an unusual stylised manner, with individual hairs delineated. The Augustan comb-over is of thick, full-bodied hair, again somewhat stylised in the clumping of locks. He looks straight ahead into the distance. He seems both real and yet somehow unreal at the same time. This head is less easy to date than some of the others and probably was carved sometime between AD 324 and AD 337. The bronze head from Naissus, Constantine's birthplace in Serbia, which is now in the National Museum, Belgrade, bears the diadem familiar from coin portraits after AD 324, as well features such as the youthful face and short hair on the back of the neck, which probably places it before AD 332. The eyes are more upraised than is the case with the New York head, for instance, and the face altogether blockier and less rounded.

The massive cast bronze head of the emperor in the collections of the Musei del Palazzo dei Conservatori in Rome is generally accepted as being part of a five-times-larger-than-life-size work, of which the left hand and a globe surmounted by a spike, also in the museum's collections, were also part (plate 7). It has been suggested that this work may have been a reworking of an earlier imperial statue, perhaps even the colossus of Nero from the Domus Aurea, or Golden House,[31] although frankly this seems highly unlikely in the case of this bronze head. Rather, it should perhaps be accepted that this is a Late Antique work on a par with any other cast bronze portrait from the Roman world in terms of the skill required to produce the finished work and indeed in the artistic merit of the finished work itself. It is difficult to talk about a broad decline in artistic production in the late third and fourth centuries when a piece as vital and powerful as this could still be modelled and cast. The face is of a man older than the one portrayed in the colossal stone statue from the Basilica Nova. His eyes and pupils are still pronounced, but not as much, and his nose is smaller, more in keeping with the small closed lips. The chin is still pronounced, the eyebrows rendered abstractly. The hair has become even more elaborate. It falls down over the forehead to end in a wavy fringe, it covers the ears, again with that same fringe, and it comes down over the neck at the back. The ageing face and abundant hair in a style that is some way distant from the Augustan comb-over finds parallels on certain coin issues of the later AD 330s, and this work therefore probably represents the older emperor, but one who is still much younger in appearance than he would have been in the flesh; in AD 335, for instance, he would have been sixty-three or sixty-four years old.

Quite a significant number of cameos and gemstones are known that bear portraits of Constantine or his family, a number of which will be discussed here, as their imagery has interesting affinities to the image of the emperor as conveyed by portrait sculpture and coin portraits.[32] Even if luxury items such as cameos and other gems had a very specific context and limited circulation beyond the imperial family and close followers, nevertheless they are important signifiers of imperial ambition and self-image at all periods when the cutting of gemstone portraits was popular. The cameos are particularly interesting in that to some extent the Constantinian use of this medium to present individual or family portraits to others at court, or as diplomatic gifts, harks back to the time of Augustus and the Julio-Claudian emperors, and to such famous examples as the Gemma Augustea and the Grand Camée de France. The three best-known Constantinian cameos are known respectively as the Ada Cameo, the Dutch Great Cameo, and the Hermitage Cameo. Each of these will now be discussed in turn.

The so-called Ada Cameo, now mounted on the cover of the Ada Gospels in the Stadtbibliothek, Trier, Germany, depicts a dynastic family group thought to be Constantine, Helena, Constantius II, Fausta, and Constantine II. Dated to between AD 318 and 323, the family group appear as more or less head-and-shoulder portraits in the background of the cameo, with two large imperial eagles with outstretched wings dominating the foreground. The claustrophobic nature of the scene, with the figures bunched together as if in an enclosed space, probably reflects the fact that they are most likely depicted in an imperial box at the circus in Rome. Most interestingly, it has been suggested that the Ada Cameo is not an original Constantinian era piece, rather that it represents the recutting of a Julio-Claudian cameo of Claudius; his fourth wife, Agrippina the Younger; their son Nero; his daughter Claudia Octavia; and his son Britannicus, reused and recontextualised in a manner not unlike the use of *spolia* in the Arch of Constantine.[33] The recutting of this particular cameo will be discussed further below in Chapter Six.

In a similar vein, it has been suggested that the small aquamarine head of the empress Sabina, wife of Hadrian, in the Museo Archeologico Nazionale in Venice, has been reworked to become a portrait of Helena, and indeed that the best-known full-length, seated stone portrait sculpture of Helena in the Musei Capitolini in Rome is itself a reworking of a portrait of an Antonine empress, perhaps Faustina or Lucilla.

The large agate cameo in the Royal Dutch collection known as the Great Cameo takes the form of a fully classicising scene of imperial triumph and harmony that surely owes a stylistic debt to Augustan and Julio-Claudian gem cutting. The imperial family – Constantine, Fausta, Crispus and a second female figure who might be identified as Constantine's grandmother Claudia – rides in a triumphal chariot pulled by two bearded centaurs, one of whom holds a trophy over his shoulder while trampling underfoot two bare-headed and clean-shaven enemies, one of them appearing to be wearing a Roman military tunic. In the foreground a *cantharus* or wine vessel lies on its side on the ground. In the background a winged Victory spectacularly shoots across the sky in the direction of the imperial party; she holds out in both hands a victor's garland with which to crown the emperor. Constantine, caught in profile, appears on the gem wearing a laurel wreath and civilian rather than military garb, he holds in his right hand a spear or thunderbolt aimed at the enemies ahead of the chariot. Fausta is shown with veiled head, holding a corn ear or poppy head in her hand, perhaps as a symbol of dynastic fertility and continuity. Crispus, though clearly still a boy, is dressed in a military cuirass and helmet, and holds his left hand ready on his sword scabbard. Again, this might be taken as an individual image of dynastic readiness even into the next generation. The final figures to need identification are the two men being trampled by one of the centaurs drawing the chariot. This is obviously a standard way to portray the fate of enemies of Rome and the power of the emperor; however, on most occasions the enemies being killed and humiliated in this way are quite obviously barbarians, even at this period most commonly bearded northern barbarians. But given the appearance of the two overcome foes it can only be assumed that they are intended in this context to represent Maxentius's army defeated by Constantine at the Battle of the Milvian Bridge in AD 312 and shown being decimated by Constantine's forces on the contemporary frieze on the Arch of Constantine.

The sardonyx cameo now in the Hermitage Museum, St Petersburg, Russia, carries a depiction of Constantine being crowned by a female personification of a Tyche of Constantinople (plate 14). The emperor appears dressed in a cuirass, in other words he is represented here as a soldier emperor, and looks quite youthful and not unlike the young Augustus. Constantine is here both a powerful military figure and a city builder, as indicated by the presence of the Tyche, a dual role that he was keen to be associated with in both Rome and Constantinople. The piece is purely classical in conception and composition.

In addition to these three canonical cameos there are a number of other significant cameos and gemstones that probably date to the era of the Constantinian dynasty. An amethyst intaglio in a collection in Berlin could bear the portrait either of Constantine or, more favoured by academics, Constantius II. In either case, the rich imperial purple of a gem such as this was obviously highly significant. In the National Museum in Belgrade, Serbia, is a fragmentary sardonyx cameo depicting a mounted emperor riding his horse over a battlefield strewn with corpses of barbarians and with a Roman soldier taking a prisoner to one side, possibly to execute him. Though the cuirass-wearing emperor is bare-headed, he can be seen to be wearing a diadem. He brandishes a spear as if joining the battle himself. The imperial personage on the Belgrade cameo is most usually suggested to be Constantius I, but there is still the possibility that this Alexander-style figure could in fact be his son Constantine. The Content Collection agate cameo is another fragmentary gemstone that emphasises the solidarity of the imperial Tetrarchy in all likelihood, by the depiction of two emperors meeting, their hands locked in a symbolic handshake while an imperial eagle stands by to emphasise the imperial nature of the scene. A later inscription identifies the men as Augustus and Mark Antony, though the gem is quite obviously of a much later date. While there is the possibility that the two men meeting could be Constantine and Licinius, proving this would not be possible.

If the image of Constantine presented to us by the history of Eusebius shows a devout and serious man driven in his later life by his admiration of the Christian message, a striking vision, and a deathbed conversion, then the portraits of the emperor present another, less complex though equally interesting, picture to us. Eusebius's Constantine is a man of certainty and singular purpose. The Constantine represented by images in Roman imperial portraits is a man of initial uncertainty and in denial. Thus the evidence provided by the portrait sculptures, the images on coins and medallions, and those on cameos and gemstones would seem to indicate a number of different stages in the development of Constantinian image making as well as in the progressive development of the image of the emperor. In his early political career as a Tetrarch, when he was a Caesar he would have had little veto over the type of image of himself, produced at the behest of his more senior Augustus. If we had been able to see the now lost heads of the imperial Tetrarchic figures on the Arch of Galerius and Diocletian's Decennalia Monument, it is likely that we would not be able to distinguish Constantine from his fellow Caesar of the time. When more able to exert some authority in the field of imperial image making, he oversaw the creation of a hybrid image that was partly Tetrarchic, and partly classicising in terms of its looking back to the Augustan era for inspiration; together, the tension created by these two strands of influence would have allowed the viewer to discern some degree of individualism in the person of the emperor and thus perhaps in his political agenda. That the Tetrarchic influence was soon sloughed off and the model of the youthful Augustus accepted as the template for Constantinian portraiture for most of the rest of his reign would probably have come as no surprise to the astute viewer of Roman imperial art as a lightning conductor for changing political ideology. It was only relatively late in the emperor's reign that some acceptance was made of the inevitable passage of the years and of the consequent ravages made by time to the human body. This older Constantine still possessed the bearing and gravitas of an Augustus or an Alexander; he was simply slightly older, if not actually portrayed as being as old as the emperor was at the time. The manipulation of time and memory in this way was a very public form of denial that had nevertheless worked as a stratagem for both Augustus and Trajan before him and which worked equally well for Constantine.

Some of the surviving images of Constantine survive, probably for the very reason that, when rediscovered in the Middle Ages and Renaissance period, such images were seen as fitting tributes to 'a Christian emperor' in a time of great piety, and therefore they were deemed worthy of retention. The same applies to the Ada Cameo, which indeed was further recontextualised, indeed Christianised, by its incorporation into the elaborate, rich decoration of the cover of the Ada Gospels manuscript. Not all images thought to be of Constantine actually turned out to be, and indeed it is known that we owe the survival of the superb full-size gilded bronze equestrian statue of Marcus Aurelius now in the Musei Capitolini in Rome, of which there is now a convincing replica in the Campidoglio outside, to the successive Popes who mistook this image of Marcus showing clemency to a now lost barbarian foe as an image of a bearded, beatific Constantine giving a blessing.

However, it is perhaps the artistic message conveyed by the artworks on the major monument of his reign constructed in Rome that tells us more about Constantine's place in the history of the city, and this will be the theme of the next three chapters of the book.

2
Monument and Materiality

In the previous chapter the main events of Constantine's life were outlined in as much they contributed towards the creation of an image of the emperor for readers of the main Roman historical accounts of his life. His image as presented through coin and statuary portraiture and through imperial portraits on carved cameos and gemstones was also examined. In this chapter attention will be concentrated on presenting a summary description of the Arch of Constantine[1] and of both its immediate setting and its broader position within the Valley of the Colosseum in Rome. It will very much draw upon the work of Mark Wilson Jones in describing the form and architecture of the monument[2] and on that of Elizabeth Marlowe in terms of assessing the value of her phenomenological approach to reconstructing the arch's place in the urban topography of this area of Rome.[3]

Fabric and Form

The Arch of Constantine is a triple-bayed arch built of a grey-white Proconnesian marble, with an attic of brickwork revetted with marble (fig. 11). It stands just short of 69 feet high, and is almost 85 feet wide and 24¼ feet deep. Its central archway is just under 38 feet high and 21¼ feet wide, the two side arches both being 24¼ feet in height and just over 11 feet in width. It contains a staircase within the thickness of the arch, accessed by a door above present ground level at the west end. All four sides of the arch bear decorative artwork, which though arranged in a symmetrical manner is relatively understated. In terms of the integrity of the overall artistic programme of the arch, as a generalisation it can be said that the south main facade is dominated by a group of military scenes and the north main facade by a group of civic scenes. The individual scenes on specific *tondi*, reliefs, or frieze fragments will be described in detail in Chapters Three and Four below. On both front and rear long faces of the arch are four detached Corinthian columns resting on pedestal bases, with projecting entablature over the columns and each topped by a figure of a Dacian captive. There is absolutely no doubt that this arch as a structure is directly modelled on the nearby Arch of Septimius Severus, as will be discussed below.

The different materials used in the construction of the arch provide contrasts in both colour and texture and thus stimulate the overall sensory viewing experience. For

11. Giovanni Battista Piranesi, *The Arch of Constantine, Rome*, 1750s–60s. (Photo: Slide Archive of Former School of Continuing Studies, Birmingham University)

instance, set against the main body of the arch, which is of grey-white marble, are a deep-green porphyry frieze on the main entablature and around the inset roundels, or *tondi*, are revetments of purple porphyry. The freestanding columns are of *giallo antico* or Numidian yellow marble, though one of these was removed to the church of St John Lateran in the late sixteenth century and replaced with a purple marble column. The Dacian statues are of purple-veined *pavonazetto* marble or Phrygian purple and stand on green-grey *cippolino* or Carystian marble bases. A detailed photogrammetric survey of the arch carried out in the 1990s, coupled with a stone-by-stone examination of its fabric, produced an even more complex picture of the sources of the white and coloured marbles selected and used.[4] However, the principal finding of this meticulous survey work was the astonishing discovery that every stone in the arch was an item of what archaeologists call *spolia*, quite literally 'plunder', that is an architectural fragment or part of a frieze, a statue or a sculpture that has been removed from its original location and context and reused in whole or in part. Artworks dating to the reigns of the emperors Trajan, Hadrian, and Marcus Aurelius were reused on the arch. The use of *spolia* was a genuine phenomenon in Late Antiquity and was widespread throughout the Roman world; this will be discussed at length in a number of sections of this book, particularly in Chapter Six.

The use of *spolia* in architecture in the later Roman period was by then such a culturally embedded practice that its use on the Arch of Constantine would have probably passed without comment in the Rome of its time.[5] Yet the use of coloured marbles on the arch was a strategy that would have resulted in the newly completed arch being a highly novel structure in the context of Roman imperial monuments in the Colosseum valley and the Roman Forum. Not only would the number of different coloured marbles have created unique effects, but in some cases it might have been expected that the veined marbles would have created abstract patterns through the direction of the veining. Unfortunately, this effect cannot be appreciated when viewing the arch today, though rain does help to bring out colour on some parts of the monument. The significance of the colours chosen cannot necessarily be articulated today, though it is undoubtedly true that, in Late Antiquity, colour perception played a significant role in cultural production and in the creation of memorable, often spiritual images. The brightly coloured *opus sectile* panels from the Mausoleum of Junius Bassus in Rome,[6] the purple-red porphyry sarcophagi of Helena and Constantina, and the sparkling wall mosaics of the early churches in Ravenna and elsewhere all attest to this.

Detailed architectural analysis of parts of the arch structure have shown that though there were evidently constructional problems that had to be sorted by *in situ* adjustments here and there, such problems may well have been inherent in the use of *spolia* for new building schemes. For instance, the imperfect fit of the columns, the discontinuity in some of the mouldings, and the mixing of Carrara and Proconnesian marble, both white marbles for sure but the latter often with blue-grey striations. Nevertheless it can be said that 'the whole building resonates with proportional elegance',[7] being built to a mathematical formula of proportions based on the column heights.

The arch as we see it today though is not complete. As has been pointed out by Jás Elsner,[8] further sculptures in bronze probably adorned its top, there would have been inlays of coloured marble around the Hadrianic *tondi*, and quite possibly a coloured marble frieze in either green porphyry or even *opus sectile* work running right round the top of the arch's middle section beneath the cornice on which the attic stands. The sheer pictorial skill of Late Antique *opus sectile* artists, as evidenced by the well-known artworks depicting a chariot parading at the circus and a tiger killing a calf from the Basilica of Junius Bassus on the Esquiline Hill in Rome,[9] could have meant that such a frieze depicted some further aspect of Constantine's life or reign to balance the story that can be put together from the surviving artworks on the arch. A battle against barbarian foes would certainly have added balance to the curious jarring juxtaposition of past emperors defeating the enemy without, in the form of barbarian peoples, while Constantine is shown only battling enemies within, in the form of Maxentius and his army.

Of course, as with all Roman sculpture the question needs to be asked if the *spolia* artworks and the Constantinian frieze were painted. As is usually the case when this question is asked, we can only really reply that it might have been but that there is no evidence that it was. Indeed it would appear that colour effects on the monument might have been created by the use of a number of different-coloured marbles and the remote possibility that there might have been a coloured *opus sectile* frieze on the lost part of the monument.

As has already been noted, the form of the Arch of Constantine was directly modelled on the pre-existing Arch of Septimius Severus in the Roman Forum, built around 100 years earlier in AD 203[10] (plate 9). Detailed comparative architectural analysis has shown that both the Arch of Constantine and the Arch of Septimius Severus 'have triple arches with four columnar ressauts [projections] on the main façades, both have the imposts [arch rests] of the central vault aligned with the keystone of the side aisles; both display a similar sculptural theme … as is particularly apparent in the reprise of the sculpted pedestals and of the torch-bearing Winged Victories in the spandrels … in addition both arches have the same column size, the same width for the central fornix [arch], and the same overall height.'[11]. In other words the architects of the Constantinian arch themselves made a highly detailed study of the Severan arch, measured and calculated its dimensions and proportions, and drew up architectural plans that produced not a direct copy but rather a new structure based on the template of the old one.

In fact, though, there were significant differences between the two arches. Firstly, the displaying of artworks in the form of the Trajanic battle scenes on the inner side walls of the central passage of the Arch of Constantine was more a reference in terms of influence to the nearby Arch of Titus. There, the passageway walls were decorated with relief panels depicting on one side the display of spoils in a triumphal parade and on the other the emperor in his triumphal chariot. The inside passage walls of the Severan arch were undecorated and the central passageway was linked to the side passages by arched openings, a feature not replicated on the Constantinian arch. The emphasis in the case of the Arch of Constantine was on the viewer to experience the artworks in the central passageway by moving through it from one end to another and there was thus no requirement for such linking openings in the Constantinian arch. Secondly, although the overall heights of the Severan and Constantinian arches were the same, the attic of the Arch of Constantine was taller, thus perhaps allowing the lengthy and highly important inscription to be seen more clearly from ground level, and for the Dacian statues and panels here again to be more clearly seen, standing well above the cornice. The Constantinian arch was also slightly slimmer in size, perhaps to allow the important propagandist artworks in the sides of the central passage to be lit more efficiently by natural light. An analysis of the Corinthian columns of the later arch, whose proportions are unusual for Late Antiquity but not for earlier times, has shown that they were evidently reused columns, perhaps intended to mimic the earlier columns on the Severan arch; the Arch of Constantine, in certain aspects of its architectural design, again provides a historical reference back to the Roman past.

While there would have been good topographical reasons for the Constantinian arch to mirror the Severan arch, it might also have been the case that the earlier arch might have been chosen as a basic design model because of Severus's reputation as a restorer of Roman imperial legitimacy by his defeat of an illegitimate regime. This is something that Constantine might also claim to have done and that the Roman Senate was certainly advertising as his achievement in the inscriptions on the arch, as will be discussed below.

Given that the Arch of Constantine was specifically designed to mirror in size the Arch of Septimius Severus and thus follow the traditional broad design of historic Roman triumphal arches in general, the bronze statues that would have stood above the attic would most likely have been either of the emperor in a triumphal four-horse chariot, or *quadriga*, or of an equestrian statue of the emperor, perhaps trampling a symbolic barbarian under the horse's front hoof or, less likely, a prostrate Maxentius. The latter image, though perhaps singularly appropriate, would have been altogether too provocative an image to display here in the very heart of Rome, where Maxentius's firm identification with the mother city of the empire would most likely at one time have been a highly popular stance. The argument that there was in fact no statue on top of the arch cannot be proven to be wrong, just as the one time presence of such statues cannot be proven either, though the further argument that there is evidence from Renaissance paintings and a later drawing that the arch was simply topped by a parapet appears unlikely.

The triumphal arch is one of the type monuments of Roman imperial material culture. Though the form of such arches might have varied, sometimes considerably, there is nonetheless a direct line that can be drawn from the arches of Augustus right up to the Arch of Constantine, the last of these monuments. It is perhaps unsurprising that the arch form was chosen to commemorate Constantine's victory over Maxentius because of its highly traditional nature. The alternative choice of a commemorative column would not have allowed the reuse of the historic artworks that form the linking narrative content of the Arch of Constantine and thus might have been deemed an unsuitable vehicle for the messages that the Senate of Rome and Constantine wished to communicate to the citizens of Rome. That the honorary column was very much a monument still seen as appropriate to Late Antique times is demonstrated by the building of the Column of Theodosius in his forum at Constantinople in the AD 380s and by the Column of Arcadius, again in Constantinople, started in AD 401.

By Divine Inspiration

It is crucial to understand that the various dedicatory inscriptions on the attic and elsewhere on the fabric of the Arch of Constantine would have been seen as equally important as the design and form of the arch itself, its architecture in other words, and the artworks that adorn it. Together, these three elements created a whole, and yet in many studies of the arch one or another of these elements is often omitted from discussion or briefly glossed over. The architecture of the monument has already been discussed above and will be returned to below, and analysis of the artistic programme of the arch will form the basis of Chapters Three and Four. Discussion here will now therefore be concentrated on the dedicatory inscriptions.

The long main inscription on the attic, which is the same on both the north side and south side, reads:

IMP CAES FL CONSTANTINO MAXIMO P F AUGUSTO S P Q R QUOD INSTINCTU DIVINITATIS MENTIS MAGNITUDINE CUM EXERCITU SUO TAM DE TYRANNO QUAM DE OMNI EIUS FACTIONE UNO TEMPORE IUSTIS REM PUBLICAM ULTUS EST ARMIS ARCUM TRIUMPHIS INSIGNEM DICAVIT. (plate 10)

This reads in translation as: 'To the emperor Flavius Constantine, the Great, pious and fortunate, the Senate and People of Rome, because by divine inspiration and his own great spirit with his army on both the tyrant and all his faction at once in rightful battle he avenged the State, dedicated this arch as a mark of triumph'.[12] This is a long inscription, though shorter than that on the Arch of Septimius Severus. However, the Severan inscription is much taken up with establishing the emperor's ancestry and the listing of his offices held, detail of a kind more or less omitted from the Constantinian inscription, which very much gets straight to the point in terms of stating the reason for the erection of the monument. There are a number of words and phrases in this inscription which need some element of analysis here. Firstly, it needs to be stressed that the arch is being dedicated to Constantine by 'the Senate and people of Rome' and that the Senate may therefore have played a highly significant role in shaping the propagandist message of the monument, in consultation with Constantine and his representatives. Such a dedication from the Senate is not in any way unique though, and it must be remembered that a similar formula was also used on the dedicatory inscription on the Arch of Septimius Severus. Secondly, the Senate describe Constantine here as 'the Great', though they do not allow him the kind of honour bestowed on Severus in the form of the recording of his lineage and offices. However, Maxentius, defeated in battle by Constantine, of course goes unnamed in the inscription and is referred to simply as 'the tyrant' and his followers as 'his faction'. It is very explicitly made clear here, as on the Arch of Severus, that the emperor is acting on behalf of 'the State'. The language used in the inscription heaps further opprobrium on Maxentius by the use of words such as 'rightful' and 'avenge' to describe Constantine's victory.

Yet it is the use of the phrase 'INSTINCTU DIVINITATIS' – by divine inspiration – that has generated the most discussion among ancient historians and archaeologists. Some have seen this as a tacit acknowledgement of Constantine's reported Christian vision ahead of the Battle of the Milvian Bridge, and therefore that the divine inspiration referred to is that coming from the Christian God. Others have quite rightly pointed out that not only was Constantine reported to have had a Christian vision but that he had also previously had a vision of Apollo while visiting a temple in Gaul some years before, and was well known for stressing his affinity to Sol Invictus, the sun god, in images on a number of his coin issues. 'Divine inspiration' in that case might equally have meant the inspiration provided by pagan deities such as Apollo or Sol. As there is a great deal of pagan imagery in the artworks on the arch and as historic scenes of pagan sacrifice are included among the reused *spolia*, it seems likely that the latter explanation for this divine inspiration is correct. Besides, the 'Christian vision' was a personal epiphanic moment for the emperor and not for the largely pagan Senate who had set up the monument in his honour.

There are also a number of much shorter inscriptions elsewhere on the arch, almost in the form of propagandist slogans of the kind that appeared on Roman coins, and these each provide further evidence about the arch designers' intent. In the central passageway, above the reset Great Trajanic Frieze panel on the eastern side, are inscribed the words 'FUNDATORI QUIETIS', literally 'founder of calm' but more likely to imply 'founder of peace', and above its pendant panel on the western side,

'LIBERATORI URBIS', 'liberator of the city'. The link between war and peace, as with Augustus's Ara Pacis monument, is explicit in the juxtaposition of 'FUNDATORI QUIETIS' and 'LIBERATORI URBIS' and, of course, in the imagery on the arch, as will be discussed in detail in Chapters Three and Four.

On the north side of the arch, above the eastern pair of Hadrianic *tondi*, is carved 'VOTIS X', and above the other, western, pair, 'VOTIS XX'. On the south side, again above the reset pairs of *tondi*, are carved 'SIC X' in the west and 'SIC XX' in the east. The X in 'VOTIS X' and 'SIC X', literally the number ten, refers to Constantine's *decennalia*, his ten years as emperor calculated from the time of his proclamation at York in 306 AD. The XX, literally twenty, refers to a future event, his *vicennalia* to come in 326 AD. These slogans, though paired on opposite faces of the arch, can therefore be read together to mean 'solemn vows for your *decennalia* and for your future *vicennalia*, as for the tenth anniversary so for the twentieth'. This is an extremely optimistic inscription in one respect in that the Senate is here hoping for such an extended period of rule by Constantine as Augustus that they have projected their message of goodwill to the emperor well into the future in a way that interrupts linear time and memory and lulls the viewer into perhaps a false sense of security. Such optimism quite surely went against the political and military reality of the time.

Doubt and Controversy

Despite the fact that the Arch of Constantine is one of the largest extant ancient monuments surviving from Late Antiquity, there still rages an academic debate about the identification of its original instigator, and some time will need to be spent here flagging up the various strands of this debate and weighing up the probability or possibility of each separate interpretation.

In the earlier part of the twentieth century the American art historian Arthur Lincoln Frothingham had suggested that the arch actually dated to the time of the Emperor Domitian (AD 81–96), and that it had been subsequently remodelled, if not necessarily completely rebuilt in the fourth century under Constantine.[13] However, the consensus view that the Arch of Constantine was indeed the Arch of Constantine held firm and indeed held sway more or less until the 1990s. Questions about the original date of the arch now resurfaced, first in conference presentations and then as a result of new archaeological fieldwork, involving limited but significantly placed excavation being carried out around the arch and a highly detailed inspection being made of the arch structure itself, involving a high level of photogrammetric recording. However, each of these important new pieces of practical research was claimed to have provided unequivocal evidence that the arch was not in fact what it seemed and what it had been accepted to be. Unfortunately the two strands of new evidence not only created two new interpretations of the history of the arch, but two diametrically opposed interpretations.

On the one hand the Italian excavators Alessandra Mellucco Vaccaro and Angela Maria Ferroni came to the conclusion that the foundations of the arch dated to the reign of the Emperor Hadrian, who reigned from AD 117 to AD 138, and that much of the above-ground structure of the arch also dated to this time, based on their inspection of the monument from the scaffolding erected around the arch during a period of cleaning and restoration.[14] On the other hand, the architectural survey team led by Patrizio Pensabene and Clementina Panella came to the conclusion that every single one of the 16,000 or so stones in the arch was an item of *spolia*, and not just the most obvious ones such as those bearing decoration and carving, somewhat of a revelation but perhaps not altogether a surprise.[15]

Since the presentation of these two extraordinary new theories in both conference presentations and publications, academic consensus has realigned itself to accept what might be called the architectural survey model for the arch's origins, and has sidelined the interpretation offered of the excavated evidence and its resulting Hadrianic origin theory. In many ways the incontrovertible similarity between the Arch of Septimius Severus and the Arch of Constantine, as discussed above, should have immediately put paid to the argument as to whether the Arch of Constantine was merely a modification of a Hadrianic arch, which would then presumably have made this Hadrianic arch a prototype for the subsequent Arch of Septimius Severus. Two distinct academic camps still exist though; one that sees the arch as a monument started by Maxentius for some reason and subsequently taken over by the Senate and Constantine after Maxentius's death, and another that sees the arch as a purely Constantinian monument from planning to dedication, the almost exclusive use of *spolia* being very much an accepted Constantinian strategy and cultural construct. I certainly find myself firmly in the latter camp, though as this book is intended to present all aspects of the study of the arch to interested students it has been thought apposite to at least flag up the existence of alternative theories to the one that forms the main narrative of this work.

However, there is one indisputable fact that is quite literally chiselled in stone, in the long inscription on the arch: that the Senate of Rome dedicated this monument to Constantine. It may have begun as a planned Maxentian monument, and construction might even have begun under Maxentius's aegis, but it was finished following Constantine's decisive victory at the Milvian Bridge. It may well be that to many of the senators the final outcome of the bloody contretemps between Constantine and Maxentius was largely an irrelevance, and that what really mattered was that this massive new triumphal monument was being erected in Rome, thus, for a while at least, returning the city to the centre of affairs in the empire.

Setting and Context

The arch cannot and must not be viewed in splendid isolation; its setting within the urban topography of Rome needs to be considered at the same time.[16] In terms of the significance of the site and positioning of the arch there are a number of factors to consider. Firstly its relationship to the Via Triumphalis and to the nearby arches of Titus and Septimius Severus. Secondly, its relationship to other nearby monuments including the Colosseum, the fountain known as the Meta Sudans, and a now vanished colossal statue of Sol, which stood nearby in front of the Temple of Roma and Venus. Each of these aspects will now be considered in turn.

Its relationship to the Via Triumphalis and to the nearby arches of Titus and Septimius Severus is relatively easy to understand. Although the arch was not formally a triumphal arch as such, its positioning sets it in a highly charged and significant political sacred landscape linked to the celebration of Roman feats of arms and imbued with numerous folk memories in the minds of the Roman populace at large. When entering the city in triumph, generals and, latterly, exclusively emperors would proceed along this route starting at the Campus Martius, by the Circus Maximus and around the Palatine Hill. The procession would turn at the point later marked by the Meta Sudans fountain and go along the Via Sacra to the Forum Romanum and thence to the Capitoline Hill, taking in both the Arch of Titus and the Arch of Septimius Severus on the way. The Constantinian arch, as described above, echoes the Severan arch in its form, shape and size but does not necessarily copy it. If anything it acted as a pendant to the Severan arch. As to the link between the Arch of Titus and that of Constantine, apart from their close proximity it might be thought that they had no particular formal relationship to discuss. However, that would be wrong. Certainly the Arch of Titus is much smaller and of a completely different form, being a simple arch with one central passageway. As has been noted above, the designer of the Arch of Constantine has quite obviously borrowed from the Arch of Titus the concept of the viewer walking through the arch and viewing artworks depicting dramatic, energetic scenes on the sides of the passageway as they progress through. The movement of the viewer helps to further animate the already busy representations.

Its relationships to other nearby monuments including the Colosseum, the fountain known as the Meta Sudans, and the colossal statue of Sol are less easy to understand. All three of these earlier monuments was standing when the arch was planned and constructed, so their presence may have had some considerable bearing on the specific siting of the arch. The Meta Sudans, which does not survive today other than as a foundation marked out on the ground, lay between the arch and the Colossus.[17] It was probably both a historical and political boundary marker, erected at the point where the Via Triumphalis turned to go up the Velian Hill to the Via Sacra. This was a monumental fountain dedicated in the reign of Domitian, some time between AD 89 and 96. The final demolition of the last upstanding part of the monument took place relatively recently, in 1936, on the orders of Mussolini who wished to ease traffic congestion around the Colosseum, and indeed part of the decaying work can be seen on two of the nineteenth-century paintings reproduced as illustrations in Chapter Seven. The original fountain was in the form of a tall cone on a cylinder, down the outside of which water would flow, surrounded by a walled pool. There is some evidence that the Meta Sudans, or rather its surroundings, was modified, perhaps at the same time as the building of the Arch of Constantine, by the addition of a parapet, perhaps topped by a colonnade. It also seems likely that when the arch was being built consideration might have been given to the demolition and clearing away of the Meta Sudans, as its presence might have been thought to potentially impact in a negative way upon the positioning and setting of the new arch. That this might have been the case is suggested by the fact that the builders of the arch eventually decided to position the central arch carriageway of the monument not directly over the line of the road but rather some 6 feet to one side of it, thus avoiding the sight line from one side of the central arch being blocked or dominated by the bulk of the fountain. Indeed this shift also allowed the central arch to frame the colossal bronze statue of Sol, something that was probably a major factor in linking some of the new Constantinian imagery on the arch to the broader urban setting here in the valley of the Colosseum.

The colossal statue of the sun god Sol, created by Zenodorus, is thought to have stood to around 350 feet in height.[18] It was sited behind the arch to the north, having been moved there by Hadrian from its original position in the vestibule of Nero's Domus Aurea on the Velian Hill. Originally a statue of Nero in the guise of Sol, after the emperor's death it was significantly altered to expunge Nero's image and to make the statue a representation of the sun god alone. Some idea of the appearance of the statue, today represented on the ground only by the position of its base, can be gauged from its appearance on a number of coin issues. The giant naked figure of Sol, wearing his signature radiate crown and in what is known as a *contrapposto* pose, leans against a pillar braced by his left arm, while in his right hand he holds a rudder which itself rests on a globe. People walking north along the Via Triumphalis and gaining a distant view of the colossal figure of Sol would, with progress along the road, eventually be presented with a viewpoint at which they would have been aware of the intended visual synchronicity between colossus and arch and thus between Constantine and Sol, a dual identification doubtless already known to many viewers from certain of Constantine's coin issues (fig. 12, see also plate 19). At first this synchronicity and relationship would have favoured the deity, with him towering over the blocky shape of the arch. Then, nearer to the arch, the head and upper body of Sol would have seemed to almost merge into a single image with the gilded bronze statue of the emperor atop the arch, if that was what had originally been in place here. Finally, at

12. A gold *solidus* of Constantine, Ticinum mint, AD 316. Obverse: busts of emperor and Sol, reverse: *Liberalitas*. British Museum, London. (Photo: Copyright Trustees of the British Museum)

around 115 feet south of the arch it has been calculated that the viewer would have been presented with a singular vision, that of the figure of Sol framed in the central opening of the arch. This was political theatre at its most sophisticated. It has been written that the arch thus 'framed the sun'[19] and indeed that must almost literally have been the case as well as being a useful metaphor for presenting Constantine's religious concerns to the Roman people. Thus in this way the arch can be seen to have created a new way to view and appreciate an old monument, in this case the Colossus, and thus almost reinvent it in the eyes of the contemporary viewer. This provides yet another example of the way in which strategies were developed in Late Antiquity to appropriate physical and material parts of the past and turn them into contemporary artefacts or pieces of material culture.

However, it must also be noted that at certain points along the road the view northwards would have appeared confusing to the viewer and indeed even ugly as the squat arch interfered with and blocked a clear view of the Colossus. This phenomenological interpretation of the arch's broader setting developed by Elizabeth Marlowe very much needs to take on board not only the pleasure and positive experience of some viewers at different points along the route but also the suggested frustration and irritation of other viewers. In the immediate few decades following the building of the arch there would doubtless always have been a few die-hard nostalgics who 'preferred the area the way it used to be' or who thought the arch now 'spoiled the view' of the colossal Sol. One person's successful merging of competing images is another person's visual clutter, jumble, and confusion. Again, while the view from the south by a northward-proceeding traveller undoubtedly would have produced a number of points of pleasurable visual juxtaposition, for most viewers views from the north backwards may not have been quite as stimulating, thought-provoking, or entertaining.

It could be argued that the hinterland and setting of the arch was designed and intended to be much broader than simply the four-monument grouping of the arch, Colosseum, colossal statue, and fountain. Indeed, if Constantine and his planners had intended this to be the case then the revamping of the Circus Maximus under Constantine some way back along the Via Triumphalis could have been part of this broader scheme to illustrate to the people of Rome how Constantine had transformed this part of the centre of Rome and imposed his authority and character on the appearance and fabric of the city to which he was largely a stranger. While I do not altogether subscribe to this theory of an overarching development plan for such a large area of the city linked to a highly complex and integrated programme of propaganda, it is nevertheless tempting to accept the fact that Constantine's original plan to install a super-huge Egyptian obelisk at the circus may have been intended to provide a soaring solar monument here that mirrored the distant colossal statue of Sol near the site of the arch. In the end the chosen obelisk was only shipped part of the way from Egypt to Rome during his reign, and indeed it did not complete its journey to the Circus Maximus until the reign of his son Constantius II. This obelisk was subsequently moved from the Circus Maximus to its present position outside the church of St John Lateran in the sixteenth century.[20]

Thus it would appear that the artworks on the Arch of Constantine illustrating the emperor's devotion to the sun god were echoed and intensified by the proximity of the nearby colossal statue of Sol, which was also framed by the arch's central opening and thus in some way integrated into its visual narrative. Probably more fortuitous would be the roar of the crowds inside the Colosseum on certain days, leaking out to pollute the ears of any viewers of the Constantinian battle scenes on the arch, providing a soundtrack to the noisy mayhem of combat depicted, and the background sound of water flowing through the Meta Sudans fountain as the viewer looked at images of Maxentius's army drowning in the fast-flowing, churning waters of the Tiber.

There can be no doubt that the juxtaposition of the Arch of Constantine to the colossal bronze statue of Sol to the north was of great significance. Equally, the framing effect created by viewing the statue through the central passageway of the arch from a specific spot to the south would without doubt have been a deliberate strategy to place the large new monument in an awkward preordained vacant space along the Via Triumphalis, and at the same time to dominate that space, to capture it, and to recontextualise the other monuments nearby by creating new visual sightlines and experiences for the viewer. As images of Sol also appear in the new Constantinian artworks on the arch, in the form of a radiate-crowned bust of a male figure with a raised right hand and globe in a niche in one of the lateral passageways, and most prominently in a *tondi*, or roundel, on the short eastern side, where he drives a four-horse chariot up to the heavens, it is likely that the viewer of the arch and Colossus would be in no doubt about Constantine's identification with the sun god. Whether he or she would have assumed, or have been right in assuming, that the 'divine inspiration' that guided Constantine to victory over Maxentius according to the long inscription on the arch was that of Sol is another question altogether, as discussed above. The ambiguity of that phrase leaves it open for others to interpret that divine inspiration to have come from the Christian god, as detailed for instance by Eusebius, but even those favouring the Christian interpretation of this phrase cannot in any way deny the weight of the evidence that shows us unequivocally that Constantine saw Sol as a powerful deity he wished to publicly associate himself with.

Elsewhere in this book, both above in this chapter and more fully in Chapter Five, I have summarised the details of the debate about the date of construction of the arch and have noted, though not necessarily agreed with, the viewpoint that the arch was in fact started by Maxentius and then subsequently usurped by Constantine after his victory over Maxentius, in the way it can be demonstrated that so many Maxentian projects in Rome were rededicated. If this were the case, then the phenomenological approach to the study of the arch's immediate and broader environs would fall apart immediately. If Maxentius had chosen this spot for an arch and started building work, then it would be *his* relationship to Sol that was being celebrated by the juxtaposition of the monuments here.

Even if the ambiguity of the phrase 'divine inspiration' on the arch leaves an open interpretation of the significance of these words which might include allusion to the Christian god rather than to a pagan deity, nevertheless the depictions of Sol Invictus on the arch suggest that its original intention was otherwise. Other pagan deities and figures also feature, including Mars, Luna, and river gods. However, it may be that only a few years after the dedication of the arch, the reception of this phrase to some viewers and readers would have significantly altered to become less ambiguous and decidedly Christian. The Edict of Milan of AD 313 had to all intents and purposes legalised Christianity, if only by ending official persecutions, and, of course, a few years later Constantine's efforts at emperor were to become heavily dominated by Christian affairs. In other words, some Roman Christians in the years following the dedication of the arch may have viewed the arch as a Christian monument, and certainly the number viewing the monument in this way probably increased exponentially following the deathbed conversion of the emperor in AD 337. I have suggested elsewhere that just such a Christianising of what was intended to be a pagan imperial monument occurred in the case of the Column of Marcus Aurelius,[21] where the occurrence of the so-called Rain Miracle, and thus the significance of its depiction on the column, became a focus for debate about the nature of the divine intervention that brought this about, this eventually in later years being attributed to the Christian god rather than to a pagan one.

In any case, if the arch represented a restating of the link between imperial power and pagan religion made by the Senate on Constantine's behalf, then there does not really need to be an investigation of the possible Christian connotations of the arch, its artworks, or inscription in relation to Constantine's own beliefs and stance. Looking elsewhere in Rome over the next few decades, the interested citizen would have seen the focus of the city of Rome shift away from the old imperial pagan centre towards the new churches springing up around the periphery as a result of the impetus given to church building by Constantine. There was no ambiguity here about what was pagan or what was Christian.

The Senate's chosen artistic and epigraphic programme for the monument, doubtless broadly if not necessarily totally endorsed by Constantine, almost exactly reflected the contemporary political agenda as they would have seen it, with a need for peace and tranquillity being the prerequisite for renewal and regeneration, particularly in the city of Rome itself but also more widely throughout the empire.

While this chapter has been concerned with describing the monument and its original setting, attention in the next chapter will be turned to the detailed description and analysis of some of the *spolia* artworks built into the arch, and an analysis of their possible significance.

3

The Good Emperors

In the previous chapter a description of the Arch of Constantine and its original setting was presented. As explained there, the arch includes in its fabric three sets of reused sculptural panels dating respectively from the reigns of Trajan (AD 98–117), Hadrian (AD 117–38), and Marcus Aurelius (AD 161–80), in addition to the Trajanic era statues of Dacian men (fig. 13). These reused artworks will now be described here and an attempt will be made to consider whether their selection for the new arch was based on the subject matter portrayed in each case or whether together they created a new, coherent narrative concerned with Constantine alone, or rather with how the Roman Senate wished to present the emperor to the Roman people. It will be suggested that the choice of artworks associated with Trajan, Hadrian, and Marcus Aurelius was a very deliberate one, forging a visual and conceptual link between Constantine and these three 'good emperors'. It must, however, also be remembered that while no images associated with Septimius Severus appeared on the Arch of Constantine, nevertheless the knowledgeable Roman viewer would have been aware of the referencing of this earlier emperor inherent in the close modelling of Constantine's arch on that of Severus, as has been already discussed in Chapter Two. Allusion is also made on the Arch of Constantine to the design of the Arch of Titus. In other words the arch was a mixture of references to the past and the then present, as well as to the future in terms of one of the inscriptions looking forward to Constantine's *vicennalia* in AD 326. The purpose of the arch was very much concerned with the manipulation of memory.

The Trajanic Sculptures

The Trajanic sculptures reused in the arch consist of four sections, each comprising two adjoining blocks, of a once much larger commemorative frieze in Pentelic marble, which is by general academic consensus considered to have been the so-called Great Trajanic Frieze that once stood in some part of the temple complex to *Divus Traianus* – the Divine Trajan – built by his successor Hadrian at the north end of Trajan's Forum.[1] Around 100 feet long and with figures around 10 feet tall, this astonishingly ambitious work in a classicising style commemorated Trajan's Dacian wars. Plaster casts made in 1937 of the four frieze sections set into the arch and of other known sections elsewhere in Rome, and in museums as far afield as Paris and Berlin, allowed

13. Positions of artworks on the arch. A) Dacian prisoners and sections of the Great Trajanic Frieze. B) Panel reliefs of Marcus Aurelius. C) Hadrianic *tondi*. D) Constantinian *tondi*, relief, and pedestal bases. The Arch of Constantine, Rome. (Photo: Graham Norrie, after Giuliani 1955)

14. Plaster cast of the Great Trajanic Frieze, Museo della Civiltà Romana, Rome. (Photo: Author)

a reconstruction of the original full frieze to be made. This is on display today in the Museo della Civiltà Romana in the suburbs of Rome and is illustrated here (fig. 14). In addition there are eight free-standing sculptural figures of male Dacian prisoners in a purple marble reset on the arch, having probably originally stood in Trajan's Forum.

The two frieze scenes set in the central opening of the arch, facing each other and on opposite sides of the passageway, both feature the emperor Trajan himself but in both cases the head has been recarved to become a portrait of Constantine. Crucially, both panels appear with a Constantinian inscription above them, the significance of which was discussed in Chapter Two. The positioning of these two panels in the passageway meant that they would not be seen at first by a casual viewer of the monument. Like the passageway panels in the nearby Arch of Titus, which they were surely intended to mimic, these were meant to be viewed by spectators walking or processing through the arch. The additional experience of viewing these already dynamic scenes while on the move and glancing from side to side to take in both panels would have only enhanced their inherent theatricality and instant narrative power.

The first frieze double panel on the west wall of the central passageway contains a complex scene of furious battle (plate 11). Surrounded by Roman troops, Trajan/Constantine is depicted wearing a cuirass and is on horseback trampling a Dacian barbarian beneath his horse's hooves. The emperor's cloak billows out from his shoulders, giving the scene a great sense of movement and instantly drawing the viewer's eyes towards the figure of the emperor, one of many figures in a great combative melee. Another Dacian kneels in supplication before the emperor's rearing horse while other Dacian fighters are shown being attacked and struck down by Roman troops. A horse falls towards the ground, his rider clinging on to his mane in desperation. A number of Roman soldiers appear from the left of the scene holding severed Dacian heads in their hands. Of course it is highly unlikely that Trajan or indeed any emperor ever took part in actual fighting as depicted here, so the scene has to be taken as a metaphor for the victory of the emperor and by extension of Rome through the valour of the Roman army and the leadership and strength of character of the emperor. Again, the emperor's clemency to the kneeling Dacian is contrasted with his warlike valour. Above the scene is set the Constantinian inscription 'LIBERATORI URBIS' – liberator of the city.

The second double panel, on the east central passageway wall, shows the *adventus* or arrival of Trajan/Constantine, with the cuirassed emperor at the head of his troops being crowned with a wreath by Victory (plate 12). He is being greeted by two figures who may be Virtus, dressed as an Amazon, and Honos shod in lion-skin boots and wearing armour. At the same time, the other half of the double panel is taken up with a scene of battle, with mounted Roman troops trampling barbarians under their horses' hooves. The presence of a scene involving rearing horses seems to be a deliberate way to mirror the scene on the other side of the passageway. This panel is also topped by a Constantinian inscription 'FUNDATORI QUIETIS' – founder of peace – making it quite explicit that peace could only have been brought by the cleansing power of war.

The two scenes were in all likelihood chosen by reason of their depicting one of the 'good emperors' and an emperor who in this case could be changed by a sculptor from Trajan to Constantine without too much trouble. The accompanying inscriptions also invited the viewer to identify the figure of the emperor in the scenes below as Constantine, the Liberator of the City and the Founder of Peace, and not as Trajan, to whom neither of those epithets was ever employed. Both scenes were completely accessible to the viewer at ground level. Confusion may have been caused for some viewers by the image of their contemporary emperor Constantine here battling with quite distinctly barbarian enemies rather than the enemies within in the form of Maxentius and his forces. We are able to suggest today that the intention was for the viewer to immediately identify Constantine as a worthy successor to Trajan, an earlier good emperor and soldier emperor, but the recarving of the two portrait heads surely removed the principal way for a viewer to know that Trajan had originally been depicted here (fig. 15). Only the presence of accurate, almost anthropological depictions of Dacian barbarians in these scenes would have alerted the knowledgeable viewer to their true age and chronological origins.

The other reused panels from the Great Trajanic Frieze were positioned in the attic of the arch on its two short sides. Both are scenes of combat between Roman soldiers and Dacian warriors; Trajan does not appear in either scene. The double panel on the west face carries a scene of rampant Roman cavalrymen trampling Dacian fighters segueing into a scene of Roman infantrymen escorting an important Dacian prisoner, this bearded figure having his hands tied behind his back. The double panel on the

15. Head of Trajan, recarved as Constantine, on the east wall of central passageway. The Arch of Constantine, Rome. (Photo: Deutsches Archäologisches Institut Rom. Faraglia, DAIR 32.51)

east face carries a scene of heavily armoured Roman cavalrymen riding triumphantly over a carpet of Dacian bodies, with musicians blowing their *buccine*, or trumpets, to sound the victory.

Of all the reused sculptures on the Arch of Constantine it is the choosing of the giant statues of Dacian male prisoners that is perhaps the hardest to understand, particularly as their prominent positioning on the monument gives them a pre-eminent appearance in the eyes of viewers both near and from afar.[2] I suggest elsewhere in the book that they might be later additions to the arch. The fact that they are free-standing emphasises their power as individual images. Yes, they would have been seen as iconic images linked to Trajan and to his forum from which these eight sculptures probably derived, but how long in the collective memory of Romans would this link have survived after they had been seen in their new setting for a number of years? Images across the whole arch continuously stress the might of Roman imperial power through the conquering of foreign peoples, through the death and enslavement of barbarian peoples, and these barbarian enemies from different regions and tribes have here merged to become a single, universal barbarian foe against whom Rome was pitched into opposition with eternally. But as a former province Dacia would have meant little or nothing to most citizens in early fourth-century Rome, and the images of conquered male Dacians here must simply have been employed as universal images of defeat. The same is true of the barbarian prisoners who appear with Victory and Roman troops on the faces of the Constantinian decorated pedestal bases for the columns in front of the two long faces of the arch. The pedestal barbarians are pathetic in their depiction, cowed, tamed and scared, facing nothing but a desperate short life as a slave. Yet the male Dacian captives, with heads bowed certainly and with their hands tied together in front of them, have an air of dignity about them that would not seem to be just a projection onto them made by this viewer; there is a general consensus amongst art historians that this is the case. Their positioning and grouping might have made them appear less prominent than they do to us today and less dignified when the bronze statue of a triumphant Constantine, now missing from on top of the arch, was *in situ*, towering over them. However, it might just be that they were intended to be employed here as generic signifiers of dignity in defeat for some, perhaps those supporters of Maxentius in Rome, whose purging would have been self-defeating for Constantine and whose value to him was greater by the fact of their being alive rather than dead.

Alternatively I would suggest that the Dacian statues might have been added to the arch sometime after its official dedication. Certainly it is generally accepted that the reuse of Trajanic artworks on the arch was consciously intended to link Constantine with Trajan in the minds of viewers of the arch, as with the memory jogging intended by the use of images of Hadrian and Marcus Aurelius as well. However, this had already been achieved by the resetting of parts of the Great Trajanic Frieze on the arch as discussed above. Placing the Dacian statues here too simply seems excessive in terms of referencing that part of the Roman past. It would seem more logical to think that the Dacian captives might have been added to the arch in or shortly after AD 336, either by Constantine's own edict or by one of his sons after his death in AD

337, when Constantine had adopted the title Dacicus Maximus. Indeed, these statues are in such a position that had there been other statues in the eight spots on which the Dacians were set, these would have been relatively easy to remove and replace.

The Hadrianic Sculptures

The Hadrianic sculptures reset in the arch comprise eight circular panels or *tondi*, known collectively today as the Hunting *tondi*, given the nature of their subject matter[3] (figs 16, 17, 18, 19, 20, 21). There has been a considerable amount of academic debate about the type of monument from which these *tondi* were removed, and it has variously been suggested that they came from an imperial monument celebrating the emperor's travels or his love of hunting, or, less convincingly, that they came from a temple or tomb dedicated to Hadrian's favourite, the beautiful Antinuous. They are of particular interest in terms of their reuse on the arch in that they depict scenes that are not linked to war, to imperial triumph, and to conquest, as were the Trajanic frieze sections, Dacian prisoners, and some of the Aurelian panels. Nor are they linked to imperial ideology as expressed through the concepts of duty and responsibility and the rites associated with the fulfilment of those things, as so well illustrated on some of the reused panel reliefs of Marcus Aurelius. However, it could be argued that they are expressions of *virtus* personified in the person of the emperor, or indeed that establishing a link of some kind between Hadrian and Constantine was pre-eminent in their choice. The fact that the scenes are set in a number of disparate locales perhaps indicates that they are illustrative of Hadrian's travels around the empire, and thus representative of the idea of the unity and diversity of the Roman Empire. An even simpler explanation would be that they were chosen as much for their shape as for any other consideration.

The eight *tondi* of Luna marble comprise scenes of the departure for the hunt, the hunt itself, and sacrifice after the hunt. The game hunted comprises the bear, the boar, and the lion. The sacrifices are shown as being to Silvanus, Diana, Apollo, and Hercules. Hadrian's young companion Antinuous appears in at least one of the scenes, most certainly to be identified taking part in the boar hunt. The portraits of Hadrian in these scenes have been recarved; in the sacrifice to Apollo on the north side and to Hercules on the south side the new portrait face may be that of Constantius I, Constantine's father, or less likely of Licinius, Constantine's fellow Tetrarch, while on the other *tondi* where the emperor's head still survives it can be seen that Hadrian is recarved to become Constantine.[4] These *tondi* are positioned four on each long side of the arch; two in a pair above each of the small side passageways. Their arrangement probably does not mirror their original disposition on the Hadrianic monument from which they came.

The *tondo* depicting the boar hunt is of particular interest in that the two main mounted figures in the middle ground in pursuit of the huge boar, their horses depicted charging at a gallop after the magnificent charging boar that dominates the foreground of the scene, almost mirror the pose of the mounted Trajan on the panels set into the sides of the main central passageway of the arch. The hunted boar replaces the prostrate barbarian foes as quarry or victim.

16. Hadrianic *tondo*, a bear hunt. The Arch of Constantine, Rome. (Photo: Graham Norrie, after Giuliani 1955)

17. Hadrianic *tondo*, Sacrifice to Diana. The Arch of Constantine, Rome. (Photo: Graham Norrie, after Giuliani 1955)

18. Hadrianic *tondo*, Sacrifice to Apollo. The Arch of Constantine, Rome. (Photo: Graham Norrie, after Giuliani 1955)

19. Hadrianic *tondo*, the aftermath of the lion hunt. The Arch of Constantine, Rome. (Photo: Graham Norrie, after Giuliani 1955)

20. Hadrianic *tondo*, Sacrifice to Hercules. The Arch of Constantine, Rome. (Photo: Graham Norrie, after Giuliani 1955)

21. Hadrianic *tondo*, a boar hunt. The Arch of Constantine, Rome. (Photo: Graham Norrie, after Giuliani 1955)

While hunting was an aristocratic, restricted pursuit at the time of Hadrian it became even more marked as a signifier of power and status in the third and fourth centuries and much further beyond. Hunting became a defining elite male leisure activity in the later Roman Empire, even in the most remote of the provinces. In the late Roman period such an activity as hunting would have been the preserve of not only the aristocratic male landowner but also of senior bureaucrats and military officers. It was to become a defining activity linked to a suite of pursuits celebrating hypermasculinity in Late Antiquity. In classical art and mythology the hunt was itself symbolic of the life course, with death inevitably waiting for all of us at the end of life's chase; this may account for the popularity of the hunt motif in Roman art in general and its ubiquity in many different media, even down to smaller items of material culture such as pottery and knife handles. The hunt also became quite regularly used as an allegorical image for life itself and was often linked to ideas reflecting salvation, something which Christianity would employ in its palette of symbolic expression. However, it is unlikely that the Senate's architect for the decorative scheme on the Arch of Constantine selected these *tondi* for their allusive content. They may simply have been selected on aesthetic grounds – that is, for their round shape, and for their links with the good emperor Hadrian.

While writing about the Hadrianic hunting *tondi* I was very much drawn towards thoughts about the Troyes Casket, in pride of place in the Treasury of Troyes Cathedral in north-central France[5] (fig. 22 and plate 13). Brought to the cathedral by its bishop Jean Langlois as booty after the sack of Constantinople in 1204, this ivory casket, subsequently repaired with metal fittings, is a richly decorated piece of Byzantine court art that probably dates from the tenth or possibly eleventh century. Of course, while accepting that this in no way provides a direct parallel for any aspect

22. The Troyes Casket. Cathedral Treasury, Troyes, France. (Photo: Slide Archive of Former School of Continuing Studies, Birmingham University)

of the decoration on the Arch of Constantine, the casket's simultaneously simple and complex ideologically motivated decoration may provide at least some ideas which can help inform the interpretation of the reuse of the Hadrianic *tondi* on the arch. The lid of the casket is decorated with a scene of two emperors in military garb mounted on richly appointed horses positioned on either side of a walled city. The emperors may be about to enter the city, some of the citizens inside being pictured greeting them with acclaim. A Tyche, the personification of the city, offers a victor's crown to the emperor on the right. On both the front and back faces are hunting scenes; on the front a lion hunt is portrayed, with the two mounted emperors confronting the beast, one armed with a bow, the other with a sword; on the back a boar is being hunted by a single individual with a lance, again in imperial military dress, and accompanied by a pack of dogs. Hunting is here, as so often in ancient art, an affirmation of the emperor's hold over the natural world, its terrain and creatures, acting as a broader metaphor for the control of the Byzantine Empire. On the two ends are depicted Chinese imperial phoenixes, suggesting either the reach and influence of the Byzantine court, or indicating that the casket might well have been an imperial or diplomatic gift to the Chinese court. There is no doubt that this precious item represents a material manifestation of Byzantine political power, of how imperial ideology was here made manifest in artistic production. The juxtaposition here in terms of images of urban and rural imperial roles and pursuits and between practical and almost existential concerns, between the concerns of the Byzantine Empire and of the world beyond, between individual and collective responsibilities, echoes, centuries later, many of the themes touched upon in the programme of artworks on the Arch of Constantine, both in the images on the Hadrianic *spolia* and in their new setting.

The Panels of Marcus Aurelius

Eight Luna marble panel reliefs depicting various aspects of Marcus Aurelius's German wars are reused on the Arch of Constantine, in the attic on both long sides of the arch. These date originally to the mid-AD 170s[6]. Though the portraits of Marcus were probably recarved to become those of Constantine, heavy restoration of the panels in 1732 under Pope Clement XII led to the replacement of the heads and we cannot be entirely certain that this was the case.[7] A further three panel reliefs, similar in size, shape, and style, have survived and are in the collections of the Palazzo dei Conservatori in Rome; these bear scenes of *clementia* or clemency, triumph, and sacrifice. On the arch panels are depicted scenes of departure (*profectio*), purification (*lustratio*), presentation of a client king (*rex datus*), an address (*adlocutio*), prisoners, submission, arrival (*adventus*), and bounty and generosity (*liberalitas*). The question as to whether all eleven panels once adorned a single monument, perhaps a triumphal arch celebrating victory over the Germans and Sarmatians in AD 176, or came from two Antonine monuments, has exercised many academics but has never really been satisfactorily answered and perhaps never will be conclusively. In a way, attempting to readdress that question again here is not strictly necessary, given that it is the recontextualisation of the eight panels by their being built into the arch that is of overriding relevance in this book. However, the subject matter of each of the reused panel reliefs on the Arch of Constantine will now briefly be considered in turn.

The four panels reset in the attic of the long north face are presented as two pairs, each pair being set in the attic above the side passageways. The *profectio* and *adventus* panels were paired together by the designers of the Constantinian arch at the east end of the north facade (figs 23 and 24). The *profectio* panel is centred on the scene of the emperor's leave-taking for the German wars in AD 169. The emperor is accompanied by his right-hand man Tiberius Claudius Pompeianus. His troops and his mount restlessly await him and military banners are animated by the wind while various personifications, including Virtus, bid him safe journey and farewell. It is noteworthy for the presence in the background of a monumental arch decorated with elephants, probably the same arch which is depicted on the *adventus* panel. The *adventus* panel, as has already been noted, includes in the background a monumental arch, probably the same arch which is depicted on the *profectio* panel, though here with a temple building, possibly the Temple of Fortuna Redux, standing next to the arch. As has been pointed out by a number of authorities this particular panel is unique among the eleven known in that here the emperor appears only with deities or mythological figures. No other human is present in the scene and Marcus stands centre-stage, flanked by the figures of Mars and Roma. The depiction on both these panels of buildings in Rome is hugely significant and will be discussed further below in Chapter Seven.

The submission and *liberalitas* panels were paired together at the west end of the north facade (figs 25 and 26). The submission panel carries a depiction of barbarian prisoners being brought before the emperor at a military camp. An elderly man is supported by a youth; they stand before the emperor who sits on a chair set up high on a podium. The panel depicting a scene of submission is simple in its depiction of barbarian submission to the emperor, but more complex in terms of the nuances in this relationship implied by the composition of the scene and the attitudes and stances of the main protagonists. The *liberalitas* panel represents a traditional event linked to an emperor's homecoming to Rome following a successful military campaign, the distribution of monies to the Roman populace in celebration of victories achieved. It is worth noting here the appearance of a woman among the citizens receiving largesse from the emperor, the only mortal Roman woman depicted anywhere on the arch. While, almost inevitably, monuments such as triumphal arches and commemorative columns dwell on war and battle, and thus are dominated by images of men, nevertheless on many such monuments, like Trajan's Column and the Column of Marcus Aurelius, female images do appear in small numbers and at least allow some kind of gendered reading of these images to be made. However, the Arch of Constantine almost constitutes an exception, in that in both the reused artworks and the contemporary Constantinian artworks there is a dearth of representations of women, even on the so-called civic facade of the arch. The exceptions would appear to be the figures of Victory in the spandrels and the female prisoners depicted on the column pedestal bases. Finally it is worth noting that the Aurelian *liberalitas* scene almost exactly mirrors in its subject matter

23. Panel relief of Marcus
Aurelius. *Profectio* – the leave
taking of the emperor from Rome.
The Arch of Constantine, Rome.
(Photo: Graham Norrie, after
Giuliani 1955)

24. Panel relief of Marcus
Aurelius. *Adventus* – the arrival
and entry of the emperor into
Rome. The Arch of Constantine,
Rome. (Photo: Graham Norrie,
after Giuliani 1955)

25. Panel relief of Marcus Aurelius; the submission of barbarian prisoners. The Arch of Constantine, Rome. (Photo: Slide Archive of Former School of Continuing Studies, Birmingham University)

26. Panel relief of Marcus Aurelius. *Liberalitas* – the distribution of largesse to the Roman people by the emperor. The Arch of Constantine, Rome. (Photo: Graham Norrie, after Giuliani 1955)

the Constantinian frieze scene below on the same face of the arch, where Constantine is depicted distributing monies to the senators and people of Rome.

The four panels reset in the attic of the long south face are again presented as two pairs, each pair once more being set in the attic above the side passageways. The so-called *Rex Datus* and Prisoners panels were paired together by the designers of the Constantinian arch at the west end of the south facade. The *Rex Datus* panel derives its present name from the scene depicted on it, the presentation by the emperor of a vassal barbarian king to the Roman army in their camp. The emperor stands on a podium to receive the king, while in the background of the scene can be seen numerous military standards billowing in the breeze. The Prisoners panel depicts another scene in camp, with Roman soldiers dragging prisoners before the emperor, who once more surveys the scene from atop a podium (fig. 27).

The *adlocutio* and *lustratio* panels were paired together by the designers of the Constantinian arch at the east end of the south facade. The *lustratio* panel carries a depiction of a purifying sacrifice before battle. The emperor drops something onto a fire held in a bowl on a tripod while soldiers look on. Musicians play their instruments to drive away any negative spirits present. A pig, sheep, and bull can be seen awaiting their imminent sacrifice (fig. 28). The *adlocutio* panel depicts the emperor on a podium addressing his troops, presumably just before battle.

The eight individual panel reliefs of Marcus Aurelius reset in the arch each carry busy and complex images, and together they represent stylistically the most complex single element of design in the arch. Yet they were placed in the attic of the monument, in a position where much of the subtlety of the imagery and its detail would simply not have been visible and apparent to most viewers on the ground. It must have been just the broad, general impression of each scene that was intended to capture the viewer's eye.

Strangely, and probably purely coincidentally, if Constantine's strategy of identifying with past emperors was somehow designed to assure the people of Rome of his devotion to the mother city of the empire, despite his possibly not having set foot there till he was almost forty years of age, then while identifying with Trajan and Hadrian made perfect sense, identifying with Marcus Aurelius, though a 'good emperor' too, was an altogether riskier strategy, as Marcus was largely away from Rome campaigning for a large part of his reign.

Curating the Past

Explanations as to why these three groups of sculptures were chosen for reuse in the programme of artworks on the Arch of Constantine are always going to involve a great deal of guesswork. At the simplest level they would have been chosen because they fitted size- and shape-wise into the already chosen design of the arch, that is, an arch modelled on the earlier Arch of Septimius Severus, as was discussed in Chapter Two. However, they must also have been chosen because of their associations with three of the five 'good emperors' of Roman history and more specifically again because

27. Panel relief of Marcus
Aurelius receiving the barbarian
prisoners in camp. The Arch
of Constantine, Rome. (Photo:
Graham Norrie, after Giuliani
1955)

28. Panel relief of Marcus
Aurelius. *Lustratio* – sacrifice.
The Arch of Constantine, Rome.
(Photo: Graham Norrie, after
Giuliani 1955)

of the universal themes they portrayed with regard to the unchanging, seamless nature of imperial power, obligation, and duty through the ages.

Whether the monuments they derived from were systematically demolished at this time for the express purpose of harvesting these stones again must remain a largely unanswerable question. If not, and the monuments had been taken down at an earlier period or periods, it is likely that the artworks and other pieces of sculpture had been stored in a depot of some kind and curated in some way. Curation implies some kind of protective code for artworks bearing imperial images, something that is not attested by documentary sources but which would be the flipside of the process of *damnatio memoriae* where images were deliberately damaged as punishment under official sanction.

It is generally accepted that the use of *spolia* became quite common under the Tetrarchy and indeed Diocletian's monument, known as the Arcus Novus, though known only to us by fragments from its structure, would seem to have been the forerunner of the Arch of Constantine in this respect.[8] It may be that a store yard for sculptural marbles existed in the Campus Martius, and indeed fragments of Dacian statues have been found there, as were indeed the so-called Cancelleria Reliefs from the reign of Domitian. The base of one of the giant Dacian statues on the Arch of Constantine bears the *graffito 'ad arcum'* – to the arch – implying that this was a transit instruction for its removal from a store yard to the site of the arch.[9]

Of course, one can look back to earlier Roman times to find numerous examples of individual emperors collecting art: Hadrian for display at his villa at Tivoli, for instance, or the collecting of works to adorn the Baths of Caracalla. In these instances many of the works collected were in fact copies of earlier Greek and Roman works, the originals then lost. In collecting copies these emperors were little different from any number of Roman aristocrats with private sculpture collections; they were simply collecting on an altogether grander scale and buying generally superior copies. But the most important point to be made is that the *spolia* artworks collected for the Arch of Constantine were not copies; they were all originals and this makes their reuse innovative rather than simply an act of pure nostalgia or an act of desperation in the face of a dearth of good contemporary sculptors, as some authorities have suggested as a motive for their reuse.

4

Inspired by the Divine

The Late Antique Decoration

Leaving aside the quite obviously reused Hadrianic, Trajanic, and Antonine artworks reset in the Arch of Constantine, there is also a considerable quantity of Late Antique decoration on the arch which may be Constantinian, or at least more or less contemporary with the arch structure in date. The view that *all* of the arch is constituted of *spolia*, including the decorative elements, would have these evidently late-decorated stones coming from a pre-Constantinian monument.

The Late Antique decoration on the arch consists of four specific elements: decorative busts, decorative *tondi* or roundels, decorated spandrels above the central arch, and a narrow continuous frieze around all four sides of the upper part of the arch. Each of these will now be described in turn. The decorated pedestal bases on which the Corinthian columns rest are also probably contemporary, though anachronistic in style.

The decorative busts are set into the two side passageways in pairs on each facing wall, making eight busts in total originally. However, not all of them survive today. In the east passageway, on its east wall, is a bust of a martial figure in armour, whose damaged face prohibits firm identification, accompanied by Victory. A second bust has been removed on this side. On the west wall of the eastern passageway is a bust of Sol wearing a radiate crown. The second bust on the west wall is no longer extant. In the western passageway, on its east wall, are two busts of figures wearing armour, one accompanied by two Victories. On the west wall only one bust survives, of a male figure, notably not wearing a cuirass like the other three males portrayed in busts. Logic dictates that the four males are emperors. However, these busts are relatively small and positioned where most viewers of the arch would not be aware of their presence without going through the side passages; this seems a curious way to celebrate imperial authority. Four imperial busts suggests the depiction of Constantine and the other three contemporary Tetrarchs together, though this would have been unlikely given that the victory celebrated by the arch's erection more or less marked the sundering of the Tetrarchy. If, as has been suggested, two of the busts depicted Constantine and his co-emperor Licinius[1] then it does not follow that the other two individuals portrayed can be easily identified. Perhaps the busts are of Constantine and the male members of his family, that is, his late father Constantius Chlorus, and two of his sons.

The two Late Antique decorative *tondi*, or relief roundels, are found one each on the east and west short faces of the arch, positioned above the narrow Late Antique relief band. The east-face *tondo* (fig. 29) depicts Sol in a long garment, stepping out of the sea, overseen by Oceanus, and being transported upwards in a four-horse chariot or *quadriga*. He holds the orb of the sun in his hand and is guided in his solar ascent by a small winged figure holding a torch. The west-face *tondo* (fig. 30) depicts Luna – the Moon, again dressed in a long, flowing garment, descending in a chariot towards the sea. The winged guide is in attendance again and once more Oceanus awaits below. Together these two images represent the relentless, inescapable passing of time, and form part of the narrative on the arch that is centred on the relationship of past, present, and future, as mediated by memory. These are accomplished pieces of classicising art; that such works could be produced at this time rather argues against the idea that the Constantinian frieze represents poor art resulting from a shortage of skilled sculptors and masons.

One of the most interesting aspects of the Constantinian sculptures on the arch is the appearance of Sol and the implications of this for our understanding of Constantine's religious beliefs in or around those crucial years when he became drawn towards Christianity either for practical or pragmatic reasons.[2] The setting of the monument is also relatable to the emperor's interest in Sol, as has been discussed in Chapter Two. The Latin Panegyric of AD 310[3] tells us of Constantine's visit to a temple of Apollo in Gaul and how this led to the adoption of Sol-Apollo as the protector deity of Constantine and his subsequent dynasty. In the temple Constantine had a vision of Apollo offering him laurels, and saw in this act a confirmation that he was somehow being anointed the new Augustus.

The decorated spandrels above the central arch on both north and south facades bear images of Victories holding trophies and accompanied by *putti*, which may represent the four seasons and thus once more the passing of time, quite obviously by now a leitmotif of the arch as a whole (plate 15). These are so similar in design to the figures of Victories on the Arch of Septimius Severus that conscious copying or referencing can be thought to have taken place in this instance. Above the smaller arches/bays are spandrel images of river gods, eight in total, something that would appear to be entirely appropriate in the context of the role played by the Tiber in the defeat of Maxentius's army and of his own drowning. These images, of course, echo the presence of the Tiber god in the frieze scene depicting the Battle of the Milvian Bridge. Figures on the keystones are very badly worn, and with the possible exception of a portrayal of Mars, these are in all honesty beyond identification.

The plinths, or socles, supporting the four free-standing columns in front of both long facades are decorated on three sides, with Victory on their fronts and scenes of Romans with barbarian captives on their side faces (figs 31 and 32). They very much duplicate the decoration of the socles on the Arch of Septimius Severus and those that survive from the otherwise destroyed Arcus Novus, and which are now located in the Boboli Gardens in Florence. Indeed, so close are these three sets of decorated socles in appearance, it has been suggested that such artworks were now accepted as a standard item to be included in any major post-Severan imperial triumphal monument.

29. A Constantinian *tondo* depicting Sol. East face of the Arch of Constantine, Rome. (Photo: Author)

30. A Constantinian *tondo* depicting Luna. West face of the Arch of Constantine, Rome. (Photo: Author)

31. Detail of the Constantinian pedestal bases decorated with barbarian captives and Victories. The Arch of Constantine, Rome. (Photo: Author)

32. Detail of one of the Constantinian pedestal bases decorated with barbarian captives and Victories. The Arch of Constantine, Rome. (Photo: Author)

The image of the barbarian captive was by now so ingrained in the vocabulary of imperial triumph that to some extent the appearance of the captive barbarians here is meaningless in terms of any historical context relating to contemporary events. Perhaps the barbarians in chains were to be taken as substitute images for defeated members of Maxentius's army, though elsewhere on the monument the issue of the defeat of Romans by Romans had certainly not been shied away from or dealt with in an allusive manner.

The narrow continuous frieze around all four sides of the upper part of the arch measures just under 4 feet in height, though its placing low down on the arch coupled with the depth of the carving makes it perfectly visible from the ground today, as it must have been in the fourth century. It depicts the emperor both carrying out his imperial duties, as might be expected to be found on any imperial monument here in Rome, and also his military campaign against Maxentius. In other words we are seeing here an extraordinary and otherwise unprecedented depiction of civil war in the Roman world. It is generally accepted that the frieze should be read starting at the short west side of the arch. It is highly novel in the context of viewing a Roman arch to achieve a coherent understanding of a frieze such as this by moving around the monument to end the viewing where it had started. This is more commonly a strategy used by an artist when decorating a column such as those of Trajan and of Marcus Aurelius. The Constantinian frieze to all intents and purposes is in the form of a visual timeline spanning the months between Constantine's invasion of Italy in the autumn of AD 312 and his victorious distribution of largesse to the Roman populace on 1 January AD 313.

The frieze begins, then, on the short west face, with the depiction of Constantine's army marching out from a camp or perhaps, as has been suggested, the city gate of Milan on their way to confront Maxentius's forces at Verona (figs 33, 34, 35). The order of march is clearly delineated. At the rear, caught just coming through the gate, is a large wagon drawn by four horses and carrying two officers wearing tunics and cloaks, on their heads are the round, brimless pillbox hat – the *pileus pannonicus* or Pannonian cap – adopted by Diocletian and the Tetrarchs as a uniform cap. Immediately ahead of them is a group of similarly clad soldiers walking with the baggage train, represented by a laden mule or donkey and, most extraordinarily, a baggage camel. Cavalry accompany the baggage train on the flanks. As is so often the case with Roman imperial friezes, a

33. The Constantinian frieze – the army on the march from Milan. West face of the Arch of Constantine, Rome. (Photo: Graham Norrie, after Giuliani 1955)

Above and below: 34. and 35. The Constantinian frieze – detail of the army on the march from Milan. West face, the Arch of Constantine, Rome. (Photo: Graham Norrie, after Giuliani 1955)

small anomalous detail has been added to this martial scene, presumably to help add a human dimension to the scene and to amuse the viewers. In front and to the side of the front-most baggage mule is the figure of a soldier sat on the ground where he seems to have fallen, as if he has just tumbled off the baggage animal or fallen over. This immediately brings to mind a similar scene (Scene IX) on Trajan's Column where a barbarian emissary to Trajan is shown having fallen off a mule, and it is difficult to believe that the Constantinian artist was not aware of that episode and its visual power. Ahead of the baggage train march heavily armed, helmeted troops with spears and shields, in amongst whom are two *signifers* or standard-bearers holding aloft standards with images of Victory and Sol Invictus on them. Soldiers with musical instruments lead the way and march to the far end of the frieze on this face.

On the south long face of the arch the frieze is in two separate sections, one on either side of the central passageway, above the side passageways. In the first, westernmost, section, the army has arrived at the city of Verona and is depicted laying siege to its walls (figs 36, 37, 38, 39, 40). Constantine appears on this part of the frieze, dismounted from his horse and resting his hand on a huge shield, attended by bodyguards and in the process of being crowned victor by Victory, who spectacularly hovers at full length above the throng of soldiers in the air beside him. Though the emperor is foregrounded in this scene he nevertheless appears to be much larger in size in relation to his surrounding troops than is altogether realistic. This is obviously a strategy employed by the artist to draw the viewer's attention straightaway to the figure of the emperor. The emperor's face does not survive today. Constantine's besieging troops are shown in two main tiers, those Roman soldiers towards the front of the scene posed with their shields up and their spears held ready in attack, looking up at the walls of the besieged city. Behind them, less clearly depicted, are perhaps Moorish auxiliary soldiers and archers firing arrows at the city's defenders. The city walls and its five crenellated towers are dramatically rendered as a solid block, seemingly impregnable examples of great Roman architecture that in other contexts would be seen as unassailable by barbarian foes. Above the parapets of the beleaguered city can be seen the defenders of Verona, brandishing shields and spears and in two instances depicted ready to hurl rocks or stones down onto the heads of the soldiers in Constantine's army.

However, this scene is further enlivened by two events happening right in front of the city walls. Over towards the main detachment of the besieging army the body

36. The Constantinian frieze – the siege of Verona. South face, the Arch of Constantine, Rome. (Photo: Graham Norrie, after Giuliani 1955)

Above and below: 37. and 38. The Constantinian frieze – detail of the siege of Verona. South face, the Arch of Constantine, Rome. (Photo: Graham Norrie, after Giuliani 1955)

Above and below: 39. and 40. The Constantinian frieze – detail of the siege of Verona. South face, the Arch of Constantine, Rome. (Photo: Graham Norrie, after Giuliani 1955)

of one of the city's defenders falls dead off the high battlements, his body caught in mid-air by the artist as he plummets headfirst towards the ground, his limp arms outstretched, his legs bent up under his falling body. If this were not dramatic enough, along the outer face of the city walls runs the solitary figure of one of Constantine's soldiers, spear in hand and shield raised up towards the walls to protect himself from the enemy missiles raining down on him from on high. We are evidently intended to understand that this man is involved in some kind of strategic manoeuvre to breach the defensive cordon and capture the city, the event that Constantine is already depicted as celebrating. The depiction of the siege of the city again brings to mind certain images on Trajan's Column, such as the Dacian assault on a Roman fort (Scene XXXII) and the Roman assault on a Dacian fortress, off whose walls falls a dead defender (Scene CXIII), and once more it makes one wonder whether such a coincidental depiction was accidental or paying deliberate artistic homage to the earlier work. It can also be asked whether, to the literate viewer, the image of the lone Roman hero making a circuit of the outside of the city walls did not somehow echo the story of Achilles pursuit of Hector three times around the walls of Troy.

The easternmost section of the south face frieze depicts the victory at the Battle of the Milvian Bridge, illustrated in quite graphic detail, again with the figure of Constantine, no longer extant, placed firmly in the action to the right of the scene, standing on a barge on the river with Victory and Dea Roma and viewing the carnage around as Maxentius's troops are slaughtered or drowned in the Tiber (figs 41, 42, 43). The river god himself rears up in the churning water in front of the imperial barge. On the far left of the scene two musicians, possibly the same two from the depiction of the exit from Milan, strike up a victory fanfare. The events of 28 October AD 312 are shown in two registers. In the background are the emperor and gods and goddesses, the musicians, and the rest of his army – infantrymen, cavalry, and bow-firing Moorish auxiliaries – and in the foreground is the fast-flowing River Tiber with its waters enveloping Maxentius's heavily armoured troops, who have fallen or been driven into the river. The body of one soldier is shown tumbling off the riverbank, killed by one of Constantine's men. The writhing, interlocked bodies of the soldiers in the river assume the character of a netted shoal of fish, agitating the waters, their scale armour flashing and glinting like fish scales. On the bank the depiction of a trio of Moorish archers, all posed in exactly the same way, suggests the regimented, methodical

41. The Constantinian frieze – the Battle of the Milvian Bridge. South face, the Arch of Constantine, Rome. (Photo: Graham Norrie, after Giuliani 1955)

Above and below: 42. and 43. The Constantinian frieze – detail of the Battle of the Milvian Bridge. South face, the Arch of Constantine, Rome. (Photo: Graham Norrie, after Giuliani 1955)

nature of the slaughter. On the far left a Maxentian soldier kneels begging for mercy.

There is no doubt that the composition of this battle scene owes a great deal in terms of inspiration to Antonine battle sarcophagi and to the intricately composed vignettes of slaughter on the Column of Marcus Aurelius, though the use of repetitively posed figures on the arch relief introduces an element of pattern into the basic equation.

Curiously, a victory procession, the entry into Rome the day after the Battle of the Milvian Bridge, starts towards the very end of the south facade, where two stray soldiers are depicted at the rear of what is subsequently discovered by the viewer to be the victorious column, the main body of the victorious marching army being depicted on the east face of the arch (figs 44, 45, 46). There, Constantine once more is clearly depicted in the processional caravan, transported on a four-horse wagon decorated with acanthus tendrils, the horses' leads being held by the figure of Victory. The now headless emperor enters Rome through an arch, presumably the Porta Flaminia. The artist has taken a great deal of care to portray the victorious Constantine as a still, seated figure in a scene otherwise dominated by the forward movement of the victory parade. Without the emperor's head surviving it is difficult to say whether the emperor's demeanour here was intended to be totally passive, although that certainly seems to have been the case. Wearing a belted tunic and a mantle-like cloak, the emperor holds a scroll in one hand, an indicator of imperial legitimacy perhaps, the other hand unfortunately being damaged. He is seated on an elaborate chair decorated with ivy leaves. The rest of the scene is taken up by the soldiers of the army, cavalry and infantry, many of the figures being duplicated to produce another pattern effect, in two or three registers to indicate depth of field. One or two of the men glance back in the direction of the emperor, but otherwise the momentum is forward-looking. One of the units carries two banners in the form of dragons – *dracones* – raised high above their heads.

A phalanx of cavalrymen canter forward, the whole procession heading through an arch along the route of the parade. It has been suggested that the decoration of elephants on this arch marks it out as being the now lost Arch of Domitian,[4] which stood in the Campus Martius.

Given the great significance of the defeat of Maxentius to Constantine, it is not altogether surprising that a possible allusion to this victory also appears on another piece of Constantinian artwork, the carved Great Cameo in the Dutch Royal Collection

44. The Constantinian frieze – Constantine's entry into Rome. East face, the Arch of Constantine, Rome. (Photo: Graham Norrie, after Giuliani 1955)

Above and below: 45. and 46. The Constantinian frieze – detail of Constantine's entry into Rome. East face, the Arch of Constantine, Rome. (Photo: Graham Norrie, after Giuliani 1955)

described in detail in Chapter One. The enemies of Constantine, here being trampled by one of the centaurs pulling his triumphal chariot, are not bearded barbarians but clean-shaven Roman soldiers, obviously defeated in a civil war.

On the north face of the arch we move from scenes of war to two scenes of peace. Just as Constantine featured as soldier emperor at Verona and the Milvian Bridge and as imperial victor entering Rome, so he now appears as an emperor attending to matters of state. But these pivotal scenes are not simply about the emperor. Rather it is to all intents and purposes about the city of Rome itself, about its Forum, streets, arches, monuments, and temples. Indeed, with the exception of the late Flavian or Trajanic Tomb of the Haterii monument now in the Vatican Museums, Rome, it is difficult to think of any other Roman monument where intertextuality of this kind and on this level occurs.

In the easternmost scene – known as the *oratio* – Constantine, once more now headless, is depicted addressing the Roman people from the Rostra or orators' platform in the Roman Forum (figs 47 and 48). The emperor is dressed in military uniform, to emphasise the establishment of his present power by force of arms and probably to reassure viewers that he was very much a soldier emperor in the mould of Trajan. He is at the very centre of the scene, symbolically placing him at the very centre of Roman life and politics, and stands in front of a Jupiter column and two military banners on either side of it. He looks directly out from the Rostra into the Forum, or rather in this case towards the viewer of this scene on the arch. The scene is crowded with around seventy figures in the emperor's audience, including three boys, though no women are present. The emperor is shown surrounded by senators in togas, the very men who would have voted for the dedication of the arch that the viewer is looking at; some of these, too, are posed frontally, but the majority turn their heads to watch the emperor deliver his oration. Crowds of men and a few boys flank the Rostra on either side.

The attention to detail is quite extraordinary and quite deliberate. The Rostra itself is depicted in some detail, with its stone screen and pilasters topped by small statue heads of *amorini*. The dais is further decorated with seated statues on pedestals on both the left and right sides, the most likely identifications of these bearded figures being Marcus Aurelius and Hadrian. While at first glance it is easy to mistake these life-size statues for members of the emperor's audience, in a way the artist responsible for placing these statues so prominently in this scene when there is no record of such statues having been permanently

47. The Constantinian frieze – *Oratio* scene. Constantine addresses the Senate and Roman people. North face, the Arch of Constantine, Rome. (Photo: Graham Norrie, after Giuliani 1955)

48. The Constantinian frieze – detail of the *Oratio* scene (Constantine addressing the Senate and Roman people). North face, the Arch of Constantine, Rome. (Photo: Graham Norrie, after Giuliani 1955)

on show on the Rostra was suggesting their presence here on that winter day in AD 312 in the form of spirits of the emperor's ancestors, his *imagines*, even though there was no bloodline or direct link between Constantine, Hadrian, and Marcus Aurelius. Yet here they were in attendance at his speech, certifying his legitimacy. Many urban monuments are shown; the triple-arched Arch of Septimius Severus, the now lost single-bay Arch of Tiberius, the Basilica Julia represented by its arcades, the Basilica Aemilia. Five columns appear in the background: atop one is a statue of Jupiter in front of which Constantine stands to deliver his oration, the four others probably carried statues of the original Tetrarchy – Diocletian, Maximian, Constantius Chlorus and Galerius. These columns were part of the Decennalia Monument set up by Diocletian in AD 303.

The westernmost scene on the north face of the arch is a scene of *congiarium*, the distribution of monies to the members of the Senate and the Roman people by the emperor, which is a historical event recorded as having taken place on 1 January AD 313 (figs 49, 50, 51). Constantine, now headless, yet again occupies a dais at the very centre of the scene. Dressed on this occasion in civilian clothes, he sits on a chair or throne raised up above the surrounding throng. In his hand he holds a coin tray, probably made of wood, out of which he is emptying money. A senator is portrayed catching some falling coins in the folds of his toga, while other senators stand by to receive their allotted share. On either side of him, on the upper level of the dais, are more senators,

49. The Constantinian frieze – *Congiarium* scene. Constantine distributes monies to the Senate and Roman people. North face, the Arch of Constantine, Rome. (Photo: Graham Norrie, after Giuliani 1955)

50. The Constantinian frieze – detail of the *Congiarium* scene (Constantine distributing monies to the Senate and Roman people). North face, the Arch of Constantine, Rome. (Photo: Graham Norrie, after Giuliani 1955)

51. The Constantinian frieze – detail of the *Congiarium* scene (Constantine distributing monies to the Senate and Roman people). North face, the Arch of Constantine, Rome. (Photo: Graham Norrie, after Giuliani 1955)

in this instance seemingly here to help oversee the distribution of money; indeed one of them appears to be passing some loose coins to the emperor. Two attendants carrying candles or torches stand on either side of the group of observers, providing both light for the ceremony and a suitably theatrical setting for the emperor's otherwise aloof presence. To the side of the imperial and senatorial party on the upper tier are depicted four rooms, two to either side, occupied by busy parties of bureaucrats whose backstage counting and sorting of money and keeping of written records of the amounts of money being handed out is helping to ensure the smooth running of this exercise in imperial largesse. Four accountants are depicted in each room seated on low benches. In the centre of each room is what appears to be a strongbox; individual accountants variously pass around coin trays or tip coins out for counting, or unfurl scrolls on which their records are being kept. Once more the audience for the *congiarium*, queuing in single file with arms upraised, is exclusively male, with just six young male children being present. A number of these children are being held aloft on the shoulders of adults, reaching out their hands in a gesture of need towards the emperor. Such poses by children are not altogether dissimilar to the poses of children receiving *alimenta* from the Emperor Trajan on his great arch at Benevento.

There can be no doubt that stylistically the Constantinian frieze is very much in the Late Antique tradition of sarcophagus art. This does not imply that only sarcophagus artists were available to work on the arch, thus second-rate work was produced. One has only to look at the sprightly figures of Victories in the spandrels and in the frieze and the representations of Sol and Luna in the *tondi* to see that skilled sculptors and stoneworkers were available for the commission and could produce work in a classicising, anachronistic style if required to do so.

Reading the Arch

Having now described the various individual decorative elements that were assembled or created to adorn the arch, an attempt will now be made to suggest how the arch may have been viewed up close from the ground by contemporary Roman citizens. How the arch might have been viewed by those approaching it from some distance away and how it related to other monuments in the viewer's sight lines has already been discussed in Chapter Two.

The most obvious way for the ancient viewer to have looked at the arch is pretty much the same as how the modern viewer might experience it, by looking at each of the four faces in turn and perhaps by then following the narrow Constantinian frieze around the arch from beginning to end, once the starting point for the narrative of the frieze had been established. With the exception of the decorated pedestal bases for the Corinthian columns and the artwork in the passageways and in the spandrels of the three arched passageways, this frieze is physically the lowest decorative element on the arch's facades, stressing its importance and significance and of course making it more clearly visible to the viewer. The majority of the reused Trajanic, Hadrianic and Aurelian sculpture appear at higher levels on the facades.

The modern visitor, without special access, cannot walk through the passageways of the arch and thus cannot experience the sensation of viewing the artworks here on the sides of the passageway or look up at the passageway ceilings. Reading the inscriptions on the two long sides and on the sides of the central passageway would also have formed an essential part of the viewing experience.

Logic dictates that viewing would have started with one of the two long faces, probably the south face, which looks away from the civic centre of Rome (plate 17). Appropriately, then, the south face of the arch is dominated by depictions of battle and siege in the Constantinian frieze. Just as we see Constantine and his army en route to the siege of Verona and then slaughtering Maxentius and his army at the Battle of the Milvian Bridge, so above we see Hadrian/Constantine setting off for the hunt, killing a bear and sacrificing to Diana in thanks. Both represent bloody ends to imperial ventures. Above in the attic Marcus Aurelius/Constantine is pictured in his campaign headquarters, treating with a client king, addressing his troops, sacrificing, bloodletting again, and receiving prisoners. Barbarian prisoners in the form of the giant Dacians line the top of the facade, barbarian prisoners on the pedestal bases for the columns catch the viewer's eye at the bottom.

On the north long face a very different message is received by the viewer, with battle and war now giving way to scenes in which civic life now predominates and the emperor's role as soldier now gives way to his role as statesman and arbiter of religious duties (plate 16). Tellingly, this face looks towards the civic centre of the city, being on the Forum side of the arch. By walking around the arch from one long side to another, or by moving through the passageways, the viewer has moved from a state of war to a time of peace, this transformation mediated by the skilful selection and juxtaposition of the disparately sourced imagery on the two opposed long faces of the arch. In the Constantinian frieze on this face the emperor addresses the Senate and people of Rome and is later seen distributing largesse. Above, Hadrian/Constantine hunts a boar and sacrifices to Apollo; he then hunts a lion and sacrifices to Hercules. Higher still, Marcus Aurelius/Constantine is shown both leaving Rome for war and returning to the city after victories. He receives barbarian prisoners, including a boy, and grants them clemency. He is finally depicted distributing largesse to the Roman people, including a woman and children. As if to underpin the message that there can be no peace, no celebratory triumphal distribution of largesse, without war the Dacian barbarians above and the bound barbarian prisoners below on the pedestal bases intrude into the viewer's line of sight.

On the short west face the Constantinian frieze catches the scene of Constantine and his forces setting off from Milan to move against Maxentius (fig. 52). Immediately above is a Constantinian *tondo* depicting the setting moon. Above in the attic is a

52. Detail of the west face of the Arch of Constantine, Rome. (Photo: Author)

Trajanic battle scene. Caught in profile in the viewer's eye are two statues of male Dacian prisoners to either side of the body of the attic, and at ground level are two faces of pedestal bases on either side, each bearing images of male and female barbarian prisoners and Roman standards. This represents a relatively harmonious and consistent message to the viewer, in which all enemies of Rome, whether enemies without, such as barbarians, or enemies within, such as Maxentius, are conflated over time to become one universal adversary, of Rome, of its emperor, and of its historical sense of self as represented by imperial duty and service to the (pagan) gods. There is a message of hope here for the viewer, who sees Constantine's army moving off to war in the depiction of the historical precedent of the victory of his predecessor against similar dark forces.

On the short east face the Constantinian frieze depicts Constantine's forces marching in triumph towards Rome after Maxentius's defeat (fig. 53). Immediately above, as on the west face, is a Constantinian *tondo*, on this occasion depicting the rising sun. Above, in the attic, is a Trajanic scene of triumph, as Roman soldiers sound instruments and cavalrymen's horses trample barbarians underfoot. Once more, caught in profile in the viewer's eye are two statues of male Dacian prisoners to either side of the body of the attic, and at ground level two faces of pedestal bases on either side, each bearing images of male and female barbarian prisoners and Roman standards. The hope held out to the viewer by the images on the west face has now been realised by the intervention of the hand of history and Roman tradition.

53. East face of the Arch of Constantine, Rome. (Photo: Author)

As arches were always intended to be structures that people would pass through, sometimes in procession, it might have been be easy for some viewers to have missed the decorative schemes on the two short faces of the arch entirely. However, in a way, their artistic messages were supplementary to the main message conveyed on the two long faces of the arch, that is, the contrasting of war and peace, and of military duty and civic duty.

Though the arch is a monument on which past and present time have been freely mixed in terms of the liberal use of decorated *spolia* of different earlier periods, there are nevertheless two clear horizontal demarcation lines on the arch. The Constantinian artworks all appear on the lower part of the monument, the past *spolia* on the upper part above the narrow Constantinian frieze. Of course the two Constantinian *tondi* on the east and west short faces are set above the frieze, but no *spolia* artworks appear beneath them, so here the horizontal line, with a looping up to take in these two *tondi*, is more or less dividing past from present. Again, if one remembers that there would have been contemporary Constantinian bronze statues on top of the arch, then once more a line could be drawn under these, separating them from the zone of *spolia* artworks. Thus we would have had three time zones of artworks representing three separate horizontal fields on the arch, starting at the lower level with Constantinian time, in the central zone with pre-Constantinian time, and in the upper zone returning to Constantinian time. A slight muddying of the waters with regard to this conscious separation of present time from past times would have been created by the recarving of portrait heads in the pre-Constantinian time zone to relocate Constantine himself there in the viewer's eye, if not necessarily in his or her mind.

Architecture, Barbarians, and Children

While I have now presented summaries of the main academic interpretations of the Arch of Constantine, there are three topics that I would like to return to briefly here, that is the representation of Roman architecture and of barbarian peoples on the arch, and the appearance there also of images of children in a few scenes. All of these groups of images contribute significantly to the overall ideological programme of the arch and their detailed study in the future would doubtless make a significant further contribution to the interpretation of the monument.

The images of warfare that appear on the arch are either of long-distant conflicts from the reigns of Trajan and Marcus Aurelius, or of civil war – of the banishing of the tyrant Maxentius by the liberator Constantine, as the arch's dedicatory inscription would have it. The depiction of scenes of civil war here was a startling novelty and represented both a break with the past, with the political consensus that for centuries had worked against such portrayals on monuments in Rome, and provided a link with the distant past when a maverick figure like Augustus had felt confident and secure enough in his power to celebrate his victory over Antony and Cleopatra with monumental commissions in the heart of the city.

The arch also marks a break with the past in that it is the last great civic monument constructed in Rome. While other commemorative imperial monuments such as

the Column of Arcadius and the Column of Theodosius may have been erected in
Constantinople, in Rome itself the emphasis in the mother city now turned towards
the building of churches, sometimes under state patronage, certainly under state
agreement. It is therefore of great significance to consider the implications of the
depiction of buildings in Rome on the Arch of Constantine.

The use of images of architecture as a signifier on the arch is quite complex in
its sophistication. I have previously written about the use of images of Romanised
buildings in various scenes depicted on Trajan's Column and on the frieze around
the later Column of Marcus Aurelius.[5] In both instances solid Roman structures
were juxtaposed and contrasted with the more rough-and-ready timber buildings of
barbarian peoples, and thus acted as metaphors for the difference between civilisation
and barbarism, between the Roman world and the world of the barbarian peoples
beyond the frontiers of the empire. I have also suggested that the longer-lasting
qualities of Romanised stone structures, their permanence if you will, in their
materiality and monumentality represented the continuing strength and longevity
of the Roman Empire, as the timber and thatch, daub and reeds of native dwellings
rotted away with time as their peoples' cultural legacy waned.

On the Arch of Constantine, images of buildings or structures appeared on both
artworks that were reset or reused here as *spolia*, that is, on some of the panel reliefs of
Marcus Aurelius, and in the so-called *oratio* scene on the Constantinian frieze. Bridges,
city walls, triumphal arches, the Rostra in the Roman Forum, and the columns of the
Decennalia Monument of Diocletian are all depicted here. The latter was erected in
AD 305 to commemorate the tenth anniversary of the Tetrarchy, and it is therefore
ironic that Constantine, who had more or less single-handedly sundered the Tetrarchy,
should now be depicted in association with this monument, an irony that would not
surely have been lost on many of the arch's viewers. In any case the intertextuality here
– of the viewer looking at a real monument in Rome on which are depicted images of
other real monuments in Rome – stresses beyond doubt the centrality and importance
of Mother Rome in the events being depicted. This was probably part of the Senate's
deliberate policy to make use of the opportunity provided by the dedication and
inauguration of the arch to reassert the primacy of Rome the city at this time.

Thus the Romanised buildings depicted on the arch seem to have played two
distinct roles there: to provide contrast with the many figures of barbarians depicted
on the arch, in terms of contrasting civilisation, as represented by Roman architecture,
with barbarity, as represented by their subservience to the power of Rome; and to
remind Constantine and the Roman viewers of the importance of Rome's architectural
heritage and thus its of its primacy among the cities of the Roman Empire.

Another of my academic interests is the way in which barbarians were portrayed
in Roman art and how images of non-Roman peoples – barbarians – were sometimes
used by the Romans to achieve the same sort of contrasting of civilisation/barbarism
as has just been discussed with regard to images of buildings and other architectural
elements such as arches, bridges, or town walls. In my extended study *Enemies of Rome:
Barbarians Through Roman Eyes* I discussed the way in which images of barbarians
became largely debased after the reigns of Marcus Aurelius and Commodus, and that

the kind of anthropological images of foreign peoples that could be seen in some earlier Roman artistic contexts, and some more sympathetic portrayals, fell away in numbers in the third and fourth centuries.[6]

It might therefore be of some interest to consider the numerous images of barbarians which appear on the Arch of Constantine, these falling into two different chronological and ethnic groups: the earliest borrowed Trajanic images are of Dacian warriors, the later group being largely Germanic tribespeople at war with the emperor Marcus Aurelius. Yet viewers of the scenes of barbarian slaughter, submission, and captivity on the arch would also have been singularly aware of the presence there also of scenes of the killing of Romans by Romans, that is troops of Maxentius's army being overcome by Constantine's forces.

As I wrote at the time in my previous book, 'The presence [of images of Dacians on the arch] must ... also have been a cautionary one, to remind the Roman viewer of the fact that, due to pressures on the empire in the later third century, the Romans had been forced to evacuate Dacia in AD 271, and that the need for vigilance against the barbarian foe was as real in the era of Constantine as it had been at the time of Trajan.'

The Aurelian images of Germanic barbarians were again not altogether without a contemporary resonance for Roman citizens of Constantine's time. Constantine's own victories against Franks and other German tribes across the Rhine were celebrated in a panegyric delivered at Trier in AD 310,[7] yet, though he had accompanied the emperors Diocletian and Galerius on a number of military expeditions, his own early reign was not marked by campaigning against barbarians on any really significant scale.

This pictorial timeline of Roman victories from the time of Trajan up to that of Constantine placed the Roman army at the very centre of the action alongside the emperor. References to the past in the artworks on the arch may have been intended as tributes to the Roman army and have helped locate Constantine in the minds of the arch's viewers as a soldier emperor in the spirit of Trajan. Constantine had been hailed as Augustus by the army in Britain at York, following the death of his father there, and it was the continuing loyalty of his troops that had brought him victory in the civil war and ensured that he entered Rome in triumph. Establishing legitimacy for these forces – they were now *the* Roman army and not *a* Roman army – could have been enhanced by reference to Trajan, that most military of emperors; to Hadrian, architect of the vast frontier works in Britain and elsewhere; to Marcus Aurelius whose reign was largely taken up by his campaigning far away from Rome and Italy; and to Septimius Severus, who put an end to contemporary civil strife and who, like Constantine's father, died on campaign in Britain. Certainly the presence of numerous barbarians on the arch, historic enemies from both the east and the north, attested to the victory of Rome against her previous enemies in general. Maxentius, while not obviously a barbarian, could nevertheless now be defined, like the barbarians, as an enemy of Rome, if only in the eyes of the new Constantinian regime and its majority supporters in the Senate. Such a conclusion is reinforced by an examination of the language used in contemporary panegyrics.

The figure of Victory also appears in a number of scenes on the arch, as might have been expected on any Roman triumphal or commemorative arch. However, the

Victories that appear in the spandrels of the arch are again not simply the Victories to represent the eternal triumph of Roman over barbarian, but are here also to represent Constantine's victory during the recent civil strife.

The co-opting and subversion of the images of timeless Roman architectural structures, of barbarians, and of Victory on the Arch of Constantine together make a very consistent and conscious statement about Constantine's place in the timeline of Roman imperial history. It need not altogether be surprising that such images of civilisation, victory, and enslavement of enemies still had a resonance, some emotional currency, even in times when sweeping geo-political and cultural change was altering the Roman Empire almost beyond recognition from what it had been in the first and second centuries AD.

The appearance of Roman children in both the *oratio* and *congiarium* scenes on the arch also deserves some further comment here, as this too could have related to concepts concerning the blurring of temporal boundaries and the interruption of linear time.[8] One authority has suggested that a lack of women on the arch and the small number of children that do appear signify the lack of importance attached to family symbolism in the art and image-building of Constantine. However, this would seem to ignore both the evidence of imperial gemstones and coins, as discussed in Chapter One, and the tone of some parts of the contemporary panegyrics. The children might be thought to appear on the arch firstly because they represent a new generation in Rome, the future of the city, and in this symbolic role images of children might be thought to fit in well with the playful manipulation of ideas relating to the relationship of past, present, and future, which underpins the use and interpretation of much of the artwork on the arch. In the *oratio* scene Constantine is addressing the present and future citizens of Rome, watched over by the images of past emperors. This scene is all about heritage, memory, and legacy. In the *congiarium* scene, the children in the queue to receive the imperial largesse are there not as individual recipients of Constantine's generosity, rather they are representative of the emperor's providing for and feeding the children of Rome. This means they too can serve their city and empire, their emperor, in the future, having grown up strong and healthy thanks to Constantine's perpetuation and continuation of this system of imperial help for the families of the city. Constantine is not quite becoming 'the father of the country', the aim of the childless Trajan, but at least he is becoming its reliable provider into the future.

If, as has been suggested in this chapter, Constantine, or more properly the Roman Senate, had attempted to manipulate time and memory in order to present the emperor to the Roman people as being in a continuum in the line of 'good emperors' that ended with Marcus Aurelius in the late second century, then an examination of other contemporary monuments might allow us to identify other instances of this occurrence. This topic will therefore be examined in the next chapter.

5

The Ghost in the Machine

That the Arch of Constantine is in a number of ways a unique and unprecedented monument in the cityscape of Rome is beyond argument. Indeed, one of its most significant characteristics is the fact that it is in effect a monument to civil war in the Roman world, in contrast to the numerous monuments in the city commemorating Roman victories over barbarian peoples. The Roman Senate who dedicated the arch to Constantine were not only apparently happy to celebrate here the defeat of 'the tyrant' Maxentius, they also appear to have taken the opportunity of choosing of the scheme of artworks on it to restate and restress the importance of the relationship between an emperor and the city of Rome itself. That this didactic message was not lost on Constantine, at least for a few years after his victory at the Milvian Bridge and subsequent rise to power, can be seen by his impact on the appearance and urban topography of Rome in the next decade. Indeed, there is a growing body of evidence and opinion to suggest that Constantine spent a great deal of his time and energy trying to exorcise the ghost of Maxentius and to drive his memory away from the streets and public spaces of Rome by his own architectural munificence. In this chapter, therefore, consideration will be given to the discussion of other Constantinian monuments in Rome and their propagandist intent, if discernible. In particular an analysis will be made of the building legacy of Maxentius in Rome, and of the growing academic opinion that his impact on Rome in terms of the commissioning of new, sometimes grandiose, building schemes was quite considerable.

The Enemy Within

In order to find any sort of parallel to the arch in terms of its commemoration of civil strife, of Roman citizens killing Roman citizens, we have to go back to the first century BC and the building of the Actian arch and other victory monuments in the Roman Forum, set up to commemorate the victory of Augustus, or rather Octavian as he then was, over Mark Antony in 31 BC[1]. However, Augustus's Actian arch was a monument that would have employed allusive techniques to inform the contemporary viewers of its message and political intentions by proposing that victory at Actium represented victory over the foreign forces of Cleopatra rather than over another Roman army. And yet, it is also known that a temporary monument in celebration of the victory was set up in the form of prows of captured warships mounted on the facade of the speaker's platform, or *Rostra*, in the Roman Forum, and other commemorative monuments were erected, including four bronze columns with ships' prows, apparently cast from bronze from captured ships. The victory was also celebrated on coins of the period and by depictions of the victory arch on some issues.

The victory at Actium was also commemorated in Greece at Nikopolis, on the coast overlooking the battle site. Here a temple was decorated with ship's rams cut off the captured boats of Antony and Cleopatra's navy, and doubtless other artworks were set up to further commemorate Augustus's triumph. It is also commemorated on at least two major monuments set up in the provinces, at Saint-Bertrand-de-Comminges, southern Gaul, in the border area between Gaul and Spain, and at Orange in Provence.[2]

At Saint-Bertrand-de-Comminges a massive Augustan trophy monument was erected, acting as a pendant to the Alpine Trophy of Augustus at La Turbie, above St Tropez. The Saint Bertrand trophy celebrated a triple triumph, with smaller 'Gallic' and 'Hispanic' trophies flanking a large central, naval trophy with attendant victories. The naval trophy consisted of a ship's prow, a female marine deity, an imperial eagle, and a Victory with palm frond and a laurel wreath held aloft in her right hand. At the base of the naval trophy were a dolphin and a crocodile, to represent Augustus's dominion over both land and sea, the crocodile also conveniently alluding to Egypt.

At Orange, the so-called Arch of Tiberius, which in all likelihood is an Augustan arch rededicated to Tiberius, is a massive, triple-bayed triumphal arch, which at first glance represents a monument to the very Roman victories in southern Gaul that led to the annexation of Provence into the Roman Empire and the foundation of a veterans' colony there. Scenes of battles between Romans and Gauls dominate the attic, while images of bound prisoners also appear on the arch, as do depictions of piles of captured Gallic weapons. However, in the present context, the most notable are the panels decorated with naval spoils, including ships' prows, ships' rams, and anchors. Images of tritons also appear. This naval and marine imagery can only really constitute a pictorial reference to Actium.

Whether the citizens of Rome in the fourth century viewed the overt depiction of a victory over Roman forces under Maxentius by Roman forces under Constantine as a historic event unprecedented since the time of Actium, and thus by association saw Constantine as a new Augustus, is open to question. That the Senate wished the Roman people to make this conceptual link is more certain. And indeed Constantine had already started to model his portrait image on that of the youthful Augustus as early as AD 310, as discussed in Chapter One.

Constantine may have felt that a more recent precedent had allowed for the celebration of the triumph of legitimate Roman power over usurpers. This was in the form of the iconography used to commemorate his own father's victory over Allectus in AD 296, thus bringing to an end the ten-year illegitimate regime established in Britain and northern Gaul by Carausius, who had himself been murdered by his right-hand man Allectus in AD 293. As best exemplified by the image on the reverse of the gold Arras Medallion, found in the Beaurains Treasure in 1922, Constantius

I is depicted on horseback approaching the walls and fortifications of the town of London. He holds a lance or spear in one hand and a globe in the other.[3] Outside the city gate kneels a figure in humble greeting, either a personification of the city or a representative of its inhabitants, while a Roman warship approaches the city by river. The legend on the coin declares Constantius to be '*Redditor Lucis Aeternae*' – the Restorer of Eternal Light. This title and acclamation is indeed remarkably similar to the title of '*Fundatori Quietis*' – the Founder of Peace – given to Constantine by the Roman Senate, as recorded by an inscription on the arch. A certain linkage with the past was obviously being attempted here. It is also worth noting that on some of his coin issues from the Rome and Ostia mints, Maxentius had styled himself as '*Liberator Urbis Suae*' – Liberator of Our City – a slogan that was to be turned around on Maxentius's memory by the Senate's also declaring Constantine on the arch to be '*Liberatori Urbis*' – Liberator of the City.

Thus, once more, it can be seen that the artworks and inscriptions on the Arch of Constantine often both attempted and succeeded in conflating the past, present, and future in a highly sophisticated manner that allowed the manipulation of time inherent in the use of *spolia* on the arch to link Constantine directly to the lineage of the 'good emperors' of the first and second centuries AD, and to celebrate victory in a civil war as if his opponent had been a barbarian enemy. The ending of civil strife by Constantine may have been comparable in the viewer's mind with the achievements of Augustus in bringing peace to a fractured Roman world by waging unforgiving war and sealing victory with efficient ruthlessness. On the arch the past may have been most clearly represented by the reused Trajanic, Hadrianic, and Aurelian artworks, and the present by the long dedicatory inscription from the Senate and the short inscription noting his present *decennalia*. The future, however, was presented as a continuum from the present, as represented by the allusion in a short inscription looking forward to years of political stability culminating in Constantine's *vicennalia* ten years hence. Such was the kind of promise of dynastic equilibrium made by Augustus to the Roman people through his presentation of his imperial ideology in artistic propaganda.

The Spectre at the Feast

The great significance of the nature of the relationship between the city of Rome and its emperor was brought home to Constantine in no uncertain terms by the Senate of Rome in their dedication of the arch that bears his name. Not only was he acclaimed there as the liberator of *the* city, that is of Rome, but he was also depicted on the arch as an active protagonist carrying out his imperial duties in the city against a backdrop of its architectural heritage, both in the contemporary Constantinian frieze and in some of the reused relief panels of Marcus Aurelius, where he was presented as Marcus/Constantine to establish a link with the distant past. There could be no more direct a plea to the emperor not to neglect the mother city of the empire than that articulated in the political programme of the arch. Constantine was probably also aware that Maxentius's had sustained his six-year reign by catering to the needs of the city and the proud heritage of its Senate and citizens. Maxentius had identified himself *with* Rome in no uncertain terms. He did not simply style himself as 'liberator of the city', rather he called himself 'liberator of *our* city.' In order to fill what some might have seen as a political vacuum following Maxentius's death, Constantine quite evidently needed to stamp his authority on the city. He needed to make his mark on the city's appearance by commissioning new building schemes and overseeing, or at least encouraging, the completion of unfinished schemes. In order to assess the nature of the Constantinian impact on the architecture and appearance of Rome, it would first seem appropriate to discuss the architectural schemes set in train by Maxentius, some of these subsequently appropriated as 'Constantinian' schemes. It is also pertinent to ask whether there was some kind of curious competition between the living Constantine and the dead Maxentius over the architectural heritage of Late Antique Rome.

Given that his formal reign was quite short, lasting only six years from AD 306 to 312, Maxentius's plans for Rome were astonishingly ambitious for their time, even though the later emperors Diocletian and Maximian oversaw large-scale building projects in the city[4] (plate 18). Indeed, it should be noted that some of Maxentius's building projects in Rome were in point of fact probably completions of unfinished schemes originally set in train by others, particularly his father Maximian. It must not be forgotten that the geographical territory for which Maxentius was responsible as emperor was the very central part of the Roman Empire, which included the city of Rome itself. Indeed, in his propaganda he quite deliberately and, it might be said, blatantly positioned himself as 'the champion of the city of Rome and the guardian of its traditions'.[5] That some of Maxentius's coin issues carried the legend '*conservator urbis suae*' – preserver of his city – seems to have been considered quite provocative, in that it garnered a contrary riposte on the inscription on the Arch of Constantine, which dubbed Constantine as liberator of that self-same city. However, some coin issues of the period also featured Constantine and Maximian, in which case all would appear as '*conservatores*' – preservers. Nevertheless, it is more often than not Maxentius who had this title attached to himself alone.[6] The very fact that under the Tetrarchy new urban centres of power were established at Milan, Trier, Nikomedia, Sirmium, and other places might have been considered a snub by many in the Senate at Rome and among many of the ordinary citizens. While many earlier emperors spent considerable parts of their reigns campaigning away from Rome, and here Marcus Aurelius springs immediately to mind, Rome as *the* centre of the empire was never questioned. Under the Tetrarchs it was becoming *a* centre, among many others.

Despite the *damnatio memoriae* declared by Constantine on Maxentius, a list of the latter's building projects in Rome can be confidently reconstructed from architectural, archaeological, epigraphic, and numismatic evidence enhanced by literary sources. It must be noted that his building projects were not all necessarily schemes to stamp his mark on the very fabric of the city by replacing old buildings with new. In some cases he was probably simply following the intentions of a number of his predecessors, who had been attempting to restore and fill those large areas of the central part of the city devastated by a great fire of AD 283 in the reign of Carinus.[7] Maxentius was also restoring buildings damaged by a fire recorded in his own reign, in AD 307.

The first group of Maxentian buildings to be considered was built on and around the Velian Hill, a complex of structures so substantial that they have been dubbed 'the Forum of Maxentius' by one Italian scholar,[8] though that epithet will not be adopted here, as its use would rather confuse discussion of the function and status of these buildings. These comprised the massive Basilica of Maxentius, the Temple of Romulus, and the Temple of Roma and Venus.

The Basilica of Maxentius, or Basilica Nova, is the grandest of these three buildings; its partial shell comprising just the north aisle of the building still dominates the Velia today. Much of the destruction is owed to the ravages of an earthquake in AD 847[9] (plate 21). Around 315 feet long by 213 feet wide, the building consisted of a central nave, roofed by three vaults supported by four large piers, ending in an apse at its western end. There were two long flanking aisles, with high coffered concrete barrel vaults perpendicular to the nave. On the east side, facing the Temple of Roma and Venus, was an outer porch, which acted as the original entrance. Alterations subsequently made to the building, comprising the addition of a second apse on the north side and a new, grander entrance facing the Palatine Hill to the south, may have been additions in progress under Maxentius, or they might have been Constantinian additions made during the completion of the basilica after AD 312.

The Temple of Romulus is a small and unusual circular building of brick-faced concrete lying at the foot of the Velian Hill and, according to an inscription, was dedicated to Constantine.[10] However, the general consensus among academics today is that this building was indeed Maxentian, but was one of several such buildings rededicated to Constantine after Maxentius's death and *damnatio memoriae*, including of course the Basilica of Maxentius as just discussed. The temple does, though, include in its build a considerable quantity of architectural *spolia*, a choice that was very much a genuine Constantinian cultural phenomenon. The Temple of Roma and Venus was a Hadrianic building, perhaps completed under Antoninus Pius and rebuilt by Maxentius after a fire, according to literary evidence.[11] It lay to the east of the Basilica of Maxentius. As the reader is probably becoming aware, in the case of the two temples there is no conclusive proof one way or another as to whether it was Maxentius or Constantine who started or finished the building works on these structures. As Maxentius was especially determined to align himself with the city of Rome and its mythological and historical past, it would have made considerable sense for him to become personally associated with rebuilding and renovation works at temples dedicated to the legendary Romulus, after whom his son was indeed named, and to Roma herself, the protective goddess of the mother city. Yet the same logic could be applied to Constantine, who immediately after AD 312 would have wished to project the image that the Senate and people of Rome desired him to adopt in terms of his dealings with Rome.

Almost inevitably, Maxentius would also appear to have had a hand in the building or restoration of a number of the large bath complexes, specifically the restoration and extension of the Severan baths in the palace on the Palatine Hill, the restoration of the Baths of Agrippa in the Campus Martius, and the initiation of the large scheme of baths known as the Baths of Constantine on the Quirinal Hill, which was completed by Constantine. Perhaps less convincingly, in the Lateran there is a suggestion from archaeological excavations that Maxentius may have built or restored a palace here, though a lack of epigraphic or literary evidence for such a major undertaking argues against this identification. Other restoration projects may have included works at the Basilica Aemilia in the Roman Forum. On the Via Appia, between the second and third milestones outside the city, an extraordinary and grand complex comprising a villa or palace, a circular mausoleum, and a circus is once again firmly tied to Maxentius by epigraphy, a literary reference, and by the brickwork of the structures themselves.[12] Why Maxentius chose to build his complex here and not in Rome itself, given his almost obsessive identification with the city, must remain a mystery. The villa was a grand extension of a pre-existing building, now including a private corridor linking the villa to the circus. The circus itself was substantial, in the Roman world second only in size to the Circus Maximus, and would seem to have had a funerary function, at least in its final incarnation. The circular mausoleum was probably built for Maxentius himself, but instead came to house the body of Maxentius's son Valerius Romulus, who died in AD 309.

It is also the case that Maxentius was one of a long line of Roman rulers to make alterations of some kind to the colossal bronze statue of Sol which stood near the Colosseum, originally dedicated by Nero and having been moved here by Hadrian, as has been discussed at length in Chapter Two. Fragments of a giant Maxentian rededicatory inscription mentioning his deified late son Romulus, thought to have once adorned the base of the Colossus, have been found built into the attic of the Arch of Constantine. This was probably a symbolic act of appropriation, which included the inscription's removal, its breaking up, and the final incorporation of some parts into Constantine's monument.[13] Constantine's desire to be somehow closely associated with Sol was demonstrated not only by this act but also by the appearance of Sol on certain of his coin issues (plate 19, see also fig. 12) and, of course, on the arch.

It would therefore seem from the presentation of this short summary of Maxentius's building works in Rome that the emperor had a dramatic impact on the appearance and fabric of the city, both in its public areas as well as in its more private spaces. This would surely have been seen by the Roman citizens themselves as a personal commitment by Maxentius to Rome the cosmopolis, to its citizens, to its history, and to the very idea of Rome, a commitment all too obviously lacking in the behaviour and policies of many of the third- and fourth-century emperors, who lived on in the city only by name rather than by deed and in the solid forms of marble and brick. Some of Maxentius's other historically attested acts could also be interpreted in this way, for example his prevention of the withdrawal of the garrison troops of Rome, the *equites singulares Augusti*.[14] Indeed, these same forces were to form the backbone of his army in battle with Constantine and, along with the defeated and humiliated Maxentius, were to suffer a form of organisational *damnatio memoriae* by Constantine's disbandment of their regiment along with the Praetorian Guard, and the destruction and building over of their barracks just outside Rome.

1. A general view of the Arch of Constantine, Rome. (Photo: Author)

2. The modern Milvian Bridge over the River Tiber, Rome. (Photo: Author)

3. An alabaster portrait head of Constantine. (Photo: Copyright Trustees of the British Museum)

Above left: 4. A portrait bust of Maxentius. Staatliche Kunstsammlungen Dresden, Skulpturensammlung (Albertinum). (Photo: Slide Archive of Former School of Continuing Studies, Birmingham University)

Above right: 5. Stone portrait head of Constantine from York. Yorkshire Museums, York. (Photo: Kate Donkin)

6. A portrait head of Constantine.
Metropolitan Museum, New York.
(Photo: Slide Archive of Former School
of Continuing Studies, Birmingham
University)

7. A bronze portrait head of Constantine.
Museo del Palazzo dei Conservatori, Rome.
(Photo: Author)

8. Full-length portrait statue of Constantine. Piazza del Campidoglio, Rome. (Photo: Author)

9. The Arch of Septimius Severus in the Forum Romanum, Rome. (Photo: Author)

10. The main dedicatory inscription on the Arch of Constantine, Rome. (Photo: Author)

Above left: 11. A section of the Great Trajanic Frieze on the west wall of the central passageway. The Arch of Constantine, Rome. (Photo: Author)

Above right: 12. A section of the Great Trajanic Frieze on the east wall of the central passageway. The Arch of Constantine, Rome. (Photo: Author)

Above left: 13. The Troyes Casket. Cathedral Treasury, Troyes, France. (Photo: Slide Archive of Former School of Continuing Studies, Birmingham University)

Above right: 14. A cameo depicting Constantine being crowned by Tyche of Constantinople. Hermitage Museum, St Petersburg. (Photo: Slide Archive of Former School of Continuing Studies, Birmingham University)

15. Victories in the spandrels of the central passageway arch. The Arch of Constantine, Rome. (Photo: Author)

16. Detail of the north face of the Arch of Constantine, Rome. (Photo: Author)

17. Detail of the south face of the Arch of Constantine, Rome. (Photo: Author)

18. Gold *aureus* of Maxentius, Ostia mint, AD 308–12. Obverse: bust of emperor, reverse: Victory. British Museum, London. (Photo: Copyright Trustees of the British Museum)

19. Gold *solidus* of Constantine. Sirmium mint AD 321. Obverse: bust of emperor, reverse: Constantine being crowned by Sol. British Museum, London. (Photo: Copyright Trustees of the British Museum)

20. Gold *solidus* of Helena, Nicomedia mint, AD 325–30. Obverse: bust of empress, reverse: *Securitas* holding branch. British Museum, London. (Photo: Copyright Trustees of the British Museum)

21. The Basilica Nova of Maxentius and Constantine, Rome. (Photo: Author)

22. The Arch of Malborghetto, near Rome. (Photo: Author)

23. The Mausoleum of Helena, Tor Pignatarra, Rome. (Photo: Author)

24. The Mausoleum of Constantina, Via Nomentana, Rome. (Photo: Author)

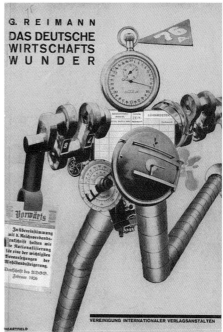

Above left: 25. Kurt Schwitters, *Bild mit heller mitte* (Picture with Light Centre), 1919. Museum of Modern Art, New York. (Photo: Slide Archive of Former School of Continuing Studies, Birmingham University)

Above right: 26. John Heartfield's book cover design for G. Reimann's *Das Deutsche Wirtschafts wunder* 1927. (Photo: Slide Archive of Former School of Continuing Studies, Birmingham University)

27. Sandro Botticelli, *The Punishment of the Rebels* (*Punizio dei Ribelli*), 1481–2. Sistine Chapel, Vatican, Rome. (Photo: Slide Archive of Former School of Continuing Studies, Birmingham University)

28. Jan Miel and Alessandro Salucci, *The Arch of Constantine, Rome*, 1647. Barber Institute of Fine Arts, Birmingham University. (Photo: Slide Archive of Former School of Continuing Studies, Birmingham University)

29. Herman van Swanevelt, *The Arch of Constantine*, 1630s. Dulwich Picture Gallery, London. (Photo: Slide Archive of Former School of Continuing Studies, Birmingham University)

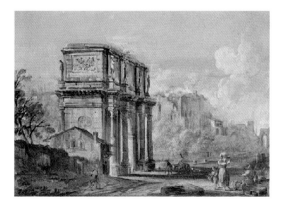

30. Jean-Baptiste Lallemand, *The Forum, with the Arch of Constantine, Peasants in the Foreground*, mid-eighteenth century. Private collection. (Photo: Slide Archive of Former School of Continuing Studies, Birmingham University)

31. Hendrik Frans Van Lint, *The Arch of Constantine, Rome*, mid-eighteenth century. British Government Art Collections. (Photo: Slide Archive of Former School of Continuing Studies, Birmingham University)

32. Anton von Maron, *Portrait of Two Gentlemen Before the Arch of Constantine in Rome*, 1767. Private collection. (Photo: Slide Archive of Former School of Continuing Studies, Birmingham University)

33. Samuel Prout, *The Arch of Constantine, Rome from the South-East*, 1830s. (Photo: Slide Archive of Former School of Continuing Studies, Birmingham University)

34. Oswald Achenbach, *The Arch of Constantine, Rome*, 1886. Alte Nationalgalerie, Berlin (Photo: Slide Archive of Former School of Continuing Studies, Birmingham University)

35. Edmond Clément Marie Duthoit, *The Triumphal Arch of Constantine, Rome*, 1862–5. Private collection. (Photo: Slide Archive of Former School of Continuing Studies, Birmingham University)

36. Jean-Baptiste Camille Corot, *The Arch of Constantine and the Forum, Rome*, 1843. Frick Collection, New York. (Photo: Slide Archive of Former School of Continuing Studies, Birmingham University)

37. Joseph Mallord William Turner, *The Arch of Constantine, Rome*, 1835. Tate, London. (Photo: Slide Archive of Former School of Continuing Studies, Birmingham University)

38. The head of a colossal statue of Constantine. Museo del Palazzo dei Conservatori, Rome. (Photo: Author)

39. General view of the Arch of Constantine, Rome. (Photo: Author)

Again, Maxentius's revocation of Galerius's tax legislation (which would have downgraded Rome's true and favoured place as the centre of the Roman Empire) was likely to have been a popular move.

Perhaps the Tetrarchic abandonment of Rome as *the* dwelling place of the emperor, and even as *a* dwelling place for one of four emperors, had been intended as a way to neutralise the power of whichever emperor would have resided in Rome (thus maybe claiming more prestige and power than his quarter-share). In this case, Maxentius's acclamation as emperor in Rome, and what might have been seen as his over-identification with the city, was perhaps a provocative and ultimately destabilising action. Maxentius may not have actually been the 'tyrant' that the Senate claimed Constantine had freed the city from, but he was not altogether without blame for the escalating crises of the years AD 310–12. Maxentius may have seen himself as the true emperor in Rome, a stance perhaps bolstered by the inability of the other Tetrarchs to band together to deal with him. The increasingly isolated operating of each Tetrarch, instead of their working cooperatively for the common good of the whole empire, was probably exacerbated by the increasingly isolationist stance adopted at Rome by Maxentius. Inevitably such a system was going to lead to Tetrarchic alliances, fallings out, clashes, and all-out war. It would be Constantine who would emerge as the last man standing from this Tetrarchic face-off, and not Maxentius. Nevertheless, Constantine would have been stalked by the ghost of Maxentius wherever he went in central Rome. His rededication of completed Maxentian buildings and the completion of others under his own aegises would have in some way allowed Constantine to exorcise the spirit of his predecessor from the urban topography of Rome, if not necessarily from the minds and memory of the Roman people.

On a purely pragmatic basis, it would have been an extraordinary move for Constantine to have demolished completed or part-built Maxentian buildings in Rome simply to physically erase him from the fabric of the city. Memory would do that job for him more quickly and ultimately more comprehensively, alongside the rites of the *damnatio memoriae* that Constantine carried out on his late rival. Likewise, to have shunned the stocks of bricks bearing Maxentian brick stamps would have appeared needlessly profligate in a city where economic crises had so badly affected the provision of raw materials and other goods, even if such an action, leading to their reuse, would cause confusion among architectural historians and archaeologists in the distant future.

Reimagining the City

In order to try and understand what can best be called the Constantinian impact on the urban topography of Rome and of its environs, it is intended here to discuss a number of buildings and structures in the city erected, completed, or somehow modified during Constantine's reign, and some beyond the city boundaries.[15] These include two further arches, the Arch of Janus in the Forum Boarium and the Arch of Malborghetto, a few miles outside of the city. Discussion of these arches is intended to throw some further light on the interpretation of the Arch of Constantine. Also of note are the Basilica of Maxentius, the Circus Maximus, and, of course, the era of church building in the city that was ushered in following Constantine's coming to power in Rome. Discussion of the great Constantinian basilica in Trier in Germany, and of buildings in Constantinople, the 'new Rome', is outside the scope of this present study and is not in any case strictly relevant.

That three monumental arches in and around Rome can be assigned to the era of Constantine is quite remarkable. Indeed, in order to find a precedent for the building of suites of interrelated arches, one would probably have to look as far back as the Augustan and the Julio-Claudian period, in particular to the arches of distant Gallia Narbonensis. The Constantinian Arch of Malborghetto lies on the Via Flaminia, about 3 miles outside the city of Rome[16] (plate 22). Now conserved and restored, and displayed as an ancient monument, the structure betrays many signs of its post-Roman incorporation into buildings, which ranged from a church to an inn to a farmstead. This *janus quadrifrons*, or four-way arch, is probably the original commemorative arch marking Constantine's victory at the Battle of the Milvian Bridge. Certainly brick stamps of AD 292–305 place the structure close in time to that event, although this identification is still circumstantial. Now simply a brick structure, it would once, in all likelihood, have been faced with marble and furnished with an inscription and artworks of some kind. Around 51 feet in height to the top of the attic, its widest side spans the Via Flaminia and is almost 49 feet long, the narrower side being around 39 feet long. It is difficult to suggest the rationale for the building of this huge arch in such a rural location, unless it does indeed mark a crucial geographical location on the route of Constantine's march to Rome.

The Arch of Janus in the Forum Boarium in Rome is also a *quadrifrons* marble arch that again may or may not date from the era of Constantine, though an early fourth-century date is generally accepted[17] (fig. 54). It has recently been suggested that once again, this arch is a Maxentian monument, though we must await full publication of the reasoning behind this dating before deciding on the merits of the argument.[18] It is unlikely, though, that new direct evidence has emerged. Built of brick and faced with marble, much of the marble in the surviving parts of the structure can be seen to be reused *spolia*. Sited in the north-east corner of the Forum Boarium, at a significant crossroads and partly over the Cloaca Maxima drain, this massive arch is around 39 feet square and stands around 52½ feet in height, though its upper part, a superstructure of brick-faced concrete forming part of an original attic containing rooms, was removed in the nineteenth century. The arches are around 35 feet high and about 19 feet wide. The *Cataloghi Regionari* lists an arch 'of the deified Constantine' in Regio IX, and it is therefore difficult not to identify this structure as being that arch. The name 'Arch of Janus' was given to this arch in the medieval period and there is no evidence to support its dedication to this deity; however, unfortunately this confusing name has stuck. It is not a triumphal arch but rather a boundary marker of a similar kind to the shrine of Janus Geminus in the Roman Forum, a small arched passageway built of bronze, with doors at either end which were left open in times of war. Depictions of this curious structure appear on coins, but nothing survives of

54. The Arch of Janus in the Forum Boarium, Rome. (Photo: Author)

it on the ground today. The Arch of Janus as it survives today is but a shadow of its original self. There is no doubt that all four faces of the arch would have been fronted by small, free-standing colonnades projecting in front of the surviving niches in two tiers. The forty-eight niches, with their carved scallop-shell domes, were probably intended to carry statues. Sadly only a carved head of Minerva on the keystone of the arch on its north side and a head of Roma on the east survive. Thus it is difficult to truly understand the significance of this huge structure, originally highly decorated and well appointed, and how it fits in with the making of the Constantinian image in Rome.

If the inscriptions on the Arch of Constantine had promoted Constantine as a liberator and bringer of peace, and cast Maxentius as a tyrant, they had also acted to dismiss Maxentius from the Roman historical continuum of emperors. Although the sentiments displayed in the inscriptions represented the official public stance of the Senate, who had dedicated the arch to Constantine, Constantine also strove to eliminate Maxentius from that continuum and erase his memory from the very streets and fabric of Rome, firstly by instigating a formal *damnatio memoriae* on his name and image, and secondly by annexing Maxentius's great building schemes for his own grandiloquence.

One of the first matters to be dealt with in prosecuting the *damnatio memoriae* was the neutralisation of those troops that had actively supported and fought with Maxentius against Constantine. This took the form of the disbanding of the Praetorian Guard and the *equites singulares Augusti*. He also had the camp and headquarters building of the *equites singulars*, which had stood on the site where now stands the church of St John Lateran before it was razed to the ground. Maxentius's memory was next assaulted and blackened through literary propaganda, and ultimately through his branding as 'tyrant' in the inscription on the Senate-sponsored arch. If such a process could be said to be extended, then that is represented by the hatchet job done on Maxentius in Eusebius's *Vita Constantini* published many years later. Statuary images of Maxentius were also doubtless destroyed almost immediately upon Constantine seizing power in Rome. The redundancy of such images had been demonstrated to the Roman people in no uncertain terms by Constantine's ceremonial display of Maxentius's severed head at the front of his victorious processional entry into Rome on 29 October AD 312. Some of the statues, though, would not have been destroyed at this time, and were probably simply removed from public display, or access to areas where such images were on display might have been temporarily restricted. Portrait heads may have been removed from statuary bodies that were otherwise left *in situ*, ready for reuse. A number of recarvings of Maxentian portraits are likely to have eventually taken place, the most famous example, of course, being the giant Palazzo dei Conservatori head of Constantine, which is generally acknowledged by academics to be a recarved portrait of this kind. The final phase of the *damnatio memoriae* process would have involved the removal of all dedicatory inscriptions to Maxentius set up on buildings in the city that he had erected or seen through to completion. The rededication of all such structures to Constantine would then have followed.

Dealing with Maxentius's architectural legacy in Rome was no small matter, for he had expended considerable energy, money, and political will over his six years of residency in Rome to try to reinvigorate the monumental centre of the city in a manner befitting the great historical cosmopolis.

A panegyric of AD 321 gushed that in Rome, following Constantine's building works, 'all the most celebrated things in the city gleam[ed] with new work', a somewhat vague formula that gives no clues as to which specific buildings were being alluded to. Indeed, as has been recently noted, were it not for a single historical source, the work of Aurelius Victor, which alerts us to the fact that the great fourth-century basilica in the centre of Rome was the work of Maxentius and was not, as the *Cataloghi Regionari* records, truly the Basilica Constantiniana, it would indeed be assumed to be a Constantinian project.[19] Its rededication to Constantine may have followed its remodelling with a new, second entrance on to the Via Sacra and a second apse. It is generally agreed that the colossal statue of Constantine, represented by the head and a number of other body parts in the collection of the Museo del Palazzo dei Conservatori, Rome, was designed to be placed in the basilica, either in the original apse or the new one added in the Constantinian remodelling. Another Constantinian rededication took place at Maxentius's Temple of Romulus, perhaps after a restoration rather than any major rebuilding works or remodelling.

Constantine, perhaps mindful of the need to keep the people of Rome onside, and not only the Senate, also made significant improvements to the Circus Maximus, perhaps by adding a new tier of seats around the circus to increase its seating capacity. While he would also have taken control of the Circus of Maxentius on the Via Appia, it would not appear that this was brought into use as a ceremonial venue again, and certainly not as a public entertainment venue.

A new building project undertaken by Constantine, this time not started by Maxentius, was the complex now quite correctly known as the Baths of Constantine, sited between the Forum of Trajan and the great Baths of Diocletian on the Quirinal Hill. Work here would appear to have begun before AD 315 and the dedication of this grandiose project may have been intended to be the centrepiece of his *decennalia* year, along with the dedication of the arch to him by the Senate. Unfortunately none of this complex survives today, though it has been suggested that the modest, as opposed to colossal, statue of Constantine, which now stands in Campidoglio, along with statues of three of his sons, were displayed here, as discussed in Chapter One.

Whether they were new commissions by Constantine, or old ones taken over by him after Maxentius's death, there is no doubt that these building projects in central Rome together demonstrate Constantine's complete awareness of the importance of the visible expression of imperial ideology through architectural munificence. Bricks, mortar, and marble quite literally, as well as metaphorically, formed the foundations for the transmission and espousal of the imperial programme to the citizens of Rome, and even the peoples of the broader empire and those beyond its frontiers, at all eras in Rome's history. Constantine had demonstrated as much in his commissioning of the palace complex in Trier, of which the massive basilican hall known as the Aula Palatina formed a part. Built around AD 310, today this structure represents the largest extant hall to survive from antiquity, and it must have been a landmark building at the time of its construction, ably demonstrating to the Treveri Constantine's own soaring ambition and imperial aspirations.

It would not appear to be true that Constantine did little in the way of imposing his architectural legacy on the pagan centre of Rome as a sop to the still-powerful pagan elite of Rome, and instead concentrated his energies on promoting the creation of an alternative, Christian power focus for the city away from the historic centre. As has already been discussed in Chapter One, Constantine is also credited with the move towards the initiation of church building in Rome.[20] It is certainly known that building work began on the church of Christ the Saviour, and also a complex comprising a basilica, baptistery, and residence for the Bishop of Rome at the Lateran in late AD 312. Several enormous funerary basilicas to house martyrs' graves were also begun in the Christian cemeteries on the outskirts of Rome, that is at St Peter's at the Vatican, St Sebastian's on the Via Appia, and St Laurence's on the Via Tiburtina, probably with imperial support, as it is certainly known that in AD 326 Constantine provided endowments for the church of St Peter's, then under construction in the Vatican. Just as Constantine strove to create a new Roman dynasty of his family, so some members of the family also became actively involved in the Christianising of the city and its environs by sponsoring, supporting, or initiating building projects of one kind or another. His mother, Helena (fig. 55 and plate 20), had a church built in the grounds of the Sessorian palace to house the supposed fragments of the true cross with which she had returned from the Middle East. She also had built, or had built for her, a massive funerary basilica and mausoleum on the Via Labicana, at a place known today as

55. Portrait head of Helena set on earlier body of seated statue. Museo Capitolino, Rome. (Photo: Author)

Tor Pignatarra, partially over part of the cemetery of the hated, disbanded *equites singulares*.[21] His daughter Constantina likewise built a circus-basilica and mausoleum on the Via Nomentana, again well outside the city boundaries.[22] If Augustus was said to have found Rome a city of brick and left it a city of marble, so Constantine used to be said to have found Rome a pagan city and left it a Christian one. This is too glib a statement though, and the real picture is far more complex and far more nuanced than the statement might suggest.

The church of Christ the Saviour, now known as St John Lateran (S. Giovanni in Laterano), was partly built on imperial land and partly over the demolished barracks of the *equites singulares*, the imperial guard who had fought with Maxentius. The present-day church, probably of the same basic plan, has its origins in the fourteenth century, with numerous subsequent accretions including a new east facade in the eighteenth century. The choice of the barracks site was no doubt highly symbolically loaded and was an attempt to manipulate memory and time. The complex comprised a basilica, baptistery, and residence for the Bishop of Rome and was without doubt the first Christian church commissioned and endowed by Constantine, though exactly how early after AD 312 is unknown.

The Basilica of Saint Peter on the Vatican Hill became the largest building constructed during Constantine's reign, and the only one with a cross-shaped plan. The basilica incorporated the shrine of St Peter, and was thus also a *martyrium*. The complex also included the provision of a very large cemetery. The building work here is believed to have begun in the second half of Constantine's reign but not to have been finished until after his death in AD 337.

Though it is unlikely to have been part of a formal policy, one unexpected consequence of the Constantinian programme of church building on peripheral sites in the city was that the urban topography of Rome was refocused, and it was done so in a way that would considerably accelerate the relocation of imperial patronage and religious liturgy away from the pagan centre on to what would have been thought of as fringe sites such as the Vatican and St John Lateran. While there was an internal logic to the building of Constantinian structures at the Lateran and Tor Pignatarra on sites associated with the disgraced and disbanded *equites singulars*, that logic did not dictate that they should necessarily have been Christian buildings. While Constantine was evidently set on emphasising his personal patronage in sponsoring the building of Christian churches and other related structures, he seems to have taken great care to do so on what was either confiscated land or imperial property in seemingly marginal or liminal locations. Perhaps it was intended that the making of such choices would not cause friction with the Roman Senate so soon after Constantine's acceptance as the liberator of the city of Rome.

As has been noted, both Constantine's beloved mother, Helena, and his daughter Constantina also played some part in the promotion of church building in Rome. Helena's provision of accommodation for the display of her holy relics gathered in the Middle East to all intents and purposes constituted the founding of a church. As to what became her mausoleum at Tor Pignatarra, it is highly likely that this burial place had originally been constructed for the eventual interment of Constantine himself, and indeed Helena may well have been laid to rest in what was intended to be his sarcophagus too. The large, domed mausoleum adjoined a larger complex of buildings forming a funerary and basilica complex, and would have originally been adorned with mosaics and other decoration, but what survives today is little more than a roofless, stripped shell. Today, adjacent to the mausoleum stands the church of SS. Pietro e Marcellino (plate 23). The huge, decorated porphyry sarcophagus found in Helena's mausoleum and now located in the Vatican Museums, Rome, is today generally accepted as a funerary item originally intended for a male imperial individual but then brought into service upon Helena's death in AD 329. However, this is not altogether a satisfactory explanation, and such a pragmatic solution seems somehow at odds with the status of Helena and the reverence accorded her in her later life, though of course the red-purple porphyry stone itself had now become a luxurious signifier of imperial might and transcendence. The decoration on the sarcophagus stresses the continuing link between imperial authority and Roman military power and between the defence of civilisation against barbarian peoples and barbarian cultures. It consists of a number of scenes of battle on both of the long sides and the two short sides of the sarcophagus, creating the impression of an unending and continuous struggle on both a military and metaphorical level to a viewer walking around the sarcophagus. Large, high-relief figures of Roman cavalrymen with lances ride down and trample male barbarians, some of whom are already bound and kneeling in thrall to the power of Rome. Other male barbarians are led away in chains, accompanied by a Roman cavalry escort. However, there are other elements of decoration on the sarcophagus body and on its lid. In the upper corners of the two long faces are both male and female busts, so heavily restored as to make their identification impossible. On top of the lid rests a lion and two female figures, with a garland there, and further garlands held by cupids draping the sides of the lid.

Constantina's mausoleum and circus-basilica on the Via Nomentana, in the area today known as S. Costanza, also originally contained a massive sarcophagus, which has today been replaced by a facsimile, the original now being part of the collections of the Vatican Museums in Rome. The mausoleum today stands in association with the much later church basilica of S. Agnese (plate 24). The mausoleum was probably built around AD 351 or 352 and is in use today; indeed, a wedding service had just finished inside when I last visited the building. Though the interior is heavily restored, it is nevertheless noteworthy for the quite exquisite fourth-century ceiling mosaics, which include scenes of viticulture.

The sarcophagus of Constantina, while still obviously another exclusive imperial artefact by nature of both its size and of the porphyry from which it was made, could not be more different from Helena's sarcophagus in terms of its decoration, which consists of detailed and complex scenes of cupids harvesting grapes and garlands, again as on Helena's sarcophagus lid. However on the two long sides the winged cupids, enclosed in circular fields formed by acanthus scrolls, gather grapes and place them in overflowing baskets. Above the scrolls are further vegetal tendrils and doves, and below, another cupid with grapes walks in a landscape inhabited by peacocks and rams. This abundant world of plenty almost seems to hark back to the idealised landscapes on the Augustan Ara Pacis monument. On the short sides, the cupids are depicted standing in a trough treading the grapes, the vinous juice flowing copiously into barrels or vessels beneath the press. Scrolls, tendrils, and clusters of grapes frame the central main motif. On the lid are found garlands suspended from two male and two female heads or masks. The decoration on all four sides of the sarcophagus and on its lid can be seen to some extent to mirror the themes of some of the stunning ceiling mosaics inside the mausoleum, with the emphasis being on the natural world, and its taming by agriculture as a metaphor for its control by Roman imperial authority. Of course, such lush imagery would also have had Christian connotations, though there is no overt Christian symbolism on the sarcophagus. The date of Constantina's death is uncertain and the sarcophagus could date to any time between AD 330 and 360.

Personal Priorities

In this chapter an examination has been made of the emperor Constantine's own building projects in Rome, and how his sponsorship of new buildings and renovation schemes in the centre of Rome, and his completion of unfinished earlier projects there, very much fitted in with the continuum of imperial architectural munificence that went back, not quite seamlessly, to the time of Augustus. Such concentration on the buildings of Rome and the emperor's evident interest in the city's architectural heritage would have initially reassured the Senate of his newfound commitment to the mother of all cities. However, Constantine's astonishing break with the past in not only commissioning and supporting church building away from the old pagan centre of Rome, but also realigning the axes of political power in the city through his topographical choices, may have caused as much alarm to powerful pagan senators as it brought succour to Christian senators.

It is very much the case that the dedication of the Arch of Constantine by the Roman Senate puts the ideological programme of the arch's artwork in much sharper focus than if the arch had been an imperial project from start to finish. This is not to suggest that the Senate pushed through the design, building, and unveiling of a monument that Constantine himself had never seen plans of, or on whose decoration he had not been consulted. However, given the emperor's many distractions away from Rome on imperial and Church business between AD 312 and AD 315, it is unlikely that he or his advisors on the ground in Rome would have been *au fait* with all details of the scheme. It is probably in such a situation that the Senate appears to have stamped its own political programme on the arch, even if that programme was quite obviously subservient to the imperial ideology of the overall scheme. Firstly, in the main dedicatory inscription the Senate made it crystal clear that they were dedicating this monument to Constantine, thus restating the direct relationship between the Senate *of Rome* and the emperor. Secondly, in one of the minor inscriptions, they bestowed on him the title *'Liberator Urbis'* – Liberator of the City –again stressing the significance

56. The Constantinian frieze – detail of the *Oratio* scene (Constantine addressing the Senate and Roman people). North face, the Arch of Constantine, Rome. (Photo: Graham Norrie, after Giuliani 1955)

57. The Constantinian frieze – detail of the *Congiarium* scene: Constantine distributing monies to the Senate and Roman people. North face, the Arch of Constantine, Rome. (Photo: Graham Norrie, after Giuliani 1955)

of his acts in relation to the city of Rome. Thirdly, it has already been noted in Chapter Two how the city of Rome, with its gates, arches, buildings, monuments, and Forum, is visually woven into the narrative of Constantine's achievements on the 'civil side' of the Constantinian frieze on the arch (figs 56 and 57). The presiding river god of the city's Tiber is also pictured in the Battle of the Milvian Bridge part of the frieze, on the 'war side' of the arch. The Senate had thus linked Constantine and Rome in the viewers' eyes and mind – the Senate wished to see such a link re-established in this way after the age of the largely absent Tetrarchs. The Senate was offering Constantine the same close relationship with the city of Rome that Maxentius had been building up for himself, and he would seem by his subsequent actions to have both embraced and rejected the Senate's offer.

It would be beyond belief to think that Constantine might not have approved of the image of himself being promoted on the arch by the Senate. The fact that the arch is still standing suggests that he did indeed approve, for otherwise he might well have overseen the arch's immediate demolition in a fit of pique or rage. There are not many cases of an artist's subject hating his or her sculpture or painted portrait that immediately spring to mind. However, I am forcibly reminded of the fact that in 1954 both Houses of Parliament in Britain paid for a portrait of Sir Winston Churchill to be painted by the then famous Graham Sutherland. Sutherland's stunning picture was presented to Churchill on his eightieth birthday, when it was hailed by Sir Winston as 'a remarkable example of modern art', a coded damning indictment that clearly set out Churchill's view of the work. Unable to reconcile a portrait of what he apparently saw as a finished old man with his own self-image as the indomitable scourge of Hitler, Sutherland's picture was never hung at home by Churchill and it was subsequently destroyed by his wife, Lady Clementine, probably in 1955. An earlier precedent for such an action was provided by King George V, who in the 1920s was reported to have ordered the destruction of an unflattering portrait by Royal Academician Charles Sims.

The churches and other religious buildings that have come to be interpreted as Constantinian foundations, or those built or sponsored by other family members such as Helena and Constantina, were either built over former imperial properties or on land on imperial estates. This suggests that these were very much personal projects rather than being necessarily promoted as part of the pervading Constantinian imperial ideology favoured by the Senate, which was in many respects innovatory. It has been demonstrated in this chapter that a number of the other Constantinian monuments in Rome carried on the theme so clearly articulated on the Arch of Constantine of the emperor aligning himself with past times and sometimes with the past 'good emperors.' Manipulating memory in other words. This creation of a strategy for linking the deep past and the Constantinian present very much relied on the use of *spolia*, and in the next chapter it will be considered whether the widespread use of such material in Late Antiquity in general represented artistic conservatism or was in fact again a sign of innovation.

6

Collage and Memory

As seen in Chapters Three and Four, the Arch of Constantine used a strategy of linking past and present emperors and their good works in the minds of viewers of the arch, while in Chapter Five it was seen that this strategy was to a lesser extent utilised in the presentation of other contemporary Constantinian monuments in Rome. In this chapter, then, an examination will be made of how the use of *spolia* contributed towards the construction of this false narrative. It will also be considered here whether the interpretation of the use of *spolia* on the arch can encompass the idea that this was a radical, innovative strategy and not one representing conservatism or even stagnation of some kind. In order to explore these issues it will be asked if the careful curation and selection of *spolia* for the arch contributed to the finished work being more akin to a collage, as we understand that term today, rather than simply an assembly of disparate, available parts.

The Curation of Relics

The Arch of Constantine, then, would appear to have been both an actual and a metaphorical gateway of some kind. In its metaphorical guise it was designed to act as a portal through which past, present, and future passed into contemporary memory together in fourth-century Rome. But rather than being an isolated instance of this strategy in operation at this time, it would appear that this was very much a Constantinian phenomenon and that the arch should not therefore stand alone in interpretations of the referencing of the past in Late Antique ceremony and imperial ideology.

   One of the most interesting new avenues of research on the arch in the last thirty years has been the suggestion by Jás Elsner that the collection of the *spolia* to create the arch is in many ways analogous to the collection and curation of Christian holy relics that to all intents and purposes began in Rome during the reign of Constantine, and indeed found its most renowned proponent in the figure of Constantine's mother, Helena.[1] Her journeys in the Holy Land to try and recover pieces of the true cross were recounted by Eusebius in his *Life of Constantine*, and in 1950 they provided the backdrop for one of Evelyn Waugh's least appreciated and most underrated novels. How this analogy holds up when it was in fact the Senate overseeing the design and building of the arch is uncertain. Nevertheless, it is worth summarising what are literally the bones of this argument before considering its implications for the interpretation of the arch.

Elsner's exciting dissection of the arch's history centres on the phenomenon of the use of *spolia* in Late Antiquity. He sees the phenomenon as being contiguous with and analogous to other aspects of contemporary life in this period. The highpoint of spoliation he sees as the collection and shipping of artworks to the new Roman centre of Constantinople during its inauguration in the AD 320s and 330s. This collection of artworks from Rome and from numerous other cities of the empire, predominantly in the east, was on an unprecedented scale, at least as far back as the looting of artworks from Greek cities by Republican generals, who subsequently shipped their artistic spoils back to Rome in the third to first centuries BC. In Elsner's words, 'all this *spolia* represents an urge to turn to the material culture of the past in order to bolster the present'.[2] This strategy he refreshingly sees as being innovative rather than regressive, as it has so often been seen by other academics in the past.

The need to emulate Rome, almost to duplicate its materiality and cultural world, drove Constantine and subsequent emperors based at Constantinople to not only collect artworks on an almost unimaginable scale, but also to commission and build monuments that in size and number would rival the cosmopolis mother in the West. Interestingly, these monuments would very much correspond to the types of monuments that were to a very great extent typical of Rome, that is, fora, columns, obelisks, city walls, aqueducts and other engineering works such as cisterns linked to the crucial and efficient organisation of the urban water supply.[3] This also involved bringing to Constantinople bodies and body parts, holy relics of the saints. It was quite literally an arms race, in terms of competition with Rome and other centres to secure important relics. Of course, Constantinople had a major advantage, in that Constantine himself had been buried there in a grand mausoleum in the Church of the Holy Apostles rather than brought back to Rome as was expected and indeed originally intended for his remains. His mausoleum was to act as a focus for the collection of other Christian relics and may indeed have been designed as a mausoleum providing space for the eventual interment of the remains of the twelve apostles, with the emperor occupying an exalted thirteenth place. The collecting of holy relics to go in the mausoleum probably began during Constantine's lifetime, being attested as first occurring in AD 336. In AD 357 Constantius II is recording as bringing the relics of Saint Andrew from Patras in Greece to Constantinople, along with relics of Saint Luke, and in AD 365 he brought the body of Timothy to the city. In AD 391 the reputed head of John the Baptist arrived to join the collection here.

Elsner has convincingly argued that the *spolia* artworks reset in the Arch of Constantine, leaving aside the free-standing statues of Dacians and the decorated pedestal base reliefs, were chosen for one reason only. It was not their shape – indeed, their differing sizes and shapes were somewhat problematic for the arch's designers to properly incorporate – nor was it necessarily their link to a trio of 'good' emperors, though that was likely to have been a very important consideration. Rather, it was probably the fact that they each included portraits of one of the three emperors shown undertaking tasks that underpinned the very role of the Roman emperor, that is, defending Rome and Roman interests by defeating foreign foes, negotiating, forming treaties, imposing terms on foreign peoples, and fulfilling a suite of civic and religious duties by being present or officiating at various state or religious ceremonies or events. Constantine stressed his own role in this continuum by not only presenting himself in a similar way in the narrow Late Antique frieze on the arch, though in a purely contemporary style rather than an archaic and anachronistic one, but also by placing himself in the past by having the heads of Trajan, Hadrian, and Marcus Aurelius recarved to become himself. As Elsner has pointed out, such recarving in other contexts might have been linked to the process of *damnatio memoriae*, though such recutting or defacing usually took place on artworks *in situ*.[4] Here, the act is an appropriation of the very person of these past emperors, an assumption of their character, a co-opting of their deeds and achievements.

The great contemporary significance of signs and symbols, of images of all kinds, is stressed quite heavily in Eusebius's account of Constantine's life. The account of the removal of valuable statues and other items from pagan temples, and the display of these looted cult statues in prominent public locations in Constantinople, is most instructive in telling us about the continued power of images in an age dominated by ceremony and political subterfuge. The purpose of their redisplay was not intended to be in any way didactic, it would appear. Rather, they were placed there to be mocked and laughed at. It should therefore perhaps be considered whether any motive linked to mockery can be detected in the selection of imperial *spolia* depicting pagan sacrifice, and its being placed on the Arch of Constantine.

This process of disaggregating objects, statues and other artworks, monuments in whole or in part, and even bodies represents an attempt to use the fragment as a way of returning to the whole or even as a way of creating a new whole. I have written at length elsewhere about the significance of the fragment in relation to psychoanalytical theory and practice, and how we might interpret instances of the subconscious desire to engage with the part as opposed to the whole in past societies.[5]

Exactly the same process, but quite literally in miniature, undoubtedly occurred with the Late Antique trend for the recarving of earlier imperial cameos and gemstones, and in Chapter One a number of examples of this very process were discussed. It is extremely interesting to note here the enchainment of memory that subsequently, much later, was created by the incorporation of the so-called Ada Cameo and other precious stones into the decoration adorning the gold binding added to the eighth- or ninth-century Carolingian book of the Gospels, the Ada Gospels, dedicated to Charlemagne's sister Ada, in 1499. It is almost certainly the case that the binders of the book found the cameo portrayal of Constantine and part of his family a suitably Christian image to adorn such a sacred and valuable text. The fourth century, the eighth or ninth century, and the late fifteenth century all met here at a single point in time. Indeed, the quite commonly attested act of incorporating Roman gems into crosses, reliquaries, or book covers, found in some Byzantine, Carolingian, Lombardic and medieval contexts, appears to be a phenomenon driven by the same desire to manipulate time and memory as is found in the fourth-century Roman imperial contexts, where *spolia* was used in a systematic manner.

Curation and Collage

There are a number of possible ways to interpret the Arch of Constantine, but whichever framework of interpretation is chosen there is no avoiding the fact that it was intended to be first and foremost a single, indivisible work of art and propaganda. It was not a copy of any kind, even though its form was closely modelled on the Arch of Septimius Severus, as has been discussed in Chapter Two. It was certainly not a pastiche, the word implying imitation, though it can also simply mean a mixing of styles and materials. It might perhaps be thought of an example of bricolage, the concept of bricolage being first espoused by the anthropologist Claude Lévi Strauss in his 1962 book *The Savage Mind*, and defined as a cultural practice in which thoughts or ideas could be expressed through the selection and synthesis of elements from the cultural milieu; it was, he wrote, 'a reversal of ends and means'. In theoretical terms this concept was extended by Jacques Derrida in 1966 to apply to literary and linguistic situations, so that in his mind all discourse could be seen to be a form of bricolage. Yet bricolage would seem to imply the use of whatever materials were available at any particular moment in time or at a single time, rather than the kind of phenomenon exemplified by the arch in which a culture of curation and selection was married to ideological imperatives and political realities. While it was undoubtedly the case that the transport and supply of marble to Rome became increasingly difficult and perhaps prohibitively expensive from the third century onwards, such a situation alone cannot account for the growing use of *spolia* and of recarving of older statues, portraits, and other sculpture. These were probably as much to do with a quite dramatic shift in the reception of portrait and historical sculpture in Late Antiquity, as a result of broader socio-political, cultural and religious changes.[6]

The arch does certainly represent some kind of act of appropriation, a popular term today in conceptual and gallery art, but once more this term still seems somehow wrong when applied to the extended process of appropriations, selections, and rejections that had to have taken place before the assembly of the new monument, with parts of different older monuments collected at different times and from different locations, probably with no concrete idea as to their eventual use.[7] Perhaps the best way to analyse the arch seems to me to be to view it as a monumental work of collage. Collage is an art form that utilises found or curated objects and items and turns these individual, sometimes disparate, items into a new whole by their juxtaposition together. Collage as a recognised artistic practice is a twentieth- to twenty-first-century phenomenon. However, this does not negate the value of analysing how the practical processes leading to the creation of such artworks were, and are, often underpinned by theoretical stances that, while culturally specific to their time, may nevertheless contain some more universal application in terms of revealing the essence of certain artistic motivations.

While perhaps Picasso and Braque are the fathers of the art of collage, it is the work of two other twentieth-century artists, Kurt Schwitters and John Heartfield, that is of particular interest to me here. Schwitters because of the theoretical justifications underpinning his work, set down for us in numerous articles and lectures, and

Heartfield because of the political nature of his collages, and the imagery employed there to achieve his complex propagandist aims.

Kurt Schwitters (1887–1948) was a German artist forced to flee to Norway away from Hitler's regime in 1937, and who subsequently settled in England in 1940, first in London, after being interned for a while as an enemy alien, and then in the Lake District, where for many years he worked on his great architectural art project, the *Merzbarn*, at Ambleside.[8] He is perhaps best known for his collages – *Merz* pictures – of the first quarter of the twentieth century, often made by utilising a wide variety of materials and artefacts, including, for instance, train tickets, postage stamps, coins, newspaper clippings and advertisements, printed numbers and fragmented words and phrases, found objects, and pieces and fragments of wood, metal, glass, paper, card, and cloth (plate 25). Schwitters created his collages through a process of what he called *Entformung*; a process involving, through assembly, both the metamorphosis and the dissociation of fragmentary or fragmented objects and materials. He viewed these objects and materials as possessing what he called *Eigengift*, 'their own special essence or poison'. This *Eigengift* would be lost during, and as a result of, their *Entformung*. The intention was not that these materials should now function as if they were transformed into some other kind of material, rather that they now formed part of a new whole, a collage that was more than simply the sum of its parts. The crucial thing to Schwitters was that through the creation of art he could order and rationalise the world and thus understand how art and the processes of creation could work against the decay of meaning in things, and how timeless order could be created out of temporal chaos. Unlike Surrealist collage, which aimed to create a dichotomy between the real and the unreal, the collages created by Schwitters aimed to present the past and present together, but in a new version of the present where temporal boundaries had become blurred. When studying art and artefacts from the Roman world, time and time again it is possible to find instances of both contemporary and older objects being used in some way to create just such a new reality, often in a religious or ritual context, and at all periods from the time of the Republic up to and including Late Antiquity. This almost collagist process can be discussed in terms of the use of fragments and fragmented images to create a new whole in these instances, and would appear to me to make the conceptual framework behind Schwitters' collages a useful framework for viewing and interpreting the Arch of Constantine.

However, elsewhere in this book I have followed the traditional art historical approach to the study of the Arch of Constantine by presenting a systematic description of the artworks adorning the arch by chronological period of their creation: first the Trajanic *spolia*, then the Hadrianic, followed by those from the time of Marcus Aurelius, ending the exposition with a description of the contemporary Constantinian frieze and other decorative elements. This atomisation of the arch might be a useful way to *describe* the monument but perhaps it is not after all an appropriate way to *interpret and understand* it. If we do look at the arch as a single unified work, a collage, then the kind of analysis presented in Chapter Two might be thought of as misguided. Using Schwitters' terms, the original *Eigengift*, or inherent individual quality of each item of *spolia*, had become transformed by their *Entformung*, in this case their incorporation into the arch. After all, one would not begin the description of a German-era collage of Schwitters that incorporated a used tram or bus ticket by presenting an extended exposition on the public transport infrastructure of pre-war Hanover.

John Heartfield was born in Germany in 1891 in Schmargendorf, Berlin. Originally Helmut Herzfeld, he subsequently changed his name to the anglicised name by which he is best known today.[9] He is most famous for his collages created using photomontage, thus making his source material less obvious in its origins than the materials used by Schwitters, and allowing him to create collages that had a clean-lined unity of appearance, anathema to Schwitters. However, the appeal of photomontage as opposed to other types of collage lies in its exclusive use of photographs or parts of photographs, either in the form of prints or of photographic images in reproduction; the very precise nature of photographs place them perhaps closer to reality than other types of images or objects. Initially linked to the Dada movement and critical of the Weimar regime in Germany, after 1933 Heartfield's ire was firmly focused on Hitler and the Nazi party. Forced to flee to Czechoslovakia in 1933, he was subsequently forced to escape to England in 1938. His best known single work is *Hurrah, die Butter ist alle!*, translated as 'Hurray, the Butter Is All Gone!', completed in 1935. In this striking photomontage Heartfield depicts a German family seated around a dinner table laden with items of metal rather than food. The father is poised to eat a metal key, the son a length of metal chain, and the mother the metal handlebars of a bicycle. In a pram in the foreground lies a baby biting on an iron cleaver while a dog lies on the mat chewing a huge nut and bolt in lieu of a proper bone. The family's dining-room walls are nattily adorned with swastika wallpaper. This curious mealtime scene is explained by a quotation from a speech by Hermann Göering in which he informs the German people that, in translation, 'iron has always made a country strong, butter and lard only make people fat'. So firmly associated are we with his anti-Nazi art it is perhaps surprising to find that Heartfield died in 1968. In London a blue plaque has recently been unveiled at 47 Downshire Hill, Hampstead, where he lived between 1938 and 1943.

I have chosen to illustrate Heartfield's work not with the well-known 'Hurrah' photomontage but rather with a book cover he designed in 1927 for G. Reimann's *Das Deutsche Wirtschafts wunder* (plate 26). A close examination of this picture reveals that the image of the robot-like German worker is created from a montage of photographs of different kinds of tools and machine parts, a watch, and some newspaper cuttings. The point to be made here once more is that an analysis of the picture today would not include an attempt to track down the trade or technical journals from which these photographs originally derived, nor is it relevant as to which tasks the tools were designed for or from what kind of machines the metal parts were derived. Who made the watch, when it was made, and where are also irrelevant in the same way. Atomising the work almost instantly negates or confuses a proper understanding of its overall meaning.

In the works of both Schwitters and Heartfield, collage was a signifier of modernism, of innovation, and this was also reflected in contemporary poetry and prose. Anyone who has studied English literature as a subject at school will have used or have been aware of the volumes of study notes that dissect poems, plays, or novels line by line, scene by scene, or chapter by chapter until one almost feels as if one has lost sight of the whole work in the analysis of its minutest parts. In many ways T. S. Eliot's *The Wasteland* is a unified work composed almost entirely out of fragments. Eliot unapologetically made the whole creative process at once opaque and apparent to the reader, by presenting fragmentary images one after another in such a seamless manner as to make the poem appear clinically united.

It might then seem to be both incorrect and contradictory to attempt to describe an ancient monument such as the Arch of Constantine as analogous to a modernist artwork of some kind; however, it is true to say that in many ways the arch may well have been seen as a metaphor for modernity in its time. It was both traditional and innovative at one and the same time. To some extent how the arch was viewed and understood would have depended on whether the arch's use of *spolia* in such a well-integrated manner was at that time novel. In other words was it the first such monument in Rome?

Some authorities believe that the monument known as the Arcus Novus might have held that honour, in which case the Arch of Constantine might then have been seen simply as part of a continuum in a line of such monuments.[10] Because of this, it is worth briefly examining what we know of the now lost arch, which was finally demolished in the late fifteenth century without a full record being made of it. The Arcus Novus, which stood on the Via Lata, was probably dedicated in the year of Diocletian's *decennalia* in AD 293, and was intended to not only commemorate that event but also acknowledge the creation of the Tetrarchic system of imperial rule, though it may be as late as AD 303 in date (fig. 58). A collection of sculpture derived from the arch came into the hands of Cardinal de Medici via the Delle Valle-Capranica Collection in 1584; some of it remained in Rome at the Villa Medici, other pieces were taken to Florence in the later eighteenth century to be set up as decoration in the Boboli Gardens.

The earliest classical sculptural *spolia* represented in this collection are thought to have come from the Ara Pietatis Augustae – the Altar of Augustan Piety – a monumental altar in the Campus Martius, planned and commissioned by Augustus but completed under Claudius. The later pieces included two large pedestal bases decorated on their side faces with images of Victories, barbarian captives, and Dioscuri. It is difficult to think what kind of coherent and programmatic narrative about the Tetrarchy might have been put across by the bringing together of these and other images here as part of a single monument. Perhaps the bringing together was seen as an end in itself, a connecting with past times through the stimulation of the memory of its viewers. Maybe the use of *spolia* in a fully integrated and successful artistic and architectural scheme did not really occur until the building of the Arch of Constantine.

In contemporary art the term collage is often now used almost interchangeably with the term appropriation. I have otherwise avoided this term here as it implies the action of an individual artist acting somehow subversively, or at least covertly, to undermine some element of the cultural or political status quo by seizing some material or

58. A plaster cast of one of the pedestal bases from the Arcus Novus. Museo della Civiltà Romana, Rome. (Photo: Author)

element of the dominant ideology, and manipulating its meaning in relation to their own or group beliefs by so doing. Such appropriation can be profound or it can be shallow and meaningless, it can be didactic or it can simply be dogmatic, often it can be mere entertainment. True collage depends upon careful curation and selection as a precondition of creation.

Detailed architectural analysis of the Arch of Constantine, particularly with regard to defining and understanding the proportions chosen as the mathematical basis for the design of the monument, has shown that its great similarity to the nearby earlier Arch of Septimius Severus was the result of a formal choice of the latter arch as a model for the new structure. The new arch was not, however, a mere copy of the old arch; rather, certain changes were made at the design stage to modify its bulk. The new arch was made thinner, and adaptions were evidently made on site during construction works.

The *spolia* on the Arch of Constantine were not simply selected for their shape or the reused artworks for their images, though both were undoubtedly important factors driving their selection. Once the arch was assembled, a term that might in this case be more appropriate than built, a certain amount of reworking of the older images was undertaken to place the portrait image of Constantine both in contemporary scenes and in past scenes from eras long before his birth. The kind of reworking seen here can be found in all periods of Roman art and in all kinds of contexts. Heads and faces were recarved on statues for all sorts of reasons, even as mundane as the non-payment of a bill for a portrait of one client and its subsequent need to be modified – resulting in a cheaper product to be sold to another. And yet modification or reworking of portraits would appear to be something particularly significant in the art of Late Antiquity even at the level of imperial commissions (plate 38).

It is unlikely that the Arch of Constantine when unveiled to the Roman people was subject to the kind of debate about authenticity that dogged the analysis of early twentieth-century collage, nor is it likely that its astonishing formal resemblance as a structure to the earlier Arch of Septimius Severus, as discussed in Chapter Two, created discussion about its being simply a simulacrum.

Whether one views the arch as a collage, an architectural montage, the calculated sum of appropriated parts, or less graciously as a poorly cobbled together assemblage of disparate parts, the latter being an old view that holds little or no sway in academic circles today, there is no doubt that its interpretation needs to take account of the workings of memory in Roman and Late Antique society.[11] Indeed, there could be much to be learned about the arch and its contemporary reception by analogy to memory studies more broadly. If the arch was in some way intended to be a repository of memories, of the works and deeds of past emperors, of past lives, of the more stable past history of Rome, then it could only succeed as such by the cooperation and collusion of the viewers of the arch; it was through their individual and group interactions with the monument that memories were created. This was an active experience for the viewer and not simply an encounter with a meaningless static form. Each viewer would need to find his or her own personal pathway through the display of a complex network of signs on the monument, either guided by the layout of the monument and its prearranged programme for viewing, or in some random manner that might or might not connect at various points to the sequence of the programme. The monument was part of its contemporary culture and, unlike much modern collage, not a comment on it. Without the viewer having to engage with the artist, as is the case today, their direct engagement with the artwork on the arch would have allowed the art to become simply about interrelationships and memory within a network that was situated firmly in the continuum of Roman art. However, all of these viewings would have been fixed in time, and mediated through the impact of the passing of time and the fluctuating political events in the late Roman world. A viewer of the arch in AD 315 may well have had a vastly different interpretation of the monument to a viewer after AD 337 when Constantine died following his baptism into the Christian faith and so on.

However, there is one jarring factor concerning some of the *spolia* artworks that is difficult to comprehend in terms of its intended meaning. As was noted in Chapter One during a broad discussion of Constantine's portraiture, there are instances recorded on the arch of the recarving of the heads of Trajan, Hadrian, and Marcus Aurelius to turn them into portraits of Constantine. This would appear to be a simple strategy to interpret; the designer of the arch wished the viewer to think, even if only momentarily, that Constantine had become Trajan, that he had become Hadrian, and that he had become Marcus Aurelius. In other words that he was one of the so-called 'good emperors', or at least in a line traceable back to these historic figures. The past and present were therefore linked in the viewer's eye and mind. Of course, to some extent this presupposes that the viewer might know whose portrait had been replaced. If not, he or she would certainly have been somewhat confused by the figure of Constantine appearing in what presumably would have looked like anachronistic clothes. Likewise, the soldiers present particularly in the Trajanic scenes appear very different in terms of their uniforms, even compared to the soldiers in the relief panels of Marcus Aurelius, and both groups of soldiers are most certainly more different still from the troops in the Constantinian frieze. Constantine's recarved portrait faces on the bodies of these earlier, long-deceased emperors were indeed little more than masks that would have done little to fool the vast majority of the arch's viewers, had they indeed been able to clearly view these new faces, many of which were on artworks reset quite high up on the arch.

It is worth noting here the recorded existence through inscriptions and other sources of a Roman official known as the *curator statuarum*, an office that appears to have been created around the time of Constantine, or shortly before.[12] However, we do not know the exact role of this *curator* and whether he was concerned with the upkeep of works of art in Rome, their protection, repair and conservation in other words, or whether the role allowed for the more active collecting of statuary from sites or monuments being cleared in the city and their safe storage, perhaps for future reuse. In an age when the use of *spolia* had become a cultural norm it is very tempting to want to view the *curator*'s job as encompassing the latter, more active role and responsibility. The existence of the *curator statuarum* at this time might be seen as evidence that careful curation and facilitating of the collection of *spolia* was a prerequisite for the use of such material in new contexts, where the processes of selection and curation became subservient to the act of the creation of a new work of art or building. Past and present were thus merged instantly to forge a new reality cognisant of the contemporary Roman political agenda.

If the use of *spolia* of all kinds in the Constantinian period, and Late Antiquity in general, constituted a radical artistic innovation in the service of political expediency, as discussed above, perhaps some aspects of this hypothesis might be apparent in the later reception of the arch and its artworks, and in innovative theoretical schemes of interpretation of it by modern scholars. These aspects will be considered in the final chapter of the book.

7

A Metaphor for Modernity

In the five preceding chapters consideration has been given to the creation of a Constantinian image, both literary and visual, during the life of the emperor. How the Arch of Constantine and other contemporary monuments were intended to contribute towards the maintenance of his image has also been discussed. That *spolia* was used to link the distant, deep Roman past with the Rome of the early to mid-fourth century is beyond debate, though whether the creation of architectural collages using such material was viewed as innovative or conservative at the time is unknowable. In this chapter the reception of the arch as represented in Renaissance and later paintings and drawings will be considered, alongside an examination of the more recent academic strategies for studying the art on the arch, which to some extent divide themselves into two camps, seeing either innovation or conservatism in its creation. The arch as a metaphor for the decline of art at this time and thus for the wider decline of the Roman Empire itself is now thankfully an academic strategy consigned to history, but the origins of this theory also need to be explored.

Reception, Image, and the Stern Arcade

It is perhaps not altogether surprising that the Arch of Constantine became a favoured subject for artists between the fifteenth and twentieth centuries, particularly during that part of the period that corresponded with the era of the Grand Tour and an obsession with the Romantic and picturesque in European art. Frescos, drawings, prints, and watercolour or oil paintings of the arch can be studied from two main perspectives today. Firstly, such images can be viewed simply as historic documents in their own right, providing in many cases a record of the state of the monument at a particular and often quite specific point in time. Dated pictures therefore allow archaeologists and architectural historians to analyse these images in chronological order so as to chart in detail the history of the monument's decline into a partially ruinous state, and its subsequent repair and restoration at various times.[1] From the mid- to later nineteenth century onwards, photographs of the arch have also, of course, contributed significantly to the historiography of its conservation. This is an aspect of the study of the arch that I will not be pursuing further here. The second area of study of historic images of the arch relates to the information that such images can provide with regard to the contemporary reception of the arch, and the opportunity will be taken here to follow this line of inquiry further.

During research for this book I came across nearly forty artist-attributed images of the arch and have seen in addition quite a number of anonymous paintings of it, generally categorised as being of the School of Rome. A number of these pictures of the arch are reproduced here. The frescos, paintings, and drawings known to me, and my knowledge on these, which will in no way be exhaustive, can be grouped into a number of categories, each of which perhaps mirrors, and therefore illuminates, some aspect of the arch's original purpose and meaning, and is therefore of considerable interest and highly germane to the main thesis of this book.

The first category is of pictures where the arch's, and therefore Constantine's, Christian connection is brought out and even overemphasised. I have called these here Christianising Images. The arch became a backdrop for biblical events, existing out of both its time and place and underpinning human dramas which took place in the foreground. Secondly, there is a group of pictures in which the arch is portrayed in its broader architectural setting, stressing its obvious spatial connection with the Colosseum in particular, again perhaps linking in the viewer's mind the scene of the martyrdom of many Christians with a monument to a Christian convert of an emperor. Most of the images in this second category of scenes omit human figures and contemporary structures, and I have called these pictures as a group Landscape and Topographical Images. The third category is again mainly concerned with the architecture of the arch, but here it takes centre stage and acts as the focus of the composition. Sometimes contemporary human figures are used to bring the past firmly into the present, though most often in this category they are included to provide some sense of the scale of the monument for the viewer. This third group I have called Contemporary Illustrative Images. Overlapping to some extent with this is a fourth group, where the arch is once more the centre of the composition, but the presence of human figures in the pictures is here intended perhaps as some form of social comment, hence the category being dubbed here Social Commentary Images. The fifth and final group is less easy to define, especially as it includes only two paintings, one by Turner and the other by Corot, two artists whose grouping together will perhaps be problematic in its own right for some readers. This fifth group might best be called Past Metaphorical Images, for in each picture the ancient arch is being used as a prop in what are in some ways modernist visions of the present past; the arch is here acting as a metaphor for modernity. Interestingly, Turner also produced a number of more illustrative views of the arch as well as his more speculative, metaphorical picture.

The first category of what might best be called Christianising Images of the arch includes two of the fresco paintings on the side walls in the Sistine Chapel in the Vatican in Rome, painted in 1481–2 at the behest of Pope Sixtus IV. This particular fresco cycle, painted by a group of the leading Florentine and Umbrian artists of the day, contrasted scenes from the Old and New Testaments and the lives of Moses and Jesus, the main linking theme being temporal continuity. Though the Arch of Constantine itself bore no Christian images it is likely that after Constantine's deathbed conversion to Christianity and his death, the arch came to be linked to Christian heritage in the minds of many viewers. Certainly by the fifteenth century when these frescos were painted the monument had all but been co-opted as a Christian building. The arch appears in both a fresco by Sandro Botticelli (1445–1510), *The Punishment of the Rebels*, illustrated here (plate 27), and in one by Pietro Perugino (*c.* 1446/50–1523), *Christ Giving the Keys to St Peter*. In the Botticelli fresco a scene from the rebellion of Korah and others against Moses during the flight from Egypt is played out against a backdrop provided by the arch, here transported to both a different country and a different time. In the Perugino fresco the arch appears twice, each portrayal being from a slightly different perspective, the monument appearing to either side of a large octagonal temple. In both pictures the artist had provided a setting that would have both surprised and proved reassuringly familiar to contemporary Romans. In their minds the picture would have restressed the significance of this historic Roman emperor, and by association his arch, in the early history of Christianity. It would also have highlighted the seamless continuity between past and present in a way that is familiar from the artistic programme on the arch itself.

The second category, Landscape and Topographical Images, is a group of pictures in which the arch is portrayed in its wider setting within Rome's urban topography, in relation to the Forum or the Palatine Hill, and in particular its spatial connection with the Colosseum is brought out in some of the works in this group. Once more this may have been part of a Christianising tendency on the part of the artists, perhaps intentionally in many cases contrasting Constantine's monument with the former venue for the bloody martyrdom of many Christians. Paintings in this category include works by Jean Lemaire-Poussin (1598–1659), Claude Lorrain (1600–82), Filippo Gagliardi (?–1659), Viviano Codazzi (*c.* 1606–70), Giovanni Paolo Panini (1691–1765), Giovanni Battista Busiri (1698–1757), Louis Ducros (1748–1810), and J. M. W. Turner (1775–1851) who produced at least three traditional, perhaps preparatory, graphite and watercolour studies of the arch. As most of these pictures, with the exception perhaps of the two latest works by Corot and Turner, simply use the arch as one element in a wider historic landscape, none of these are illustrated here. Two of the pictures here are in any case described in their titles as being a *capriccio*, that is, an architectural fantasy. A number of them date to the period when philosophical ideas about the relationship of man, landscape, and nature were crystallising into an intellectual stance. The idea of the picturesque owed its formulation to the eighteenth-century British cleric William Gilpin and the publication of his theories and meditations on landscapes and ruins in 1782. This was very much in the mainstream of the ideas coalescing around the Romantic sensibility that was prevalent among the upper classes in eighteenth-century Europe.

The third category of Contemporary Illustrative Images is again concerned with the architecture of the arch, but here it takes centre stage and acts as the focus for the composition, often with little or no desire or attempt by the artists to locate the arch with regard to its relationship to other Roman monuments. Some of the pictures in this category are little more than illustrations of the monument, although in some, contemporary human figures appear, the purpose for their presence seemingly being to act as scales, while also bringing the past firmly into the contemporary present. Some of the pictures in this category show structures built up against or close to the arch, painted in almost as much detail as the arch itself, which betrays their documentary intent. In the early thirteenth century the arch was incorporated into the central Roman stronghold of the powerful Frangipane family, who, along with the Annibaldi family, turned the Colosseum into a fortress. The incorporation of such iconic Roman imperial monuments into these stronghold structures spoke highly of the status and expectations of the Frangipanes, but also indicated how low the relics of Rome's formerly glorious past had fallen in the estimation of its own people. It was really only the interest in the ancient Roman monuments reactivated by the adherents of the Grand Tour that led to the rescue and renovation of many of the key monuments of Rome's past in the eighteenth and nineteenth centuries. The Contemporary Illustrative Images represent the largest and one of the most significant groups of paintings of the arch, in that the paintings span the era from when the Grand Tour was in full swing, and ideas about the picturesque and the Romantic sensibility were giving way to more realistic, socially and politically engaged views of the contemporary world. For that reason the paintings and other images in this group will be discussed in broadly chronological order. Because of the great interest inherent in this group I have chosen to illustrate many of the pictures in this category which I discuss at any length below.

Nicolas Poussin (1593–1665) produced drawings of the Hadrianic Sacrifice to Silvanus and also the Lion Hunt *tondi* on the arch, not illustrated here, and their existence shows that he studied and drew the monument, but I believe that these two sketches, now in the collections of the British Museum, constitute the only surviving examples of his visit there.

One of the most powerful portrayals of the arch appears in Jan Miel and Alessandro Salucci's oil painting *The Arch of Constantine, Rome*, painted in the 1640s, now in the collection of the Barber Institute, Birmingham University, a painting I came to know intimately during numerous lunchtime visits to the Barber when I worked at the university in the 1990s (plate 28). Miel (1599–1663), a Flemish painter working in Rome in the mid-seventeenth century, was a regular collaborator with the Florentine-born artist Alessandro Salucci (1590 – *c.*1660). Salucci is responsible for at least one other picture of the arch, *View of the Arch of Constantine with Figures*, painted in 1647. Miel and Salucci's picture, illustrated here, shows the arch as a rather sad monument in a state of decay, with weeds and shrubs growing on its top, with evident damage to the monument in the form of a number of holes in the area of the large inscription, some Dacian statues missing their heads, and one of the free-standing pillars removed. A house right next to the arch, with figures standing in its doorway, acts to temporarily distract the viewer's eye from the monument itself. The surroundings of the arch appear almost rural in their tranquillity, a point made by the depiction of a shepherd driving a small flock through the once grand central opening. The arch here now seems like the gateway to the Roman countryside rather than a portal to some brave new world of Constantinian benevolence. While two gentlemen stand in front of the arch seemingly discussing it, daily life in contemporary Rome goes on around them, as represented by numerous figures going about their everyday business.

Dutch artist Herman van Swanevelt (1603–55) worked in Rome from 1629 until the late 1630s and his oil painting *The Arch of Constantine*, now in the Dulwich Picture Gallery, London (plate 29), must date from that period and be broadly contemporary with the Miel and Salucci oil. However, as can be seen in the illustration here, his picture, painted from an altogether different perspective, has less of the brooding quality that can be seen in that other work. While still quite obviously in a dilapidated state, the arch appears more imposing and luminous in the brighter light conditions chosen by the artist. The setting looks more suburban and less rural and the arch appears to be attracting more attention from both passers-by and visitors, some of whom are shown sketching or drawing the monument. Van Swanevelt is perhaps capturing the moment when the antiquarian tourists on the Grand Tour first started to visit Rome and its major monuments in numbers, both in honest homage to the Roman past but also in deference to their private classical educations and privileged social positions. The Rome they wished to see was that of the Caesars and not the Rome of their own day. The past of Rome was more important in this instance than its present.

Also dating from the mid- to late eighteenth century are two oil paintings of the arch, both illustrated here, by Dijon-born French artist Jean-Baptiste Lallemand (1716–1803) and Dutch painter Hendrik Frans Van Lint (1684–1763). Lallemand's painting *The Forum, with the Arch of Constantine, Peasants in the Foreground* sold at Christie's in London in 1998 and is now presumably in a private collection (plate 30). Van Lint's painting *The Arch of Constantine, Rome* is in the Government Art Collections (plate 31). Both pictures were painted from quite remarkably similar perspectives, though Lallemand's composition and colour palette suggest the arch to be in more of a state of decay and appear less grand than in Van Lint's picture. However, it is possible that the monument had been partially renovated between the painting of the two pictures, as by the time of Van Lint's work the house that once stood directly adjacent to the arch appears to have been demolished. Van Lint's beautifully clear sky casts an orange glow on the arch, on the Meta Sudans fountain in front of it, and on the Arch of Titus and other buildings on the hill behind. Both pictures include human figures, those in the earlier work being both more numerous and more aimlessly busy. In the central foreground of Van Lint's painting are two men either sawing a very large tree trunk or indeed cutting a large section of column drum, something that again might suggest conservation work on the arch caught in progress. An eighteenth-century gouache picture by Charles-Louis Clerisseau (1721–1820), *The Triumphal Arch of Constantine, Rome*, not illustrated here, was painted in 1781 and is now in the collections of the Hermitage Museum, St Petersburg. It represents an unusual view in that the arch is painted from quite close up and is therefore only partially in the picture, though its full height is included, allowing it to loom over the figures below, who include a number of peasants, one walking through one of the side passageways. Two women look on, one pointing towards the arch. A well-dressed man on horseback rides through the central passageway, almost as if processing, looking to one side as if at the Trajanic artworks reset there.

In the nineteenth century three of the most notable individual studies of the arch, two of which are illustrated here, were painted by the highly regarded British architectural watercolourist Samuel Prout (1783–1852), Swiss painter Franz Kaisermaan (1765–1833), and Edmond Clément Marie Duthoit (1837–89) from Amiens. Prout's watercolour *The Arch of Constantine, Rome from the South-East* is of great interest, not only by reason of its meticulous draftsmanship, but also because of its unusual perspective view of the monument, seen here from one side (plate 33). At least two versions of this picture were engraved and made into prints, each with a different configuration of male figures talking in the foreground. Kaisermaan's watercolour of 1810 *The Arch of Constantine and Colosseum*, not illustrated here, recently sold at auction, provides a detailed, quite traditional view of the arch with some peasant activity in the foreground, the figures quite dwarfed by the bulk of the arch. The Colosseum looms in the background. Duthoit painted his watercolour *The Triumphal Arch of Constantine* around 1862/1865 and it is now in a private collection (plate 35). Its face-on view of the arch, juxtaposed with the Colosseum, is more traditional than Prout's original view but is nonetheless more than simply an illustration of the monument. Rather than cluttering his foreground with numerous figures in the manner of Lallemand he includes a single female figure walking towards one of the side passageways of the arch, and a cart being driven at a stately progress towards the viewer through the central main archway.

The eighteenth and nineteenth centuries were also periods when the commercial artist's print came to popularity, particularly in collected portfolios and illustrated books. This was very much as a consequence of the growing tradition of the Grand Tour, when aristocrats were able to pursue their interests in topography and landscapes, or in classical civilisation, architecture, and history, or perhaps birds and animals, insects, trees, plants and the natural world in general, or in fossils and minerals, and so on, either through travel or through the purchase of such educational volumes. The printmakers art was particularly strong in Italy in the eighteenth century and it is therefore of no surprise that the great architectural draftsman Giovanni Battista Piranesi (1720–78) produced a number of illustrations of the Arch of Constantine (see fig. 11) among his many hundreds of drawings subsequently engraved and reproduced as prints. I am aware of quite a number of prints illustrating the arch based on the work of artists including Agostino Veneziano (1509–36), Alo Giovannoli (1550–1618), Stefano della Bella (1610–64), Matteo Piccioni (1615–71), Alessandro Specchi (1668–1729), Giovanni Paolo Pannini (1691–1765), Luigi Rossini (1790–1857), Giulio Ferrario (1767–1847), who included a print of the arch in his *Il Costume Antico e Moderno* (Ancient and Modern Costume) of the 1820s–30s, and Antonio Sarti (1797–1880). There will certainly be many more by lesser artists.

The fourth group of Social Commentary Images uses the depiction of the arch almost as a vehicle for social comment on contemporary society. The three pictures in this grouping span the period 1742–1886, from when the Grand Tour was in full swing and ideas about the picturesque and the Romantic sensibility were still rife, up to a time when such notions were giving way to more realistic socially and politically engaged views of the contemporary world.

The oil painting *Rome: the Arch of Constantine* of 1742 by Giovanni Antonio Canal, or Canaletto (1697–1768), not illustrated here, appears in a number of versions. The best-known version of the picture, now in the Royal Collection at Windsor Castle, London, shows the arch with contemporary buildings seen in the distance through the passageways. The Colosseum can just be seen towards the edge of the painting. Boundary walls line the approach to the arch and seem to be abutted against its face. The foreground is taken up by largely well-off figures, one seated in the foreground sketching the arch, three gentlemen conversing with a lady, their attention on anything but the monument, and others inspecting the stonework. In another version of around 1744, now in the Getty Museum, Los Angeles, his view is lined up on the central passage of the arch, through which he depicts the looming Colosseum, the use of his artistic licence having moved this building to accommodate this dual view of both arch and Colosseum. In all of them, while the arch is the pre-eminent subject of the painting, Canaletto has filled the scene in the foreground with contrasting groups of poor peasants and well-off visitors. Daily life is shown to go on as figures converse. A servant carries a bundle on his head for his master. Canaletto, as an Italian, seems to be contrasting too the gap between Rome's glorious past and its present.

Among my personal favourites of the paintings that I have chosen to reproduce here is an oil painting by Anton von Maron (1733–1808), painted in 1767, *Portrait of Two Gentlemen Before the Arch of Constantine in Rome*, which is in a private collection (plate 32). This is a splendid example of the linking of Italy's archaeological and architectural heritage with the broader concerns of the Western European aristocrats on the Grand Tour. The two smartly dressed and bewigged gentlemen are caught in intense conversation as they rest from their exertions engaging with Rome's past heritage. One of them sits on a large block of stone to recuperate, while the other stands up and continues to gesture and converse about some aspect of their day's site-seeing. A white dog lies on the ground at the feet of the resting man. Both men have their backs to the Arch of Constantine, which looms up behind them like some ever-present shadow of the past. It is interesting to note that von Maron, an Austrian painter active in Rome from the 1760s till his death, also painted the portrait of Johann Joachim Winckelmann, the father of German classical art history, in Rome in 1768 – another foreigner there in Rome to connect with the city's distant past. The Grand Tour was undertaken not only by younger Britons of the upper class but also by their social equivalents from a number of other Northern European countries. Its origins possibly go as far back as the later seventeenth century, though its heyday was very much the eighteenth and early nineteenth century. While it could be seen as an educational endeavour and a way of paying reverence to the civilising legacy of the classical world, it could also nevertheless be interpreted as a form of class-based cultural hegemony that had little or nothing to do with the everyday realities of life for most of the people living in places like Rome and Naples, which marked the traditional stations of progress for the travellers.

Düsseldorf-born Oswald Achenbach (1827–1905) painted two pictures titled *The Arch of Constantine, Rome*, the oil painting reproduced here dating from 1886 and now in the Alte Nationalgalerie, Berlin (plate 34). The painting provides a sense of the monument as an active part of contemporary Roman life. The cart carrying people in the foreground proceeds towards the arch, giving a sense of movement to this portrayal, a sense that is sorely lacking in some of the other paintings discussed here. There is almost an element of late nineteenth-century Italian social realism in this painting, even though it is painted by a German. It could easily be mistaken for a work by the great Telemaco Signorini (1835–1901) or other members of the Macchiaioli group. It is interesting to see that the arch is here being situated in contemporary Italy, in the lives of the Romans riding on the cart in the foreground. It is not just a ruinous relic of the past. This picture was painted not that long after the Risorgimento – the unification of Italy – and the later capture of Rome in 1870, and the monument here is not being presented in the manner of the van Maron painting discussed above, where it seems to 'belong' to the educated upper classes of England and Germany on the Grand Tour. Rather, it is almost presented here as a symbol of the new Italy, much as the original arch must have appeared as a symbol of the new Rome in AD 315. The forward movement of the laden cart seems symbolic of the political momentum pushing a unified Italy forward at this time.

The fifth and final group is less easy to define, especially as it includes only two paintings, one by Corot and the other by Turner. This fourth group, Past Metaphorical Images, can be defined by the way that both artists have used the ancient arch as a prop in what were in some ways modernist visions of the present past; the arch was indeed here being brought into play as a metaphor for modernity. Jean-Baptiste Camille Corot (1796–1875) painted his small oil *The Arch of Constantine and the Forum, Rome*, now in the Frick Collection, New York, in 1843 (plate 36). Some authorities consider it a sketch rather than a finished work as such. It represents a magnificent study in form and colour, the luminosity of the late afternoon sun giving coherent form to the blocky shapes of the Roman arch and other buildings in the vicinity and beyond. Details of the arch are indistinct and frankly unimportant in this instance. The arch is still identifiable by its outline and shape, its grandeur impossible to ignore within the immediate urban environment represented by other structures such as the Meta Sudans and buildings on the Campidoglio behind. The absence of figures gives the picture a sense of timelessness and optimism for both the contemporary present and future of Rome, something that has been missing from many of the paintings discussed above. The Corot painting is not concerned with illustration or documentation, it is more concerned with feeling and experience. The immediacy of this sketch and its quite modernist composition contrasts greatly with some of Corot's larger oils based on his visits to Rome, such as *The Forum Seen from the Farnese Gardens* and *The Colosseum Seen from the Farnese Gardens*, both now in the Louvre in Paris.

Joseph Mallord William Turner (1775–1851) painted *The Arch of Constantine, Rome* in 1835, now in the Tate collections (plate 37). As noted above, the Tate also holds a number of other, much more straightforward and traditional, Turner drawings and watercolours of the arch that were made in 1819, presumably preliminary sketches for future use. In the 1835 picture the arch appears in the distance to one side of the canvas, recognisable as in the Corot painting by its shape and outline. A tall umbrella pine, that quintessential Roman tree, dominates the foreground on the other side of the picture, behind which the sun appears through wispy cloud like a fireball. The Arch of Constantine is not here a redundant ruin or a paean in stone to Rome's former glory; rather it is being reborn here in a new light. This painting too looks to the future by referencing the past, as had been achieved so wonderfully by Corot. When writing the discussion on these two paintings I was forcibly reminded of the last two stanzas of Gérard de Nerval's mystical poem of 1854, 'Delfica':[2]

> The gods you weep for shall return at last,
> Time will restore the order of the past,
> Prophetic winds have shuddered through the lands,
>
> And still the Sybil with a Latin mien
> Sleeps on beneath the arch of Constantine
> And undisturbed the stern arcade yet stands.

It would thus appear that we can take fragments of the apparent inspiration and motives of the various artists who over the centuries have depicted the Arch of Constantine, as discussed above, and incorporate them into our collage of interpretation of that monument. The changing reception of the arch also helps to demonstrate how experiencing the monument was not a static affair, tied down by linear time, but rather an experience mediated by time and memory, and altered by contemporary and changing cultural perceptions and political and religious realities.

Writing the Arch

If those artists for whom the Arch of Constantine constituted an interesting, relevant subject can be assumed to have also appreciated the monument as a significant late Roman structure in itself, indeed imperial Rome's final great commemorative or triumphal arch, then this consensus was not necessarily shared by some of their contemporaries. Having extolled here the positive role played by the artists discussed above in deliberately or inadvertently providing insights in their work into the meaning of the Arch of Constantine, it may come as a surprise to some readers to learn that other artists saw little to interpret or celebrate. Indeed, in a well-known letter written by the painter Raphael (1483–1520) to Pope Leo X around 1519, the artist was totally dismissive of the contemporary sculpture on the Arch of Constantine, labelling it 'very feeble and destitute of all art and good design' (figs 59, 60, 61), in contrast to the reused earlier sculptures, which he saw as being 'extremely fine and done in perfect style'.[3] For Raphael, the Arch of Constantine was symptomatic of a decline in Late Antiquity of all the arts – 'literature, sculpture, painting' – but not of architecture. Indeed he saw the arch as being 'well designed and well built', which indeed it was. The opinion of Giorgio Vasari (1511–74) writing in the preface to his *Le Vite de Più Eccellenti Pittori,*

59. The Constantinian frieze – detail of the *Congiarium* scene (Constantine distributing monies to the Senate and Roman people). North face, the Arch of Constantine, Rome. (Photo: Graham Norrie, after Giuliani 1955)

60. The Constantinian frieze – a lone horseman. South face, the Arch of Constantine, Rome. (Photo: Graham Norrie, after Giuliani 1955)

61. Plaster cast of the Tetrarchs scene on the Arch of Constantine, Rome. Museo della Civiltà Romana, Rome. (Photo: Author)

Scultori ed Architettori of 1568, generally known in translation today as *Lives of the Artists*, very much echoed the views of Raphael, contrasting the 'beautifully finished' earlier sculptures with the 'complete botch' of the fourth-century ones.[4]

As has been demonstrated in the preceding chapters, our knowledge and appreciation of the Arch of Constantine has increased greatly in the fifty years or so since Bernard Berenson used the monument as the central motif and case study in his book on what he saw as a deleterious 'decline of form' in late Roman art. It has increased exponentially since the publication of the results of the archaeological excavation of the arch's foundations, and a revelatory full photogrammetric survey of its fabric in the 1990s. Old certainties have been thrown aside and new avenues of enquiry have suddenly been opened up around a monument about which it might have been thought everything to be said had indeed now been said. Not only that, but in some cases by returning to first principles in terms of examining the architectural structure of the arch itself and its inscriptions, much new light has since been shed on the genesis and meaning of the project of commemoration personified in stone by the arch. By placing the arch in its topographical setting within the city of Rome, as well as in its chronological and artistic ones, a deeper understanding of its symbolic value has been gained, along with a deeper understanding of its role in the context of urban political discourse centred on late imperial ideology, display, ceremony, and presentation.

Bernard Berenson's 1954 short book *The Arch of Constantine or the Decline of Form* now, like much of his critical writing, appears dated and curiously elitist; his prose style as decorous as a classical frieze. Nevertheless, the book still succeeds in being provocative and challenging. The whole work is predicated on the thesis that the whole history of

'Eurasian' art from the time of Constantine to the reign of Charles V of France (1338–80), a period of around a thousand years, represented a complete cycle from 'decline and recovery of Form and what can be expressed through Form'.[5] Bereson's concentration on 'competence' as a driver of 'Form' in his interpretation of the arch immediately condemned in his eyes much Late Antique art, which he saw as poorly executed in contrast to earlier classical art. That the Constantinian art on the arch was simply an aesthetic reflection of contemporary late Roman culture and society was not seriously considered. Berenson's stance had moved on little, if at all, from those of Raphael and Vasari quoted above, and yet he would have been familiar with the writings of the Austrian art historian Alois Riegl, who around the turn of the twentieth century had argued that the Constantinian sculpture on the arch was stylistically different from the earlier reused sculpture there *by choice* and not because of a decline in competence among late Roman artists and a decline in taste among the commissioners of such work.[6]

Again, Berenson did not at all appreciate the concept of the use of *spolia* on the arch; indeed, he wondered if its use – 'this curious procedure' – was not simply part of a strategy 'to hurry to get things ready in time ... [and] that nothing could be done there and then as worthy of the occasion'.[7] It was for him 'a confession of inferiority to the past'.[8] Even when his observations were significant he would often then muddy the waters by returning once more to the question of competence. For instance, he astutely observed that the section of the Constantinian frieze depicting the Battle of the Milvian Bridge 'with horses and riders struggling in the water, sappers and trumpeters pell-mell, reminds one (not to the advantage of the frieze) of sarcophagi of this period'.[9] Though he claimed to have made extensive use of Hans Peter L'Orange and Armin von Gerkan's invaluable 1939 monograph on the arch, there is little evidence in his essay that Berenson's own interpretations of the artwork were influenced by their readings of the ideological content of the reliefs on the arch.[10]

Throughout this book I have tried to avoid making the kind of aesthetic judgements on the Arch of Constantine that so flaw Bernard Berenson's book on the subject and which place the newer artworks on the arch in a narrative linked to ideas of decline. It has been suggested that Berenson's thesis of decline was very much a product of the time when he first started thinking about this topic, the 1940s, when the forces of barbarism in Europe were very much knocking on the doors of civilisation.[11] This may be so, but it hardly accounts for the highly blinkered nature of his views, no matter how eloquently expressed. If Berenson saw himself as the successor to Vasari in decrying the nature of the Arch of Constantine and pointing out its stylistic defects to contemporary society, then in so doing he had no need to adopt the additional position that modernism as a movement in his own time produced nothing but bad art too. This anti-modernist stance was indeed quite ironic, given the fact that an argument could have been made from the opposite standpoint, that the arch was both novel and revolutionary rather than conservative or even retrogressive.

An argument in favour of the originality of Late Antique Roman art in general was made by the Marxist Italian art historian Ranuccio Bianchi Bandinelli in the 1960s and 1970s.[12] His thesis was that late Roman art was the unique product of the merging of two streams of influence from what he called 'plebeian art', what we might term popular art today, and to a lesser extent provincial art, feeding back into the mainstream of Roman art. The stranglehold of classical style on elite art he now saw broken by this phenomenon, which to him appeared to reflect broader social and political shifts in power in the later Roman world. This shift he thought was even reflected in the choice of artworks for an imperial or senatorial monument such as the Arch of Constantine. To some extent Bianchi Bandinelli's work was the last word in the style argument that had so dominated much of the discussion of the Arch of Constantine, and, as seen in the preceding chapters of this book, study of the arch is now very much dominated by matters relating to dating, topographical location, context, fragmentation, memory, and the possible significance and meaning of the use of *spolia* on the arch.

One of the main issues concerning academics today is whether the image of Constantine presented to the Roman people by the Senate through the inscriptions and artwork on the Arch of Constantine can be seen to have in any way differed from the image that the emperor himself may have been responsible for creating and promulgating, both in Rome and more broadly throughout the empire. The most significant evidence for studying this is provided by portraits of the emperor on coins and medals, on cameos, and in the form of portrait sculptures.

Constantine appeared quite early on to promote himself as a family man with dynastic ambitions and not simply as a Tetrarch. Certainly, in the naming of his sons and heirs, and they of theirs, there was a reassuring familiarity about the emperors' names – Constantine II, Constantius II, Constans – and some hint of a promise of stability was surely implied by this lack of variation in their names and by the creation of a dynasty. The idea of a stable, calculable future was also implied by the Senate's referencing of Constantine's *vicennalia* in inscriptions on the arch, an event that was at the time of the arch's completion still ten years in the future. The fact that there is a certain amount of confusion today when art historians try to identify and distinguish between portraits of Constantine and other male members of his family suggests that there was even a policy to make successor emperors not only sound similar to their illustrious predecessor through their names, but also to resemble him in official portraits. There is a growing body of opinion among academics that Constantine's reputation in Rome immediately after AD 312 was to some extent created on the back of the achievements of Maxentius, who had refocused the attention of the imperial courts on events at Rome, and made a significant mark on the urban topography of the city through his sponsoring and promotion of new building projects and renovation schemes.

All books need to stake a claim to some element of originality to justify their existence. In this book a conscious attempt has been made to present to the reader in an accessible form what is hoped to have been an up-to-date and even-handed exposition of the history of the study of the Arch of Constantine and to bring together theories, both ancient and modern, about this highly significant monument and to weigh up their validity against the present-day body of archaeological evidence. Further to this, the concept that the arch represented an architectural collage, the blending of the selected old with the new to thereby create a unique and indissoluble whole, has been presented here as a new way perhaps to view the use of historic architectural and artistic *spolia* in the creation of the arch.

This strategy of linking past and present, and indeed the future, as represented by the inscription on the arch looking forward to Constantine's *vicennalia*, represented a way of blurring the individual, group, and social memories of the arch's viewers, and might have been a conscious strategy adopted to mitigate for the memory of the civil strife that had led to the ascendancy of Constantine and the erection of the monument. However, the depiction of civil war in the Constantinian frieze on the arch was there to always bring the viewer back to reality. The overt tinkering with the linearity of time in the service of imperial ideology was a strategy that can be seen in the art of many emperors, examples including the preternaturally youthful images of Augustus that continued to be produced in the emperor's middle age and later life, and the images of Trajan as the ageless adult who changed little in his portraits throughout his reign. Memory was here created by the individual viewers in their personal interaction with the monument.

The Arch of Constantine is a monument that should no longer be atomised during its study, that is reduced to its parts or even simply to a sum of its parts. Again, it is almost impossible now to claim to view the arch in isolation. Instead it should be seen both as part of a continuum – in the use of civic and honorific arches as part of the ideological make-up of Roman and Roman provincial life – and as a very specific part of the integrated topography of Late Antique Rome.

Rome's Final Arch

In recent years academic debate about chronology has swirled around and about the Arch of Constantine in a way that might be thought surprising for such a major monument in the heart of Rome. All of these arguments have been discussed to a greater or lesser extent in this book. Surely the Arch of Constantine was built by Constantine? If not, then by whom? At one stage some of the debaters suggested that the origins of the arch could even lie as far back in time as the reign of Hadrian. Subsequently that idea was successfully countered by the now generally accepted idea that the arch was Late Antique in date, built almost entirely of *spolia*, and perhaps was originally started as a monument under Maxentius. If certainties such as this could be questioned, then what other aspects of the monument's history could also be open to discussion?

As it has turned out, these aspects have included whether the arch can really be classed as an imperial monument, or if it is rather the Roman Senate's vision of how they would have liked imperial authority to be presented to the Roman people in a period of great uncertainty and political and religious upheaval. Was the artwork on the arch innovative in almost a modernist way, including the use of *spolia*, or was it in fact terminally regressive in some way? Was the contemporary artwork on the arch an example of bad, degenerate art, incompetently executed, or was it simply what it was, art in a contemporary style competently executed to fulfil a brief? Was the harking back to the past, exemplified on the monument by the elements of *spolia* that depicted the past, 'good' emperors Trajan, Hadrian, and Marcus Aurelius, simply retrograde nostalgia, a form of bankruptcy of ideas, or was it in fact a brilliant example of the harnessing of memory in the service of the moral good of the Roman state? (plate 39)

Finally, there is the issue of which theoretical frameworks of interpretation might be appropriately deployed when considering the widespread use of *spolia* in Late Antiquity and on the Arch of Constantine in particular, and the assembly of the monument from such seemingly disparate parts to create a new whole. As it turns out, the using of *spolia* might have been both a practical necessity and a conscious choice, linked to other strands of reuse of cameos and gemstones and perhaps also the so-called cult of relics. In other words, some kind of public and social engagement with fragmented objects, ranging from small artefacts to architectural fragments and human remains, might have all been part of the same contemporary phenomenon. The arch as a repository of memories, some kind of mnemonic device for triggering reactions in its contemporary viewers, for establishing an unbroken imperial timeline, or rather presenting such in opposition to historical reality, is certainly a useful way to view the monument. If the arch constitutes the sum of its parts rather than simply being an accumulation of parts to be disassembled for analysis by scholars, then theories relating to the arts of collage and photomontage, and indeed to a lesser extent to the more modern concept of appropriation, obviously seem to be highly pertinent to the interpretation of the monument.

But after all of this, we must not ever lose sight of the fact that the Arch of Constantine is a monument dedicated by the Senate of Rome to Constantine, and not a monument erected under Constantine's own authority. The Senate may have unequivocally set out its stall in terms of what kind of emperor they would like Constantine to be through harking back to the times of three of the so-called good emperors, by including carefully chosen *spolia* artworks from each of their reigns. Maybe it was a cry for stability in contemporary political affairs that had been sadly missing during the years of the violent disintegration of the now discredited Tetrarchic system. Maybe it represented a wish-list of imperial qualities that they hoped Constantine would possess or would adopt. Maybe it was the ultimate vehicle of senatorial propaganda, utilising memory and manipulating linear time to restate the primacy of the city of Rome itself through the strength of its Senate, and placing Rome back at the very centre of the empire.

It is certainly not true, as with any artwork, that if you look at the arch for long enough it will reveal its secrets. Again, like most artworks there is no secret; it is what it is. The arch must certainly have been viewed as an excitingly different monument when first dedicated; it was both of its time and somehow out of time because of its almost exclusive use of *spolia*. Yet it must also have looked strangely and reassuringly familiar, in terms of its similarity to the Arch of Septimius Severus and its place in the continuum of Roman triumphal and commemorative arches. Some parts of the dedicatory inscription may appear ambiguous to us today, but there is absolutely no evidence to suppose that at the time this was viewed as the first Christianised Roman imperial monument, though it might certainly have come to be viewed that way at a later date. As the discussion above has indicated, there is now no need to try and understand the arch in terms of it marking some form of terminal decline in form in the Roman world, or in terms of it being a tentative harbinger of a new form of art, which would evolve into what we understand today to be Byzantine art and subsequently medieval art. In the case of the Arch of Constantine, it is as if the whole of its contemporary world can be described by looking at just this one monument.

Appendix:
Visiting Constantine's Rome

This short appendix has been provided to allow those visiting Rome to see some of the sites and artworks discussed in the main body of this book. Because a number of the sites are outside the city proper, in different directions, it would not be feasible to take in all of them in a single day, and I recommend a more leisurely tour spread over several days or even a week. I have provided details of public transport links to the sites, though most of the sites and museums in the centre of Rome are relatively accessible on foot from Colosseum (Colosseo) Metro (Metropolitana) station.

In Rome

Arch of Constantine
The last major public monument of imperial Rome, dedicated to Constantine by the Senate and people of Rome. Nearest Metropolitana stop: Colosseo.

Basilica Nova
The great basilican hall in the Roman Forum, started by Maxentius and finished by Constantine. Nearest Metropolitana stop: Colosseo.

St John Lateran (S. Giovanni in Laterano)
Site of the first Christian church complex in Rome built under the aegis of Constantine. A statue of Constantius II stands at one end of the entrance porch to the church. Nearest Metropolitana stop: San Giovanni.

Egyptian Obelisk, Piazza S. Giovanni
Brought here from the Circus Maximus where Constantine had originally planned for it to stand. Finally set in place there after his death by Constantius II. Nearest Metropolitana stop: San Giovanni.

Arch of Janus
Massive arch in the Forum Boarium on Via del Velabro, possibly the 'Arch of the Deified Constantine' listed in the Regionary Catalogues. Nearest Metropolitana stop: Colosseo.

Milvian Bridge
Mainly modern bridge, heavily restored in 1850, on or near the site of the original Roman bridge which gave its name to the decisive battle of AD 312 at which Constantine defeated Maxentius. Nearest Metropolitana stop: Flaminio. Then either walk northwards for around 30–40 minutes alongside the Tiber or catch the number 2 tram from Piazzale Flaminio in the direction of Mancini.

Museo del Palazzo dei Conservatori
Part of the Capitoline Museums (Musei Capitolini). In the entrance courtyard are the marble head, hand, foot, and other fragments of the colossal statue of Constantine that originally stood in the Basilica Nova. Inside the museum the collections include the giant bronze portrait head of Constantine, along with a hand and spiked globe from the same statue. Nearest Metropolitana stop: Colosseo.

Museo Capitolino (Capitoline Museum)
On the other side of the piazza from the Museo del Palazzo dei Conservatori, in the Museo Capitolino can be found the best known portrait head of the Empress Helena, mother of Constantine, the head having been attached in late Roman times to an earlier statue of a seated female figure. Nearest Metropolitana stop: Colosseo.

Piazza del Campidoglio
On the balustrade around this piazza between the Museo Capitolino and the Museo del Palazzo dei Conservatori can be seen two cuirassed statues of Constantine and his son Constantine II. Nearest Metropolitana stop: Colosseo.

Vatican Museums (Musei Vaticani)
In the Museo Pio Clementino in the Vatican Museums complex can be found the huge, highly decorated porphyry sarcophagi of Helena, Constantine's mother, and of Constantina, his daughter. Nearest Metropolitana stop: Cipro-Musei Vaticani.

In the Suburbs and Countryside

Arch of Marlborghetto
A massive arch, dating to the time of Constantine and possibly marking some significant stop en route to the battle site at the Milvian Bridge. Travel to Metropolitana stop Flaminio. Exit station and cross to station Ferrovie Roma Nord right nearby. Take Ferrovie Urbane train for Civitacastellana-Viterbo and alight at Sacrofano. There is no signposting to the monument, so cross the train tracks onto a path on the side opposite the station building and walk around 50 metres back in the direction of Rome. The arch, now built into an old farmhouse, is on the left.

Mausoleum of Helena

Great circular mausoleum, probably originally intended for Constantine, in which the emperor's mother Helena was buried in the porphyry sarcophagus now in the Vatican Museums. Part of a larger complex which included a basilican hall. From Roma Termini bus station catch bus number 105 as far as Tor Pignatarra. Alight at the major crossroads here. There is no signposting to the monument, but walk around 500 metres up the hill away from Rome on the left-hand side of the road. Towards the top of the hill on the left is the church of SS. Pietro e Marcellino; the mausoleum can be accessed by the entrance road at the side of the church. In summer 2012 access into the mausoleum was restricted due to ongoing building works.

Mausoleum of Santa Costanza

Part of a larger complex that included a circus-basilica, the mausoleum was built for Constantine's daughter Constantina (S. Costanza). Decorated with stunning ceiling and vault mosaics, the mausoleum is in use today as an adjunct to the nearby church. A replica of Constantina's huge porphyry sarcophagus is on show inside. The original can be seen in the Vatican Museums. From Roma Termini bus station catch the number 310 bus and alight at Piazza di S. Costanza. There is no signposting to the monument, but walking a short distance back towards Rome from the piazza and turning left onto Via Nomentana will bring you shortly to the entrance to the church of S. Agnese Fuori Le Mura, which in turn gives access to the mausoleum behind.

Glossary of Latin Words and Terms

adlocutio	an address or speech, in this case the formal address of an emperor to his troops.
adventus	arrival, in this case the formal arrival of an emperor.
alimenta	food, in this case formally given by an emperor.
buccina/buccine	a military trumpet/trumpets.
cantharus	a wine vessel.
Cataloghi Regionari	the Regionary Catalogues, fourth-century listings of monuments and buildings in Rome.
clementia	clemency, often formally given by an emperor.
congiarium	a gift, in this case formally given by an emperor.
consecratio	a consecration or deification, in this case of an emperor.
corona civica	an oak-leaf crown.
curator statuarum	literally 'curator of the statues', a fourth-century official post in Rome.
damnatio memoriae	a formal process of damnation after death by the erasing of memory.
decennalia	a ten-year anniversary, normally of an emperor's coming to power.
divus	divine, a god.
dracones	military standards in the form of a dragon's head.
equites singulares (Augusti)	an elite cavalry unit stationed in Rome to protect the emperor. Disbanded by Constantine.
imagines	images of the ancestors.
janus quadrifrons	a four-way arch.
largitio	a distribution or giving away of something, often formally carried out by an emperor.
liberalitas	kindness or generosity.
lustratio	purification, often by sacrifice.
martyrium	a mausoleum for a Christian martyr.
opus sectile	literally 'cut work', a type of mosaic inlay for walls and floors.
oratio	a speech or oration.

pileus pannonicus	a Pannonian hat, popular in Late Antiquity.
principia	a military headquarters building.
profectio	departure, in this case the formal departure of an emperor.
quadriga	a four-horse chariot.
quinquennalia	a five-year anniversary, normally of an emperor's coming to power.
rex datus	a client king.
signifer	a military standard bearer.
spolia	collected and reused architectural fragments and artworks.
tondo/tondi	a roundel/roundels.
tricennalia	a thirty-year anniversary, normally of an emperor's coming to power.
via triumphalis	the Triumphal Way.
vicennalia	a twenty-year anniversary, normally of an emperor's coming to power.
virtus	manhood, strength, courage, or worth.

Notes

Preface

1. Sein and Prusac 2012.

1 Life and Times

1. The academic literature on Constantine's life is extensive and I will only recommend a few titles here. See principally: Alföldi 1932; Bardill 2012; Barnes 1981, 1982, 2007, and 2011; Bonamente and Fusco 1992; Burkhardt 1956; Cameron and Hall 1999; Carla and Castello 2010; Demandt and Engemann 2007a and 2007b; Dörries 1972; Ehling and Weber 2011; Elliot 1996; Fowden 1993; Girardet 2006 and 2010; Grigg 1977; Hartley *et al.* 2006; Herrmann-Otto 2007; Holloway 2004; Jones, A. H. M. 1962; Lenski 2006; Lieu and Monserrat 1998; MacMullen 1968 and 1987; Marlowe 2006, 2010, and Forthcoming; Odahl 2010; Pohlsander 2004; Schmitt 2007; Schuller and Wolff 2007; Stephenson 2009; Van Dam 2007 and 2011; Veyne 2007; Ward-Perkins 1999; Ward-Perkins 2012; and Woods 1997.
2. Cameron and Hall 1999, 1–53.
3. Cameron and Hall 1999, 3.
4. Saylor Rodgers 1980.
5. Eusebius, *Vita Constantini*, 1.26 in Cameron and Hall 1999, 79.
6. Eusebius, *Vita Constantini*, 1.33–1.34 in Cameron and Hall 1999, 82–3. However, on Maxentius see: Alexander 1971; Coarelli 1986; Cullhed 1994; Curran 2000, 43–69 and 76–7; Frazer 1966; Groag 1930; Marlowe 2010 and Forthcoming; and Spiedel 1986.
7. Eusebius, *Vita Constantini*, 1.36 in Cameron and Hall 1999, 839.
8. Eusebius, *Vita Constantini*, 1.28–1.32 in Cameron and Hall 1999, 80–1. On academic writings on Constantine's visions see: Demandt 2007; Ehling and Weber 2011; Grégoire 1939; Hatt 1950; MacMullen 1968; Saylor Rodgers 1980; and Weiss 1993.
9. Eusebius, *Vita Constantini*, 1.28–1.30 in Cameron and Hall 1999, 80–1.
10. Eusebius, *Vita Constantini*, 1.31 in Cameron and Hall 1999, 81–2.
11. Lactantius, *De Morte Persecutorum*, 44.4–6.
12. Eusebius, *Vita Constantini*, 1.38 in Cameron and Hall 1999, 84–5.
13. Eusebius, *Vita Constantini*, 1.39–1.40 in Cameron and Hall 1999, 85–6.
14. *Panegyrici Latini*, 12 (9), 18.3.
15. On Constantine and Christianity see: Alföldi 1932 and 1948; Bruun 1962; Cameron 2006; Carla and Castello 2010; Demandt 2007; Diefenbach 2011; Ehling and Weber 2011; Elliot 1996; Girardet 2010; Grégoire 1939; Grigg 1977; Krautheimer 1992; MacMullen 1968; Marcone 2002; Odahl 2010; Roldanus 2006; Saradi-Mendelovici 1990; Storch 1970; and Veyne 2004.
16. Lactantius, *De Morte Persecutorum*, 24.6.
17. Aurelius Victor, *De Caesaribus*, 41.2 in Smith 1997, 201.
18. Eusebius, *Vita Constantini*, 2.45–2.46 in Cameron and Hall 1999, 110–11.
19. Eusebius, *Vita Constantini*, 3.47 in Cameron and Hall 1999, 139.
20. Eusebius, *Vita Constantini*, 3.25–3.38 in Cameron and Hall 1999, 132–6.
21. Eusebius, *Vita Constantini*, 4.69 in Cameron and Hall 1999, 180–1.
22. On the *consecratio* coins see Bruun 1954.

23. Smith 1997, 184.
24. Smith 1997, 185–6.
25. On Constantine's coinage see principally: Bruun 1954, 1958, 1962, and 1997; Harrison 82–91; Kleiner, D. E. E. 1992, 434–5; and Kraft 1954–5.
26. On the Constantinian portrait see principally: Calza 1959–60; Evers 1991; Gliwitsky 2011; Grigg 1977; Hannestad 2001, 2007a, and 2007b; Harrison 1967; Kinney 2001; Kleiner, D. E. E. 1992, 433–41; Knudsen 1988; L'Orange 1953; Petersen 1900; Presicce 2005; Rohmann 1998; Romeo 1999; Smith 1997, 185–7 and 201–2; and Wright 1987.
27. Dr Sandra Knudsen, pers. comm.
28. Holloway 2004, 160 note 75.
29. For a splendid colour, computer-generated reconstruction of the colossal statue of Constantine see Demandt and Engemann 2007a, 131.
30. Ammianus Marcellinus, *Res Gestae*, 16.10.9–10. Translation by S. P. Ellis in E. K. Gazda (ed.), *Roman Art in the Private Sphere* (Ann Arbor: University of Michigan Press, 1991), p. 129.
31. Holloway 2004, 157 note 1.
32. On Constantinian cameos and gems see: Entwistle and Adams 2011; Gagetti 2011; Henig 2006, 71–2 and 138–40; Kleiner, D. E. E. 1992, 441–2; Krug 2007 and 2011; Nolden 2007; Sande 2001; and Zwierlein-Diehl 2011.
33. Sande 2001, 151–2.

2 Monument and Materiality

1. On the Arch of Constantine see: Berenson 1954; Bianchi Bandinelli 1970, 73–85; Buttrey 1983; Calza 1959–60; Capodiferro; Cirone 1993–4; Claridge 1998, 272–6; Conforto *et al.* 2001; Curran 2000, 86–90; Elsner 1998, 2000, and 2006, 257–260; Engemann 2007; Fehl 1985; Ferris 2000, 132–5; Frothingham 1912–15; Giuliani 2000; Giuliano 1956; Di Giuseppe 2000; Gradara 1918; Holloway 1985 and 2004, 19-53; Iacopi 1977; Jones, H. S. 1906; Kähler 1953; Kinney 2012; Kleiner, D. E. E. 1992, 444–55; Kleiner, F. S. 2001; Knudsen 1989 and 1990; Kuttner Forthcoming; Koeppel 1990; Liverani 2004, 2005, and 2007; L'Orange and Gerkan 1939; Magi 1956–7; Marlowe 2006; Massini 1993; Peirce 1989; Pensabene 1988, 1993, 1995, and 1999; Pensabene *et al.* 2002; Pensabene and Panella 1993–4 and 1999; Prusac 2012; Punzi 1999; Richardson 1975; Rohmann 1998; Ruysschaert 1962–3; Schmidt-Colinet 1996; Sein and Prusac 2012; Steiner 1994; Vaccaro 2001; Vaccaro and Ferroni 1993–4; Waelkens 1985; Walton 1924; Wilson Jones 1999 and 2000; Wohl 2001; Zanker 2012; and Zeggio 1999.
2. Wilson Jones 1999 and 2000.
3. Marlowe 2006.
4. On marble samples see; Bruno *et al.* 1999; and Pensabene 1988 and 1999b. On the overall results of the photogrammetric survey and its contextualisation see the papers in Pensabene and Panella 1999.
5. On *spolia* see: Alchermes 1994; Brandenburg 2011b; Brenk 1987; Brilliant and Kinney 2011; Elsner 2000; Fabricius Hansen 2003; Holloway 1985; Kinney 1995, 1997, and 2001; Knudsen 1989 and 1990; Liverani 2004 and 2011; Saradi 1997; and Wohl 2001.
6. On the Basilica of Junius Bassus see: Elsner 1998a, 192–3; and Sapelli 2000.
7. Wilson Jones 2000, 58.
8. Elsner 2000, 152–3 and 153 note 11.
9. See Chapter Two, note 6 above.
10. On the Arch of Septimius Severus see principally Brilliant 1967.
11. Wilson Jones 2000, 65.
12. The translation of the inscription is from Claridge 1998, 272.
13. Frothingham 1912–15.
14. Vaccaro 2001; and Vaccaro and Ferroni 1993–94.
15. Pensabene and Panella 1999.
16. On the phenomenological approach to the arch and its setting see Marlowe 2010.
17. On the *Meta Sudans* see, for instance, Claridge 1998, 271–2.
18. On Constantine and Sol see: Bergmann 2007; Bruun 1958; Ehling and Weber 2011; Marlowe 2006; Wallraff 2001 and 2011; and Wienand 2011. On the colossal statue of Sol see principally Marlowe 2010, 225–8.
19. As in the title of Marlowe 2010.

20. On the Circus Maximus obelisk see Claridge 1998, 264–5.
21. Ferris 2009, 88 and 96.

3 The Good Emperors

1. On the Great Trajanic Frieze see: Ferris 2000, 74–7 and Ferris 2003, 58–9; Kleiner, D. E. E. 1992, 220–3; Leander Touati 1987; and Pallottino 1938.
2. On the Trajanic Dacian statues see: Ferris 2003, 60; Packer 2001, 178–9 figure 150; and Waelkens 1985.
3. On the Hadrianic *tondi* see: Calcani 1996–7; Kleiner, D. E. E. 1992, 251–3; Schmidt-Colinet 1996; and Turcan 1991.
4. Holloway 2004, 21–2.
5. On the Troyes Casket see, for instance, Walker 2012, 45–79.
6. On the panel reliefs of Marcus Aurelius see: Angelicoussis 1984; Ferris 2000, 98–9; Kleiner, D. E. E. 1992, 288–94; and Ryberg 1967.
7. Ross Holloway 2004, 25.
8. On the Arcus Novus see, for instance, Kleiner, D. E. E. 1992, 409–13.
9. For a photograph of this inscription/*graffito* see Pensabene and Panella 1999, 35 fig. 25.

4 Inspired by the Divine

1. An idea of L'Orange and Gerkan, quoted in Holloway 2004, 33.
2. On Constantine and Sol see Chapter Two, note 18 above.
3. *Panegyrici Latini*, 6.21.4–6.
4. Holloway 2004, 37.
5. Ferris 2009, 153–7. On architecture as a signifier on Roman monuments see also Thill 2011.
6. Ferris 2000. The literature on Romans and barbarians is extensive, but see also the following and their bibliographies: Bradley, K. 2004; Ferris 2003, 2009, and 2011; and Levi 1952.
7. De Souza 2011, 56.
8. On children on Roman imperial monuments see principally Uzzi 2005, and on the Arch of Constantine specifically Uzzi 2005, 47–50.

5 The Ghost in the Machine

1. On Augustus's Actium Arch and Actium Monument at Nikopolis see, for instance, Kleiner 1992, 82.
2. On the Saint-Bertrand trophy see Ferris 2000, 41–4 and bibliography; and on the arch at Orange see Ferris 2000, 53–4 and bibliography.
3. On the Arras medallion see, for instance, MacCormack 1981, 29–31.
4. On Maxentius's building projects in Rome see principally: Cullhed 1994, 50–60; Curran 2000, 54–63; Kerr 2002; and Marlowe 2010 and Forthcoming. On Maxentius see Chapter One, note 6 above.
5. Cullhed 1994, 45.
6. Cullhed 1994, 46.
7. Cullhed 1994, 50.
8. Cullhed 1994, 50 note 215.
9. On the Basilica Nova see principally: Claridge 1998, 115–6; Cullhed 1994, 50–2; Curran 2000, 57–8 and 80–2; Marlowe 2010, 202–3 and 208–11; and Minoprio 1932.
10. On the Temple of Romulus see principally: Cullhed 1994, 52–5; Curran 2000, 59–60 and 82–3; and Marlowe 2010, 211–14.
11. On the Temple of Venus and Roma see principally: Claridge 1998, 113–15; Cullhed 1994, 52; Curran 2000, 57–8; and Marlowe 2010, 214–15.
12. Cullhed 1994, 57.
13. Cullhed 1994, 61 and note 279.
14. On Maxentius and the *equites singulares* see Spiedel 1986.
15. On Constantine's building projects in Rome see principally: Cullhed 2000, Curran 2000, 71–114; Holloway 2004, 19–56; and Marlowe 2010.
16. On the Arch of Malborghetto see: Holloway 2004, 53–5; Messinio 1989; and Töbelmann 1915.
17. On the Arch of Janus see: Claridge 1998, 258–9; and Holloway 2004, 55–6.
18. On the Arch of Janus being another Maxentian building see Marlowe Forthcoming.

19. *Aurelius Victor De Caesaribus*, 40.26. On Aurelius Victor see, for instance: Cullhed 1994, 50; Curran 2000, 79–80; and Marlowe 2010, 202–3.
20. On Constantine and church building in Rome see, for instance: Curran 2000, 90–115; and Holloway 2004, 57–156.
21. On the Mausoleum and sarcophagus of Helena see principally: Curran 2000, 99–102; Deichmann and Tschira 1957; Holloway 2004, 86–93; Johnson 2009, 110–19; and Kleiner, D. E. E. 1992, 455–7. On Helena see: Kleiner, D. E. E. 1992, 441–3 and 455–7; and Pohlsander 1995.
22. On the Mausoleum and sarcophagus of Constantina see principally: Brandenburg 2011a; Curran 2000, 128–9; Holloway 2004, 93–100; and Kleiner, D. E. E. 1992, 457–8.

6 Collage and Memory

1. On the proposed relationship between *spolia* and the cult of relics see Elsner 2000.
2. Elsner 2000, 155.
3. On the collecting at Constantinople see, for example: Elsner 2000, 158–162; Johnson 2009, 119–29; Mango 1990; and Ward-Perkins 2012, 57–66.
4. Elsner 2000, 174.
5. On fragmentation and archaeology see, for instance: Chapman 2000; Chapman and Gaydarska 2007; and Ferris 2012, 116–38 and 181–3.
6. On Late Antique practices see, for instance: Hannestad 1994, Prusac 2011 and Stewart 2003.
7. On appropriation at all periods see the various papers in Brilliant and Kinney 2011, especially Brandenburg on Roman *spolia*.
8. On Kurt Schwitters see, for instance: Elderfield 1985.
9. On John Heartfield see, for instance: Willett 1997; and Zervigón 2012.
10. On the Arcus Novus see Chapter Three, note 8 above.
11. On memory in Rome and the ancient world more broadly see: Alcock 2001, 2002, and 2003; Baroin 2010; Boardman 2002; Bradley, R. 1987; Bradley and Williams 1998; Brilliant 2012a; Connerton 1989; Dasen 2010; Dasen and Späth 2010; Dignas and Smith 2012; Farrell 1997; Ferris 2012, 23–5, 30–1, and 86–93; Flower 1996; Hallam and Hockey 2001; Le Goff 1992; Rutledge 2012; Sande 2012; Small and Tatum 1995; Strong 1973; Van Dyke and Alcock 2003; and Wace 1949.
12. On the *curator statuarum* see Stewart 2003, 155.

7 A Metaphor for Modernity

1. On the later history of the arch and the use of pictorial sources in its conservation see Punzi 1999.
2. Translation of *Delfica* by A. Z. Foreman on: http://poemsintranslation.blogspot.co.uk.
3. The text of Raphael's letter can be found in translation in E. G. Holt, *A Documentary History of Art, Volume 1: The Middle Ages and the Renaissance* (New York: Doubleday, 1957) 289–96.
4. Giorgio Vasari, *Le Vite de Più Eccellenti Pittori, Scultori ed Architettori, Proemi*, 5 (1568), translated by G. Bull as G. Vasari, *Lives of the Artists* (Harmondsworth, Penguin, 1965) pp. 32–3.
5. Berenson 1954, 3.
6. Riegl 1901.
7. Berenson 1954, 13–14.
8. Berenson 1954, 14.
9. Berenson 1954, 16.
10. L'Orange and Gerkan 1939.
11. On Berenson see Elsner 1998b.
12. Bianchi Bandinelli 1967 and 1970.

Bibliography

Abbondanza, L. (1997) *The Valley of the Colosseum*, Milan: Soprintendenza Archeologica di Roma, Electa.

Alchermes, J. (1994) '*Spolia* in Roman Cities of the Late Empire: Legislative Rationales and Architectural Sense' *Dumbarton Oaks Papers* 48, pp. 167–78.

Alcock, S. E. (2001) 'The Reconfiguration of Memory in the Eastern Roman Empire' in S. E. Alcock, T. N. D'Altroy, K. D. Morrison and C. M. Sinopoli (eds) *Empires: Perspectives from Archaeology and History*, Cambridge: Cambridge University Press, pp. 323–50.

Alcock, S. E. (2002) *Archaeologies of the Greek Past. Landscapes, Monuments, and Memories*, Cambridge: Cambridge University Press.

Alcock, S. E. and Van Dyke, R. (eds). (2003) *The Archaeology of Memory*, Oxford: Blackwell.

Aldrete, G. S., (1999) *Gestures and Acclamations in Ancient Rome*, Baltimore: Johns Hopkins University Press.

Alexander, S. (1971) 'Studies in Constantinian Architecture', *Rivista di Archeologia Cristiana* 47, pp. 281–330.

Alföldi, A. (1932) 'The Helmet of Constantine with the Christian Monogram', *Journal of Roman Studies*, 22, pp. 9–23.

Alföldi, A. (1948) *The Conversion of Constantine and Pagan Rome*, Oxford: Clarendon Press.

Alston, R. (1998) 'Arms and the Man: Soldiers, Masculinity and Power in Republican and Imperial Rome' in L. Foxhall and J. B. Salmon (eds) *When Men Were Men: Masculinity, Power and Identity in Classical Antiquity*, London and New York: Routledge, pp. 205–23.

Angelicoussis, E. (1984) 'The Panel Reliefs of Marcus Aurelius', Mitteilungen des Deutschen Archäologischen Instituts: *Römische Abteilung* 91, pp. 141–205.

Bardill, J., (2012) *Constantine: Divine Emperor of the Christian Golden Age*, Cambridge: Cambridge University Press.

Barnes, T. D. (1981) *Constantine and Eusebius*, Cambridge, Massachusetts: Harvard University Press.

Barnes, T. D. (1982) *The New Empire of Diocletian and Constantine*, Cambridge, Massachusetts: Harvard University Press.

Barnes, T. D. (2007) 'Constantine After Seventeen Hundred Years: the Cambridge Companion, the York Exhibition and a Recent Biography', *International Journal of the Classical Tradition* 14, pp. 185–220.

Barnes, T. D. (2011) *Constantine: Dynasty, Religion and Power in the Later Roman Empire*, Oxford: Blackwell.

Baroin, C. (2010) 'Remembering One's Ancestors, Following in Their Footsteps, Being Like Them: the Role and Forms of Family Memory in the Building of Identity' in V. Dasen and T. Späth (eds), *Children, Memory and Family Identity in Roman Culture*, pp. 19–48.

Berenson, B. (1954) *The Arch of Constantine or the Decline of Form*, London: Chapman and Hall.

Bergemann, J. (1990) *Römische Reiterstatuen: Ehrendenkmäler im Öffentlichen Bereich*, Mainz: Ehrendenkmäler im Öffentlichen Bereich.

Bergmann, B. and C. Kondoleon (eds) (1999) *The Art of Ancient Spectacle*, New Haven: Yale University Press for National Gallery of Art, Washington.

Bergmann, M. (2007) 'Wenn Konstantin und der Sonnengott. Die Aussagen der Bildzeugnisse' in A. Demandt and J. Engemann (eds), *Konstantin der Grosse* (2007b), pp. 143–62.

Bertoletti, M. and E. La Rocca. (1987) *Rilievi Storici Capitolini*, Rome: De Luca.

Besançon, A. (2001) *The Forbidden Image; an Intellectual History of Iconoclasm*, Chicago: University of Chicago Press.

Bianchi Bandinelli, R. (1967) 'Arte Plebea', *Dialoghi di Archeologia* 1, pp. 7–19.

Bianchi Bandinelli, R. (1970) *Roma. La Fine dell'Arte Antica*, Milan: Rizzoli.

Boardman, J. (2002) *The Archaeology of Nostalgia: How the Greeks Re-Created Their Mythical Past*, London: Thames and Hudson.

Boatwright, M. T. (2000) 'Just Window Dressing? Imperial Women as Architectural Sculpture' in D. E. E. Kleiner and S. B. Matheson (eds) *I Claudia II*, Austin: University of Texas Press, pp. 61–75.

Bonamente, G. and F. Fusco (eds) (1992) *Costantino il Grande*, Dall'Antichità all'Umanesimo, Macerata: Università degli Studi di Macerata.

Bradley, K. (2004) 'On Captives Under the Principate', *Phoenix* 58 No. 3/4, pp. 298–318.

Bradley, R. (1987) 'Time Regained: the Creation of Continuity', *Journal of the British Archaeological Association* 140, pp. 1–17.

Bradley, R. and H. Williams (eds) (1998) 'The Past in the Past', *World Archaeology* 30 (1).

Brandenburg, H. (2011a) *The Basilica of S. Agnese and the Mausoleum of Constantina Augusta (S. Costanza)*, Milan: Jaca Book.

Brandenburg, H. (2011b) 'The Use of Older Elements in the Architecture of Fourth- and Fifth-Century Rome: a Contribution to the Evaluation of *Spolia*' in R. Brilliant and D. Kinney (eds) (2011) pp. 53–74.

Brenk, B. (1987) '*Spolia* from Constantine to Charlemagne: Aesthetics Versus Ideology', *Dumbarton Oaks Papers* 41, pp. 103–9.

Brilliant, R. (1963) 'Gesture and Rank in Roman Art. The Use of Gestures to Denote Status in Roman Sculpture and Coinage' *Memoirs of the Connecticut Academy of Arts and Sciences* XI, New Haven.

Brilliant, R. (1967) 'The Arch of Septimius Severus in the Roman Forum' *Memoirs of the American Academy in Rome* XXIX.

Brilliant, R. (1984) *Visual Narratives. Storytelling in Etruscan and Roman Art*, Ithaca: Cornell University Press.

Brilliant, R. (2012a) 'Rome, the Site of Reverberating Memories' in T. K. Sein and M. Prusac (eds), *Recycling Rome*, pp. 11–28.

Brilliant, R. (2012b) 'Late Antiquity: A Protean Term' in T. K. Sein and M. Prusac (eds), *Recycling Rome*, pp. 29–56.

Brilliant, R. and D. Kinney (eds) (2011) *Reuse Value:* Spolia *and Appropriation in Art and Architecture from Constantine to Sherrie Levine*, Farnham: Ashgate.

Bruno, M., C. Panella, P. Pensabene, M. Preite Martinez, M. Soligo, and B. Turi (1999) 'Determinazione dei Marmi dell'Arco di Costantino su Base Archeometrica' in P. Pensabene and C. Panella (eds), *Arco di Costantino*, pp. 171–84.

Bruun, P. (1954) 'The Consecration Coins of Constantine the Great', *Arctos New Series* 1, pp. 19–31.

Bruun, P. (1958) 'The Disappearance of Sol from the Coins of Constantine', *Arctos New Series* 2, pp. 15–37.

Bruun, P. (1962) 'The Christian Signs on the Coins of Constantine' *Arctos* 3, pp. 25–35.

Bruun, P. (1997) 'Victorious Signs of Constantine: A Reappraisal', *Numismatic Chronicle* 157, pp. 41–59.

Burckhardt, J. (1956) *The Age of Constantine the Great*, London: Routledge and Kegan Paul.

Buttrey, T. V. (1983) 'The Dates of the Arches of 'Diocletian' and Constantine', *Historia* 32, pp. 375–83.

Calcani, G. (1996–1997) 'I Tondi Adrianei e l'Arco di Costantino', *Rivista dell'Istituto Nazionale d'Archeologia e Storia dell'Arte* Series 3, 19–20, pp.175–201.

Calza, R. (1959–1960) 'Un Problema di Iconografia Imperiale sull'Arco di Costantino', *Atti della Pontificia Accademia Romana di Archeologia: Rendiconti* 32, pp. 133–161.

Cameron, A. (2006) 'Constantine and Christianity' in E. Hartley, J. Hawkes, M. Henig and F. Mee (eds) (2006) *Constantine the Great: York's Roman Emperor*, pp. 96–103.

Cameron, A. and S. Hall (1999) *Eusebius. Life of Constantine. Introduction, Translation and Commentary*, Oxford: Clarendon Press.

Capodiferro, A. (1993) 'Arco di Costantino' in E. M. Steinby, *Lexicon Topographicum Urbis Romae I*, Edizioni Quasar, Rome, pp. 86–91.

Carla, F. and M. G. Castello (2010) 'Questioni Tardoantiche: Storia e Mito della "Svolta Costantiniana"', Rome: Aracne.

Chapman, J. (2000) *Fragmentation in Archaeology: People, Places and Broken Objects in the Prehistory of South Eastern Europe*, London: Routledge.

Chapman, J. and B. Gaydarska (2007) *Parts and Wholes: Fragmentation in Prehistoric Context*, Oxford: Oxbow Books.

Chenault, R. R. (2008) *Rome Without Emperors: the Revival of a Senatorial City in the Fourth Century*, U.S.A.: Proquest, UMI Dissertation Publishing.

CIL *Corpus Inscriptionum Latinarum* (Berlin).

Cirone, D. (1993–4) 'I Risultati delle Indagini Stratigrafiche all'Arco di Costantino', *Atti della Pontificia Accademia Romana di Archeologia: Rendiconti* 66 , pp. 61–76.

Claridge, A. (1998) *Rome: An Oxford Archaeological Guide*, Oxford: Oxford University Press.

Coarelli, P. (1986) 'L'Urbs e il Suburbio: Ristrutturazione Urbanistica e Ristrutturazione Amministrativa nella Roma di Massenzio' in A. Giardina (ed.) (1986) *Società Romana e impero tardo antico*, pp. 1–35.

Conforto, M. L., A. M. Vaccaro, P. Cicerchia, G. Calcani and A. M. Ferroni (2001) *Adriano e Costantino. Le Due Fasi dell'Arco nella Valle del Colosseo*, Ministero per I Beni e le Attività Culturali Soprintendenza Archeologica per il Lazio, Milan: Electa.

Connerton, P. (1989) *How Socities Remember*, Cambridge: Cambridge University Press.

Cullhed, M. (1994) Conservator Urbis Suae: *Studies in the Politics and Propaganda of the Emperor Maxentius*, Stockholm: Svenska Institut I Rom.

Curran, J. (2000) *Pagan City and Christian Capital*, Oxford: Clarendon Press.

Currie, S. (1996) 'The Empire of Adults: The Representation of Children on Trajan's Arch at Beneventum' in J. Elsner (ed.) (1996) *Art and Text in Roman Culture*, Cambridge: Cambridge University Press, pp. 153–181.

D'Ambra, E. (1993) *Private Lives, Imperial Virtues. The Frieze of the Forum Transitorium in Rome*, New Jersey: Princeton University Press.

Dasen, V. (2010) 'Wax and Plaster Memories: Children in Elite and Non-Elite Strategies' in V. Dasen and T. Späth (eds) (2010) *Children, Memory and Family Identity in Roman Culture*, pp. 109–46.

Dasen, V. and T. Späth (eds) (2010) *Children, Memory, and Family Identity in Roman Culture*, Oxford: Oxford University Press.

De Maria, S. (1988) *Gli Archi Onorari di Roma e dell'Italia Romana*, Rome: L'Erma di Bretschneider.

De Souza, P. (2011) 'War, Slavery and Empire in Roman Imperial Iconography', *Bulletin of the Institute of Classical Studies* 54 (1), pp. 31–62.

Deichmann, F. W. and A. Tschira (1957) 'Das Mausoleum der Kaiserin Helena und die Basilika der Heiligen Marcellinus und Petrus an der Via Labicana vor Rom' *Jahrbuch des Deutschen Archäologischen Institus* 72, pp. 44–110.

Demandt, A. (2007) 'Wenn Kaiser Träumen – Die Visionen Konstantins des Grossen' in A. Demandt and J. Engemann (eds) (2007b) *Konstantin der Grosse. Geschichte, Archäologie, Rezeption*, pp. 49–60.

Demandt, A. and J. Engemann (eds) (2007a) *Imperator Caesar Flavius Constantinus: Konstantin der Grosse, Ausstellungskatalog*, Trier.

Demandt, A. and J. Engemann (eds) (2007b) *Konstantin der Grosse. Geschichte, Archäologie, Rezeption*, Internationales Kolloquium vom 10–15 Oktober 2005 an der Universität Trier, Rheinisches Landesmuseum Trier.

Di Giuseppe, C. (2000) *Constantine's Arch*, Ficulle: Comosavona.

Diefenbach, S. (2011) 'Konstantin und die Christliche Sakraltopographie Roms' in K. Ehling and G. Weber (eds) *Konstantin der Grosse: Zwischen Sol und Christus*, pp. 64–81.

Dignas, B. and R. R. R. Smith (eds) (2012) *Historical and Religious Memory in the Ancient World*, Oxford: Oxford University Press.

Donati, A. and G. Gentili (2005) 'Costantino il Grande: la Civiltà Antica al Bivio tra Occidente e Oriente' *Catalogo della Mostra Rimini*, 13, Marzo–4 Settembre, Silvana, Milan.

Dörries, H. (1972) *Constantine the Great*, New York: Harper and Row.

Ehling, K. and G. Weber (eds) (2011) *Konstantin der Grosse. Zwischen Sol und Christus*, Bildbände zur Archäologie, Munich: Phillip von Zabern.

Elderfield, J. (1985) *Kurt Schwitters*, London: Thames and Hudson.

Elliot, T. G. (1996) *The Christianity of Constantine the Great*, Scranton, Pennsylvania: University of Scranton.

Elsner, J. (1995) *Art and the Roman Viewer: The Transformation of Art from the Pagan World to Christianity*, Cambridge: Cambridge University Press.

Elsner, J. (1998a) *Imperial Rome and Christian Triumph*, Oxford: Oxford University Press.

Elsner, J. (1998b) 'Berenson's Decline, or his Arch of Constantine Reconsidered' *Apollo* 148, July, pp. 20–2.

Elsner, J. (2000) 'From the Culture of *Spolia* to the Cult of Relics: the Arch of Constantine and the Genesis of Late Antique Forms', *Papers of the British School at Rome* 68, pp. 149–84.

Elsner, J. (2006) 'Perspectives in Art' in N. Lenski (ed.) (2006), pp. 255–77.

Engemann, J. (2007) 'Der Konstantinsbogen' in A. Demandt and J. Engemann (eds) (2007b), pp. 85–9.

Ensoli, S. and E. La Rocca. (2000) 'I Colossi di Bronzo a Roma in Età Tardoantica: Dal Colosso di Nerone al Colosso di Costantino: A Proposito dei Tre Frammenti Bronzei dei Musei Capitolini' in S. Ensoli and E. La Rocca (eds) (2000) *Aurea Roma: Guida Breve. Dalla Città Pagana alla Città Cristiana. Catalogo della Mostra, Roma*, Rome: L'Erma di Bretschneider, pp. 66–90.

Entwistle, C. and N. Adams (eds) (2011) '*Gems of Heaven': Recent Research on Engraved Gemstones in Late Antiquity c. A. D. 200–66*, London: British Museum.

Evers, C. (1991) 'Remarques sur l'Iconographie de Constantin: à Propos du Remploi de Portraits des 'Bons Empereurs', Mélanges de l'Ecole Française à Rome: *Antiquité* 103, pp. 785–806.

Ewald, B. C. and C. F. Noreña (eds) (2010) 'The Emperor and Rome. Space, Representation and Ritual' *Yale Classical Studies*, 35, Cambridge: Cambridge University Press.

Fabricius Hansen, M. (2003) *The Eloquence of Appropriation: Prolegomena to an Understanding of Spolia in Early Christian Rome*, Rome: L'Erma di Bretschneider.

Farrell, J. (1997) 'The Phenomenology of Memory in Roman Culture' *Classical Journal* 92, pp. 373–83.

Fehl, P. (1985) 'Vasari and the Arch of Constantine' in G. C. Garafagnini (ed.) (1985) *Giorgio Vasari tra Decorazione Ambientale e Storiografia Artistica*, Florence: Istituto Nazionale di Studi sul Rinascimento.

Ferris, I. M. (2000) *Enemies of Rome: Barbarians Through Roman Eyes*, Stroud: Sutton Publishing.

Ferris, I. M. (2003) 'The Hanged Men Dance. Barbarians in Trajanic Art' in S. Scott and J. Webster (eds) (2003) pp. 53–68.

Ferris, I. M. (2009) *Hate and War. The Column of Marcus Aurelius*, Stroud: The History Press.

Ferris, I. M. (2011) 'The Pity of War. Representations of Gauls and Germans in Roman Art' in E. S. Gruen (ed.) (2011) *Cultural Identity in the Ancient Mediterranean*, Los Angeles: Getty Research Institute, pp. 185–201.

Ferris, I. M. (2012) *Roman Britain Through Its Objects*, Stroud: Amberley Publishing.

Flower, H. I. (1996) *Ancestor Masks and Aristocratic Power in Roman Culture*, Oxford: Clarendon Press.

Fowden, G. (1993) 'The Last Days of Constantine', *Journal of Roman Studies*, 83, pp. 146–70.

Frazer, A. (1966) 'The Iconography of the Emperor Maxentius' Building in the Via Appia', *Art Bulletin* 48, pp. 385–92.

Fredrick, D. (ed.) (2002) *The Roman Gaze. Vision, Power, and the Body*, Baltimore: The Johns Hopkins University Press.

Frothingham, A. C. (1912–15) 'Who Built the Arch of Constantine? Its History from Domitian to Constantine', *American Journal of Archaeology* 16, pp. 368–86; 17, pp. 487–503; 19, pp. 1–12, 367–85.

Gagetti, E. (2011) 'Three Degrees of Separation: Detail Reworking, Type Updating and Identity. Transformation in Roman Imperial Glyptic Portraits in the Round' in C. Entwistle and N. Adams (eds) (2011), pp. 135–48.

Giardina, A. (ed.) (1986) *Società Romana e Impero Tardo Antico*, Rome: Laterza.

Girardet, K. M. (2006) *Die Konstantinische Wende. Voraussetzungen und Geistige Grundlagen der Religionspolitik Konstantins des Grossen*, Darmstadt: Wissenschaftlicher Buchgesellschaft.

Girardet, K. M. (2010) *Der Kaiser und Sein Gott: das Christentum im Denken und in der Religionspolitik Konstantins des Grossen*, Berlin: De Gruyter.

Giuliani, A. (2000) 'L'Arco di Costantino Come Documento Storico', *Rivista Storica Italiana* 112, pp. 441–7.

Giuliano, A. (1956) *L'Arco di Costantino*, Milan: Istituto Editoriale Domus.

Gliwitsky, C. (2011) 'Zwischen Vergangener Grösse und Glückbringender Zukunft – zum Porträt des Kaisers Konstantin' in K. Ehling and G. Weber (eds) (2011), pp. 118–29.

Gradara, C. (1918) 'Restauri Settecenteschi Fatti all'Arco di Costantino', *Bullettino della Commissione Archeologica Communale di Roma* 46, pp. 161–4.

Gradel, I. (2002) *Heavenly Honours. Roman Emperor Worship, Caesar to Constantine*, Oxford: Oxford University Press.

Grégoire, H. (1939) 'La Vision de Constantin "Liquide"', *Byzantion* 14, pp. 341–51.

Gregory, A. P. (1994) '"Powerful Images": Responses to Portraits and the Political Uses of Images in Rome' *Journal of Roman Archaeology* 7, pp. 80–99.

Grig, L. and G. Kelly (eds) (2012) *Two Romes: Rome and Constantinople in Late Antiquity*, Oxford: Oxford University Press.

Grigg, R. (1977) 'Constantine the Great and the Cult Without Images', *Viator* 8, pp. 1–32.

Groag, E. (1930) 'Maxentius' in *Pauly-Wissowa Realencyclopädie der Classischen Altertumswissenschaft* XIV, 2, Stuttgart, pp. 2417–84.

Gruen, E. S. (2011) *Rethinking the Other in Antiquity*, Princeton: Princeton University Press.

Guberti Bassett, S. (1991) 'The Antiquities in the Hippodrome of Constantinople' *Dumbarton Oaks Papers* 45, pp. 87–96.

Hallam, E. and J. Hockey (2001) *Death, Memory and Material Culture*, Oxford: Berg.

Hannestad, N. (1988) *Roman Art and Imperial Policy*, Aarhus: Aarhus University Press.

Hannestad, N. (1994) 'Tradition in Late Antique Sculpture. Conservation, Modernization, Production', *Acta Jutlandica* LXIX:2, *Humanities Series* 69, Aarhus: Aarhus University Press.

Hannestad, N. (2001) 'The Ruler Image of the Fourth Century: Innovation or Tradition' in J. R. Brandt and O. Steen (eds), *Imperial Art as Christian Art – Christian Art as Imperial Art*, Acta ad Archaeologiam et Artium Historiam Pertinenda XV, pp. 93–107.

Hannestad, N. (2007a) 'Die Porträtskulptur zur zeit Konstantins des Grossen' in A. Demandt and J. Engemann (eds) (2007b), pp. 96–116.

Hannestad, N., (2007b) 'Skulpturenausstattung Spätantiker Herrschaftshäuser' in A. Demandt and J. Engemann (eds) (2007b), pp. 195–208.

Harrison, E. B. (1967) 'The Constantinian Portrait', *Dumbarton Oaks Papers* 21, pp. 79–96.

Hartley, E., J. Hawkes, M. Henig, and F. Mee (eds) (2006) *Constantine the Great: York's Roman Emperor*, Aldershot: Lund Humphries.

Hatt, J. J. (1950) 'La Vision de Constantin au Sanctuaire de Grand et l'Origine Celtique du *Labarum*', *Latomus* 9, pp. 427–36.

Henig, M. (2006) 'Art in the Age of Constantine' in E. Hartley, J. Hawkes, M. Henig and F. Mee (eds) (2006), pp. 65–76.

Herrmann-Otto, E. (2007) *Konstantin der Grosse*, Darmstadt: Wissenschaftlicher Buchgesellschaft.

Hill, P. V. (1989) *The Monuments of Ancient Rome as Coin Types*, London: Seaby.

Holland, L. A. (1961) 'Janus and the Bridge', *Papers and Monographs of the American Academy in Rome* 21, pp. 212–23.

Holloway, R. R. (1985) 'The *Spolia* on the Arch of Constantine', *Quaderni Ticinesi Numismatica e Antichità Classiche* 14, pp. 261–9.

Holloway, R. R. (2004) *Constantine and Rome*, New Haven: Yale University Press.

Hölscher, T. (2003) 'Images of War in Greece and Rome: Between Military Practice, Public Memory, and Cultural Symbolism' *Journal of Roman Studies* 93, pp. 1–17.

Hölscher, T. (2005) 'The Public Monumentalisation of the Roman Republic' *Journal of Roman Archaeology* Fasc. 2, pp. 472–8.

Iacopi, P. (1977) *L'Arco di Costantino e le Terme di Caracalla, Rome*, Rome: Istituto Poligrafico dello Stato/Libreria dello Stato.

Johnson, M. J. (2006) 'Architecture of Empire' in N. Lenski (ed.) (2006), pp. 278–97.

Johnson, M. J. (2009) *The Roman Imperial Mausoleum in Late Antiquity*, Cambridge: Cambridge University Press.

Jones, A. H. M. (1962) *Constantine and the Conversion of Europe*, Second Edition, London: Collier.

Jones, H. S. (1906) 'The Relief Medallions of the Arch of Constantine' *Papers of the British School at Rome* III, pp. 216–71.

Kähler, H. (1953) *Römische Gebälke 2.1: Die Gebälke des Konstantinsbogen*, Heidelberg: C. Winter.

Kampen, N. B. (1991) 'Between Public and Private; Women as Historical Subjects in Roman Art' in S. B. Pomeroy (ed.) (1991), pp. 218–48.

Kampen, N. B. (1994) 'Material Girl: Feminist Confrontations with Roman Art', *Arethusa* 27/1, pp. 111–49.

Kampen, N. B. (ed.) (1996) *Sexuality in Ancient Art*, Cambridge: Cambridge University Press.

Kampen, N. B., E. Marlowe and R. M. Molholt (2002) 'What is a Man? Changing Images of Masculinity in Late Antique Art', Reed College, Portland: Douglas F. Cooley Memorial Art Gallery.

Kerr, L. (2002) 'A Topography of Death: the Buildings of the Emperor Maxentius on the Via Appia, Rome' in M. Carruthers, C. van Driel-Murray, A. Gardner, J. Lucas, L. Revell, and E. Swift (eds) (2002) TRAC 2001 Proceedings of the Eleventh Annual Theoretical Roman Archaeology Conference Glasgow 2001. Oxford: Oxbow Books, pp. 24–33.

Kinney, D. (1995) 'Rape or Restitution of the Past? Interpreting *Spolia*' in S. C. Scott (ed.), *The Art of Interpreting*, University Park, Pennsylvania: Pennsylvania State University, pp. 52–67.

Kinney, D. (1997) '*Spolia*: *Damnatio* and *Renovatio Memoriae*', *Memoirs of the American Academy in Rome* 42, pp. 117–48.

Kinney, D. (2001) 'Roman Architectural *Spolia*' *Proceedings of the American Philosophical Society* 145, pp. 138–161.

Kinney, D. (2012) 'Hans-Peter L'Orange on Portraits and the Arch of Constantine: a Lasting Legacy' in T. K. Sein and M. Prusac (eds) (2012), pp. 11–28.

Kleiner, D. E. E. (1992) *Roman Sculpture*, New Haven: Yale University Press.

Kleiner, D. E. E. (2000) 'Now You See Them, Now You Don't: The Presence and Absence of Women in Roman Art' in E. R. Varner (ed.) (2000), pp. 45–57.

Kleiner, F. S. (1998) 'The Roman Arches of Gallia Narbonensis' *Journal of Roman Archaeology* 11, pp. 610–12.

Kleiner, F. S. (2001) 'Who Really Built the Arch of Constantine?' *Journal of Roman Archaeology* 14, pp. 661–3.

Knudsen, S. E. (1988) 'The Portraits of Constantine the Great: Types and Chronology A. D. 306–337', unpublished PhD thesis, Santa Barbara: University of California.

Knudsen, S. E. (1989) '*Spolia*: the So-Called Historical Frieze on the Arch of Constantine', *American Journal of Archaeology* 93, pp. 267–8.

Knudsen, S. E. (1990) '*Spolia*: the Pedestal Reliefs on the Arch of Constantine', *American Journal of Archaeology* 94, pp. 313–4.

Koeppel, G. (1990) 'Die Historischen Reliefs der Römischen Kaiserzeit VII: der Bogen des Septimius Severus, die Decennalienbasis und der Konstantinsbogen' *Bonner Jahrbücher* 190, pp. 1–64.

Kraft, K. (1954–55) 'Das Silbermedaillon Constantins des Grosses mit dem Christusmonogram auf dem Helm' *Jahrbuch für Numismatik und Geldgeschichte* 5–6, pp. 151–78.

Krautheimer, R. (1992) 'The Ecclesiastical Building Program of Constantine' in G. Bonamente and F. Fusco (eds) (1992), pp. 509–52.

Krug, A. (2007) 'Gemmen und Kameen' in A. Demandt and J. Engemann (eds) (2007b), pp. 132–9.

Krug, A. (2011) 'The Belgrade Cameo' in C. Entwistle and N. Adams (eds) (2011), pp. 186–92.

Kuttner, A. (Forthcoming) 'Acclaiming the New Augustus: Text and Image in the Arch of Constantine', *Word and Image*.

La Regina, A. (2004) *Archaeological Guide to Rome. Ministero per i Bene e le Attività Culturali Soprintendenza Archeologica di Roma*, Milan: Electa.

Leander Touati, A. M. (1987) *The Great Trajanic Frieze*, Stockholm: Svenska Institutet I Rome/ Astroms Forlag.

Le Goff, J. (1992) *History and Memory*, trans. S. Rendall and E. Claman, New York: Columbia University Press.

Lenski, N. (ed.) (2006) *The Cambridge Companion to the Age of Constantine*, Cambridge: Cambridge University Press.

Levi, A. C. (1952) 'Barbarians on Roman Imperial Coins and Sculpture', *Numismatic Notes and Monographs* N. 123. New York: The American Numismatic Society.

Lexicon Topographicum Urbis Romae (Rome: Qasar).

Lieu, S. N. C. and D. Monserrat (eds) (1998) *Constantine: History, Historiography and Legend*, London: Routledge.

Liverani, P. (2004) 'Reimpiego senza Ideologia. La Lettura Antica degli Spolia, dall'Arco di Costantino all'Età di Teodorico', *Mitteilungen des Deutschen Archäologischen Instituts: Römische Abteilung* 111, pp. 383–444.

Liverani, P. (2005) 'L'Arco di Costantino' in A. Donati, and G. Gentili (eds) (2005), pp. 64–9.

Liverani, P. (2007) 'L'Architettura Costantiniana, tra Committenza Imperiale e Contributo delle Élites Locali' in A. Demandt, and J. Engemann (eds) (2007b), pp. 235–44.

Liverani, P. (2011) 'Reading *Spolia* in Late Antiquity and Contemporary Perception' in R. Brilliant and D. Kinney (eds) (2011), pp. 33–52.

L'Orange, H. P. (1953) *Studies in the Iconography of Cosmic Kingship in the Ancient World*, Cambridge, Massachusetts: Harvard University Press.

L'Orange, H. P. (1965) *Art Forms and Civic Life in the Late Roman Empire*, Princeton: Princeton University Press.

L'Orange, H. P. and Gerkan, A. (1939) *Der Spätantike Bildsschmuck des Konstantinsbogen*, Berlin: Verlag Walter de Gruyter.

MacCormack, S. G. (1981) *Art and Ceremony in Late Antiquity*, Berkeley: University of California Press.

MacMullen, R. (1968) 'Constantine and the Miraculous', *Greek, Roman and Byzantine Studies* 9, pp. 81–96.

MacMullen, R. (1980) 'Women in Public in the Roman Empire', *Historia* 29, pp. 208–18. Reprinted 1990 in R. MacMullen, *Changes in the Roman Empire. Essays in the Ordinary*, Princeton: Princeton University Press.

MacMullen, R. (1981) *Paganism in the Roman Empire*, New Haven: Yale University Press.

MacMullen, R. (1987) *Constantine*, New Edition, London: Croom Helm.

Magi, F. (1956–57) 'Il Coronamento dell'Arco di Costantino', *Atti della Pontificia Accademia Romana di Archeologia: Rendiconti* 29, pp. 83–110.

Mango, C. (1990) 'Constantine's Mausoleum', *Byzantinische Zeitschrift* 83, pp. 51–62.

Marcone, A. (2002) *Pagano e Cristiano, Vita e Mito di Costantino*, Rome: GLF Editori Laterza.

Marlowe, E. (2006) 'Framing the Sun: the Arch of Constantine and the Roman Cityscape', *Art Bulletin* LXXXVIII No. 2, pp. 223–42.

Marlowe, E. (2010) '*Liberator Urbis Suae*: Constantine and the Ghost of Maxentius' in B. C. Ewald and C. F. Noreña (eds) (2010), pp. 199–220.

Marlowe, E., (Forthcoming) *Customary Magnificence: Emperor and City on the Arch of Constantine*.

Massini, A. (1993) 'The Arch of Constantine Revisited: a Study of its Critique, Use and Interpretation in the Renaissance. Can the Arch of Constantine Be Seen as a Positive Monument?' Unpublished M.A. Thesis, Courtauld Institute of Art, University of London.

Messinio, G. (1989) 'Malborghetto', *Lavori e Studi Archeologia* 15, Rome.

Minoprio, A. (1932) 'A Restoration of the Basilica of Constantine, Rome', *Papers of the British School at Rome* XII, pp. 1–25.

Nolden, R. (2007) 'Das Ada-Evangeliar' in A. Demandt and J. Engemann (eds) (2007b), pp. 498–500.

Odahl, C. M. (2010) *Constantine and the Christian Empire*, Second Edition, London: Routledge.

Packer, J. E. (2001) *The Forum of Trajan in Rome. A Study of the Monuments in Brief*, Berkeley: University of California Press.

Pallottino, M. (1938) 'Il Grande Fregio di Traiano', *Bullettino della Commissione Archeologica Comunale di Roma* 66, pp. 17–56.

Peirce, P. (1989) 'The Arch of Constantine: Propaganda and Ideology in Late Roman Art', *Art History*, 12/4, pp. 387–418.

Pensabene, P. (1988) 'The Arch of Constantine: Marble Samples' in N. Herz and M. Waelkens (eds), *Classical Marble; Geochemistry, Technology and Trade*, Dordrecht: Kluwer Academic Publishers, pp. 411–18.

Pensabene, P. (1993) 'Il Reimpiego nell'Età Costantina a Roma' in G. Bonamente and F. Fusco (eds) *Costantino il Grande* 2, Macerata: Università degli Studi di Macerata, pp. 749–68.

Pensabene, P. (1995) 'Reimpiego e Nuovo Mode Architettoniche nelle Basiliche Cristiane di Roma tra IV e VI Secolo', *Jahrbuch für Antike und Christentum Ergänzungsband* 20 (2), pp. 1076–96.

Pensabene, P. (1999a) 'Progetto Unitario e Reimpiego nell'Arco di Costantino' in P. Pensabene and C. Panella (eds) (1999), pp. 13–42.

Pensabene, P. (1999b) 'Parte Superiore dell'Arco: Composizione Strutturale e Classificazione dei Marmi' in P. Pensabene, and C. Panella (eds) (1999), pp. 139–56.

Pensabene, P. and C. Panella (1993–4) 'Reimpiego e Progettazione Architettonica nei Monumenti Tardo-Antichi di Roma', *Atti della Pontificia Accademia Romana di Archeologia: Rendiconti* 66, pp. 111–283.

Pensabene, P. and C. Panella (eds) (1999) *Arco di Costantino: Tra Archeologia e Archeometria*, Rome: L'Erma di Bretschneider.

Pensabene, P., L. Lazzarini and B. Turi (2002) 'New Archaeometric Investigations on the Fragments of the Colossal Statue of Constantine in the Palazzo dei Conservatori' in J. J. Hermann, N. Herz and R. Newman (eds), *Interdisciplinary Studies on Ancient Stone: Asmosia 5*, pp. 250–55.

Petersen, E. (1900) 'Un Colosso di Costantino Magno', *Atti della Pontificia Accademia Romana d'Archeologia* Series II, VII, pp. 157–82.

Pohlsander, H. A. (1995) *Helena: Empress and Saint*, Chicago: Ares Publishers.

Pohlsander, H. A. (2004) *The Emperor Constantine*, Second Edition, London: Routledge.

Pomeroy, S. B. (ed.) (1991) *Women's History and Ancient History*, Chapel Hill: University of North Carolina Press.

Presicce, C. P. (2005) 'L'Abbandono della Moderazione. I Ritratti di Costantino e della Sua Progenie' in A. Donati and G. Gentili (eds) (2005), pp. 138–55.

Prusac, M. (2011) *From Face to Face. Recarving of Roman Portraits and the Late-Antique Portrait Arts*, Leiden: Brill.

Prusac, M. (2012) 'The Arch of Constantine: Continuity and Commemoration Through Reuse' in T. K. Sein and M. Prusac (eds) (2012), pp. 127–58.

Punzi, R. (1999) 'Fonti Documentarie per una Rilettura delle Vicende Post-Antiche dell'Arco di Costantino' in P. Pensabene and C. Panella (eds) (1999), pp. 185–228.

Richardson, L. (1975) 'The Date and Program of the Arch of Constantine', *Archeologia Classica* 27, pp. 72–8.

Riegl, A. (1901) *Spätrömische Kunstindustrie*, Vienna: Hof und Staatsdruckerie.

Rivière, Y. (2008) 'The Restoration of Order to the Roman Empire: from the Tetrarchs to Constantine' in J-J. Aillagon (ed.) *Rome and the Barbarians: The Birth of a New World*, Milan: Skira, pp. 186–93.

Rohmann, J. (1998) 'Die Spätantiken Kaiserporträts am Konstantinsbogen in Rom', *Mitteilungen des Deutschen Archäologischen Instituts: Römische Abteilung* 105, pp. 259–82.

Roldanus, J. (2006) *The Church in the Age of Constantine*, London: Routledge.

Romeo, I. (1999) 'Tra Massenzio e Costantino: il Ruole delle Officine Urbane ed Ostiensi nella Creazione del Ritratto Costantiniano', *Bollettino della Commissione Archeologica Comunale di Roma C*, pp. 197–228.

Ronning, C. (2007) *Herrscherpanegyrik unter Trajan und Konstantin: Studien zur Symbolischen Kommunikation in der Römischen Kaiserzeit*, Tübingen: Mohr Siebeck.

Rutledge, S. H. (2012) *Ancient Rome as a Museum: Power, Identity and the Culture of Collecting*, Oxford: Oxford University Press.

Ruysschaert, J. (1962–63) 'Essai d'Interprétation Synthétique de l'Arc de Constantin', *Atti della Pontificia Accademia Romana di Archeologia: Rendiconti* 35, pp. 79–100.

Ryberg, I. S. (1967) *The Panel Reliefs of Marcus Aurelius*, New York: Archaeological Institute of America.

Sande, S. (2001) 'The Iconography and Style of the Rothschild Cameo' in J. Fleischer, J. Lund and M. Nielsen (eds) *Late Antiquity: Art in Context*, Acta Hyperborea 8, pp. 145–58.

Sande, S. (2012) 'The Art of Memory and Roman Art' in T. K. Sein and M. Prusac (eds) (2012), pp. 57–76.

Sapelli, M. (2000) 'La Basilica di Giunio Basso' in S. Ensoli and E. La Rocca (eds) (2000), pp. 137–39.

Saradi, H. (1997) 'The Use of Ancient *Spolia* in Byzantine Monuments: the Archaeological and Literary Evidence', *International Journal of the Classical Tradition* 3, pp. 395–423.

Saradi-Mendelovici, H. (1990) 'Christian Attitudes Towards Pagan Monuments in Late Antiquity' *Dumbarton Oaks Papers* 44, pp. 47–61.

Saylor Rodgers, B. (1980) 'Constantine's Pagan Vision', *Byzantion* 50, pp. 259–78.

Schmidt-Colinet, A. (1996) 'Zur Ikonographie der Hadrianischen Tondi am Konstantinsbogen' in Blakolmer, F. (ed.) *Fremde Zeiten. Festschrift Jürgen Borchardt II*, Vienna: Phoibos, pp. 261–73.

Schmitt, O. (2007) *Constantin der Grosse: Leben und Herrschaft*, Stuttgart: Kohlhammer.

Schuller, F. and H. Wolff (eds) (2007), *Konstantin der Grosse. Kaiser einer Epochenwende*, Lindenberg: Kunstverlag Josef Fink.

Sein, T. K. and M. Prusac (eds) (2012) *Recycling Rome*, Institutum Romanum Norvegiae, Acta ad Archaeologiam et Artium Historiam Pertinentia Volume XXV (New Series 11).

Small, J. P. and J. Tatum (1995) 'Memory and the Study of Classical Antiquity', *Helios* 22, pp. 149–77.

Smith, R. R. R. (1997) 'The Public Image of Licinius I: Portrait Sculpture and Imperial Ideology in the Early Fourth Century' *Journal of Roman Studies* 87, pp. 170–202.

Smith, R. R. R. (2000) 'Nero and the Sun-God: Divine Accessories and Political Symbols in Roman Imperial Images', *Journal of Roman Archaeology* 13, pp. 532–42.

Spiedel, M. P. (1986) 'Maxentius and His "*Equites Singulares*" in the Battle at the Milvian Bridge', *Classical Antiquity* 5(2), pp. 253–262.

Spivey, N. (1995) 'Stumbling Towards Byzantium: the Decline and Fall of Late Antique Sculpture', *Apollo* 142, July, pp. 20–3.

Steiner, A. M. (1994) 'Cui Costrui l'Arco di Costantino? Rivelazioni su un Monumento Simbolo del Mondo Romano', *Archeo* 1994, pp. 38–45.

Stephenson, P. (2009) *Constantine: Unconquered Emperor, Christian Victor*, London: Quercus.

Stewart, P. (2003) *Statues in Roman Society: Representation and Response*, Oxford: Oxford University Press.

Storch, R. (1970) 'The Trophy and the Cross: Pagan and Christian Symbolism in the Fourth and Fifth Centuries', *Byzantion* 40, pp. 105–17.

Strong, D. E. (1973) 'Roman Museums' in D. E. Strong (ed.) (1973) *Archaeological Theory and Practice: Essays Presented to Professor W. F. Grimes*, London: Seminar Press, pp. 247–64.

Stuart-Jones, H. (1926) *A Catalogue of the Ancient Sculptures Preserved in the Municipal Collections of Rome: the Sculpture of the Palazzo dei Conservatori*, Oxford: Clarendon Press.

Temple, N. (2011) *Renovatio Urbis: Architecture, Urbanism and Ceremony in the Rome of Julius II*, London: Routledge.

Thill, E. W. (2011) 'Depicting Barbarism On Fire: Architectural Destruction on the Columns of Trajan and Marcus Aurelius', *Journal of Roman Archaeology* 24, pp. 283–312.

Töbelmann, F. (1915) 'Der Bogen von Malborghetto', *Abhandlungen der Heidelberger Akademie der Wissenschaften* 2.

Toynbee, J. M. C. (1974) 'Some Pagan Mythological Figures and Their Significance in Early Christian Art', *Papers of the British School at Rome* XLII, pp. 68–97.

Turcan, R. (1991) 'Les *Tondi* d'Hadrien sur l'Arc de Constantin', *Académie des Inscriptions et Belles-Lettres: Comptes* Rendus, pp. 53–80.

Uzzi, J. D. (2005) *Children in the Visual Arts of Imperial Rome*, Cambridge: Cambridge University Press.

Vaccaro, A. and A. M. Ferroni (1993–4) 'Chi Costrui l'Arco di Costantino? Un Interrogativo Ancora Attuale', *Atti della Pontificia Accademia Romana di Archeologia: Rendiconti* 66, pp. 1–60.

Vaccaro, M. A. (2001) 'L'Arco Dedicata a Costantino: Analisi e Datazione della Decorazione Architettonica con un Contributo di Dora Cirone', *Römische Mitteilungen* 108, pp. 17–82.

Van Dam, R. (2007) *The Roman Revolution of Constantine*, Cambridge: Cambridge University Press.

Van Dam, R. (2011) *Remembering Constantine at the Milvian Bridge*, Cambridge: Cambridge University Press.

Van Dyke, R. and S. Alcock (2003) 'Archaeologies of Memory: an Introduction' in R. Van Dyke and S. Alcock (eds) *Archaeologies of Memory*, London: Routledge, pp. 1–13.

Varner, E. R. (2000) *From Caligula to Constantine. Tyranny and Transformation in Roman Portraiture*, Atlanta: Michael C. Carlos Museum, Emory University.

Varner, E. (2001) 'Portraits, Plots and Politics: *Damnatio Memoriae* and the Images of Imperial Women', *Memoirs of the American Academy in Rome* XLVI, pp. 41–93.

Varner, E. R. (2004) *Mutilation and Transformation: Damnatio Memoriae and Roman Imperial Portraiture*, Leiden: Brill.

Veyne, P. (2007) *Quand Notre Monde Est Devenu Chrétien*, Paris: Albin Michel, pp. 312–94.

Vout, C. (2007) *Power and Eroticism in Imperial Rome*, Cambridge: Cambridge University Press.

Wace, A. J. B. (1949) 'The Greeks and Romans as Archaeologists', *Bulletin de la Société Royale d'Archaeologie d'Alexandrie* 38, pp. 21–35.

Waelkens, M. (1985) 'From a Phrygian Quarry: the Provenance of the Statues of the Dacian Prisoners in Trajan's Forum at Rome', *American Journal of Archaeology* 89, pp. 641–53.

Walker, A. (2012) *The Emperor and the World: Exotic Elements and the Imaging of Byzantine Imperial Power, Ninth to Thirteenth Centuries C.E.*, Cambridge: Cambridge University Press.

Wallraff, M. (2001) 'Constantine's Devotion to the Sun After 324', *Studia Patristica* 34, pp. 256–68.

Wallraff, M. (2011) 'Konstantins "Sonne" und Ihre Christlichen Kontexte' in K. Ehling and G. Weber (eds) (2011), pp. 42–52.

Walton, A. (1924) 'The Date of the Arch of Constantine', *Memoirs of the American Academy at Rome* 4, pp. 169–80.

Ward-Perkins, B. (1999) 'Reusing the Architectural Legacy of the Past. Entre Ideologie et Pragmatisme' in G. P. Brogiolo and B. Ward-Perkins (eds) *The Idea and Ideal of the Town Between Late Antiquity and the Early Middle Ages*, Leiden: Brill, pp. 225–44.

Ward-Perkins, B. (2012) 'Old and New Rome Compared: the Rise of Constantinople' in L. Grig and G. Kelly (eds) (2012), pp. 53–78.

Weiss, P. (1993) 'Die Vision Constantins' in J. Bleicken (ed.) *Colloquium aus Anlass des 80. Geburtstages von Alfred Heuss*, Frankfurter Althistorische Studien 13, Frankfurt, pp. 145–69.

Whittaker, C. R. (1997) 'Imperialism and Culture: the Roman Initiative' in D. J. Mattingly (ed.) (1997), pp. 143–64.

Wienand, J. (2011) 'Konstantin und Sol Invictus' in K. Ehling and G. Weber (eds) (2011), pp. 53–63.

Willett, J. (1997) *Heartfield Versus Hitler*, Paris: Éditions Hazan.

Wilson Jones, M. (1999) 'La Progettazione Architettonica: Riflessi su Misure, Proporzioni e Geometri' in P. Pensabene and C. Panella (eds) (1999), pp. 75–99.

Wilson Jones, M. (2000) 'Genesis and Mimesis: the Design of the Arch of Constantine in Rome', *Journal of the Society of Architectural Historians* 59 (1), pp. 50–77.

Wohl, B. L. (2001) 'Constantine's Use of *Spolia*' in J. Fleischer, J. Lund and M. Nielsen (eds) *Late Antiquity: Art in Context*, Acta Hyperborea 8, pp. 85–115.

Woods, D. (1997) 'Where Did Constantine I Die?', *Journal of Theological Studies* 48, pp. 531–35.

Wright, D. (1987) 'The True Face of Constantine the Great', *Dumbarton Oaks Papers* 41, pp. 493–507.

Zanker, P. (1988) *The Power of Images in the Age of Augustus*, Ann Arbor: University of Michigan Press.

Zanker, P. (2012) 'Der Konstantinsbogen als Monument des Senates' in T. K. Sein and M. Prusac (eds) (2012), pp. 77–106.

Zeggio, S. (1999) 'La Realizzazione delle Fondazioni' in P. Pensabene and E. C. Panella (eds) (1999), pp. 117–37.

Zervigón, A. M. (2012) *John Heartfield and the Agitated Image: Photography, Persuasion, and the Rise of Avant-Garde Photomontage*, Chicago: University of Chicago Press.

Zwierlein-Diehl, E. (2011) 'Gem Portraits of Soldier-Emperors' in C. Entwistle, and N. Adams (eds), pp. 149–62.

List of Illustrations

Figures (embedded in text)

1. A bronze *nummus* of Constantine. Constantinople mint AD 327. Obverse: bust of emperor, reverse: Christogram topped standard – the *labarum* – with shaft piercing serpent. British Museum, London. (Photo: Copyright Trustees of the British Museum)
2. A portrait head of Licinius recarved from the head of Hadrian on the Sacrifice to Hercules *tondo*. The Arch of Constantine, Rome. (Photo: Deutsches Archäologisches Institut Rom. Faraglia, DAIR 32.42)
3. A silver *argenteus* of Constantine, Trier mint, AD 306–7. Obverse: bust of emperor, reverse: fort gateway. British Museum, London. (Photo: Copyright Trustees of the British Museum)
4. A gold *solidus* of Constantine. Rome mint, AD 337. Obverse: bust of veiled emperor, reverse: Constantine ascending to heavens in a chariot. British Museum, London. (Photo: Copyright Trustees of the British Museum)
5. A gold *solidus* of Constantine. Siscia mint, AD 317. Obverse: bust of emperor, reverse: Constantine and Crispus. British Museum, London. (Photo: Copyright Trustees of the British Museum)
6. Fragments of a colossal statue of Constantine. Museo del Palazzo dei Conservatori, Rome. (Photo: Author)
7. The head of a colossal statue of Constantine. Museo del Palazzo dei Conservatori, Rome. (Photo: Author)
8. A foot from a colossal statue of Constantine. Museo del Palazzo dei Conservatori, Rome. (Photo: Author)
9. The head of Hadrian recarved as Constantine, boar hunt *tondo*. The Arch of Constantine, Rome. (Photo: Deutsches Archäologisches Institut Rom. Faraglia, DAIR 32.36)
10. The head of Trajan recarved as Constantine, west wall of central passageway. The Arch of Constantine, Rome. Plaster cast from the Museo della Civiltà Romana, Rome. (Photo: Deutsches Archäologisches Institut Rom. Schwanke, DAIR 82.1106)
11. Giovanni Battista Piranesi, *The Arch of Constantine, Rome*, 1750s–60s. (Photo: Slide Archive of Former School of Continuing Studies, Birmingham University)
12. A gold *solidus* of Constantine, Ticinum mint, AD 316. Obverse: busts of emperor and Sol, reverse: *Liberalitas*. British Museum, London. (Photo: Copyright Trustees of the British Museum)
13. Positions of artworks on the arch. A) Dacian prisoners and sections of the Great Trajanic Frieze. B) Panel reliefs of Marcus Aurelius. C) Hadrianic *tondi*. D) Constantinian *tondi*, relief, and pedestal bases. The Arch of Constantine, Rome. (Photo: Graham Norrie, after Giuliani 1955)
14. Plaster cast of the Great Trajanic Frieze, Museo della Civiltà Romana, Rome. (Photo: Author)
15. Head of Trajan, recarved as Constantine, on the east wall of central passageway. The Arch of Constantine, Rome. (Photo: Deutsches Archäologisches Institut Rom. Faraglia, DAIR 32.51)
16. Hadrianic *tondo*, a bear hunt. The Arch of Constantine, Rome. (Photo: Graham Norrie, after Giuliani 1955)
17. Hadrianic *tondo*, Sacrifice to Diana. The Arch of Constantine, Rome. (Photo: Graham Norrie, after Giuliani 1955)
18. Hadrianic *tondo*, Sacrifice to Apollo. The Arch of Constantine, Rome. (Photo: Graham Norrie, after Giuliani 1955)
19. Hadrianic *tondo*, the aftermath of the lion hunt. The Arch of Constantine, Rome. (Photo: Graham Norrie, after Giuliani 1955)
20. Hadrianic *tondo*, Sacrifice to Hercules. The Arch of Constantine, Rome. (Photo: Graham Norrie,

after Giuliani 1955)

21. Hadrianic *tondo*, a boar hunt. The Arch of Constantine, Rome. (Photo: Graham Norrie, after Giuliani 1955)
22. The Troyes Casket. Cathedral Treasury, Troyes, France. (Photo: Slide Archive of Former School of Continuing Studies, Birmingham University)
23. Panel relief of Marcus Aurelius. *Profectio* – the leave taking of the emperor from Rome. The Arch of Constantine, Rome. (Photo: Graham Norrie, after Giuliani 1955)
24. Panel relief of Marcus Aurelius. *Adventus* – the arrival and entry of the emperor into Rome. The Arch of Constantine, Rome. (Photo: Graham Norrie, after Giuliani 1955)
25. Panel relief of Marcus Aurelius; the submission of barbarian prisoners. The Arch of Constantine, Rome. (Photo: Slide Archive of Former School of Continuing Studies, Birmingham University)
26. Panel relief of Marcus Aurelius. *Liberalitas* – the distribution of largesse to the Roman people by the emperor. The Arch of Constantine, Rome. (Photo: Graham Norrie, after Giuliani 1955)
27. Panel relief of Marcus Aurelius receiving the barbarian prisoners in camp. The Arch of Constantine, Rome. (Photo: Graham Norrie, after Giuliani 1955)
28. Panel relief of Marcus Aurelius. *Lustratio* – sacrifice. The Arch of Constantine, Rome. (Photo: Graham Norrie, after Giuliani 1955)
29. A Constantinian *tondo* depicting Sol. East face, the Arch of Constantine, Rome. (Photo: Author)
30. A Constantinian *tondo* depicting Luna. West face, the Arch of Constantine, Rome. (Photo: Author)
31. Detail of the Constantinian pedestal bases decorated with barbarian captives and Victories. The Arch of Constantine, Rome. (Photo: Author)
32. Detail of one of the Constantinian pedestal bases decorated with barbarian captives and Victories. The Arch of Constantine, Rome. (Photo: Author)
33. The Constantinian frieze – the army on the march from Milan. West face, the Arch of Constantine, Rome. (Photo: Graham Norrie, after Giuliani 1955)
34. The Constantinian frieze – detail of the army on the march from Milan. West face, the Arch of Constantine, Rome. (Photo: Graham Norrie, after Giuliani 1955)
35. The Constantinian frieze – detail of the army on the march from Milan. West face, the Arch of Constantine, Rome. (Photo: Graham Norrie, after Giuliani 1955)
36. The Constantinian frieze – the siege of Verona. South face, the Arch of Constantine, Rome. (Photo: Graham Norrie, after Giuliani 1955)
37. The Constantinian frieze – detail of the siege of Verona. South face, the Arch of Constantine, Rome. (Photo: Graham Norrie, after Giuliani 1955)
38. The Constantinian frieze, detail of the siege of Verona. South face, the Arch of Constantine, Rome. (Photo: Graham Norrie, after Giuliani 1955)
39. The Constantinian frieze – detail of the siege of Verona. South face, the Arch of Constantine, Rome. (Photo: Graham Norrie, after Giuliani 1955)
40. The Constantinian frieze – detail of the siege of Verona. South face, the Arch of Constantine, Rome. (Photo: Graham Norrie, after Giuliani 1955)
41. The Constantinian frieze – the Battle of the Milvian Bridge. South face, the Arch of Constantine, Rome. (Photo: Graham Norrie, after Giuliani 1955)
42. The Constantinian frieze – detail of the Battle of the Milvian Bridge. South face, the Arch of Constantine, Rome. (Photo: Graham Norrie, after Giuliani 1955)
43. The Constantinian frieze – detail of the Battle of the Milvian Bridge. South face, the Arch of Constantine, Rome. (Photo: Graham Norrie, after Giuliani 1955)
44. The Constantinian frieze – Constantine's entry into Rome. East face, the Arch of Constantine, Rome. (Photo: Graham Norrie, after Giuliani 1955)
45. The Constantinian frieze – detail of Constantine's entry into Rome. East face, the Arch of Constantine, Rome. (Photo: Graham Norrie, after Giuliani 1955)
46. The Constantinian frieze – detail of Constantine's entry into Rome. East face, the Arch of Constantine, Rome. (Photo: Graham Norrie, after Giuliani 1955)
47. The Constantinian frieze – *Oratio* scene. Constantine addresses the Senate and Roman people. North face, the Arch of Constantine, Rome. (Photo: Graham Norrie, after Giuliani 1955)
48. The Constantinian frieze – detail of the *Oratio* scene (Constantine addressing the Senate and Roman people). North face, the Arch of Constantine, Rome. (Photo: Graham Norrie, after Giuliani 1955)
49. The Constantinian frieze – *Congiarium* scene. Constantine distributes monies to the Senate and Roman people. North face, the Arch of Constantine, Rome. (Photo: Graham Norrie, after

Plates (in separate section between pages 96 and 97)

17. Detail of the south face of the Arch of Constantine, Rome. (Photo: Author)
18. Gold *aureus* of Maxentius, Ostia mint, AD 308–12. Obverse: bust of emperor, reverse: Victory. British Museum, London. (Photo: Copyright Trustees of the British Museum)
19. Gold *solidus* of Constantine. Sirmium mint AD 321. Obverse: bust of emperor, reverse: Constantine being crowned by Sol. British Museum, London. (Photo: Copyright Trustees of the British Museum)
20. Gold *solidus* of Helena, Nicomedia mint, AD 325–30. Obverse: bust of empress, reverse: *Securitas* holding branch. British Museum, London. (Photo: Copyright Trustees of the British Museum)
21. The Basilica Nova of Maxentius and Constantine, Rome. (Photo: Author)
22. The Arch of Malborghetto, near Rome. (Photo: Author)
23. The Mausoleum of Helena, Tor Pignatarra, Rome. (Photo: Author)
24. The Mausoleum of Constantina, Via Nomentana, Rome. (Photo: Author)
25. Kurt Schwitters, *Bild mit heller Mitte* (Picture with Light Centre), 1919. Museum of Modern Art, New York. (Photo: Slide Archive of Former School of Continuing Studies, Birmingham University)
26. John Heartfield's book cover design for G. Reimann's *Das Deutsche Wirtschafts wunder* 1927. (Photo: Slide Archive of Former School of Continuing Studies, Birmingham University)
27. Sandro Botticelli, *The Punishment of the Rebels* (*Punizio dei Ribelli*), 1481–2. Sistine Chapel, Vatican, Rome. (Photo: Slide Archive of Former School of Continuing Studies, Birmingham University)
28. Jan Miel and Alessandro Salucci, *The Arch of Constantine, Rome*, 1647. Barber Institute of Fine Arts, Birmingham University. (Photo: Slide Archive of Former School of Continuing Studies, Birmingham University)
29. Herman van Swanevelt, *The Arch of Constantine*, 1630s. Dulwich Picture Gallery, London. (Photo: Slide Archive of Former School of Continuing Studies, Birmingham University)
30. Jean-Baptiste Lallemand, *The Forum, with the Arch of Constantine, Peasants in the Foreground*, mid-eighteenth century. Private collection. (Photo: Slide Archive of Former School of Continuing Studies, Birmingham University)
31. Hendrik Frans Van Lint, *The Arch of Constantine, Rome*, mid-eighteenth century. British Government Art Collections. (Photo: Slide Archive of Former School of Continuing Studies, Birmingham University)
32. Anton von Maron, *Portrait of Two Gentlemen Before the Arch of Constantine in Rome*, 1767. Private collection. (Photo: Slide Archive of Former School of Continuing Studies, Birmingham University)
33. Samuel Prout, *The Arch of Constantine, Rome from the South-East*, 1830s. (Photo: Slide Archive of Former School of Continuing Studies, Birmingham University)
34. Oswald Achenbach, *The Arch of Constantine, Rome*, 1886. Alte Nationalgalerie, Berlin (Photo: Slide Archive of Former School of Continuing Studies, Birmingham University)
35. Edmond Clément Marie Duthoit, *The Triumphal Arch of Constantine, Rome*, 1862–5. Private collection. (Photo: Slide Archive of Former School of Continuing Studies, Birmingham University)
36. Jean-Baptiste Camille Corot, *The Arch of Constantine and the Forum, Rome*, 1843. Frick Collection, New York. (Photo: Slide Archive of Former School of Continuing Studies, Birmingham University)
37. Joseph Mallord William Turner, *The Arch of Constantine, Rome*, 1835. Tate, London. (Photo: Slide Archive of Former School of Continuing Studies, Birmingham University)
38. The head of a colossal statue of Constantine. Museo del Palazzo dei Conservatori, Rome. (Photo: Author)
39. General view of the Arch of Constantine, Rome. (Photo: Author)

Image Credits

Figures (embedded in text)

6, 7, 8, 14, 29, 30, 31, 32, 52, 53, 54, 55, 58 and 61 Author; 13, 16, 17, 18, 19, 20, 21, 23, 24, 26, 27, 28, 33, 34, 35, 36, 37, 38, 39, 40, 41, 42, 43, 44, 45, 46, 47, 48, 49, 50, 51, 56, 57, 59 and 60 Graham Norrie; 2, 9, 10 and 15 Deutsches Archäologisches Institut Rom (DAIR); 11, 22 and 25 the former Birmingham University School of Continuing Studies archive slide collection; and 1, 3, 4, 5 and 12 copyright the British Museum.

Plates (in separate section between pages 96 and 97)

1, 2, 7, 8, 9, 10, 11, 12, 15, 16, 17, 21, 22, 23, 24, 38 and 39 Author; 5 Kate Donkin; 4, 6, 13, 14, 25, 26, 27, 28, 29, 30, 31, 32, 33, 34, 35, 36 and 37 the former Birmingham University School of Continuing Studies archive slide collection; and 3, 18, 19 and 20 copyright the British Museum.

I have attempted in all cases to track down the copyright holders of images used in the book. In one or two cases attributions of copyright were ambiguous. Therefore I would be happy for any copyright holders that I have inadvertently not credited or been unable to contact to get in touch with me via Amberley Publishing.

Index